Helen Pankhurst CBE i[...] to CARE International, [...] trustee of ActionAid, [...] Suffolk and Visiting Professor at MMU.

Helen is the great-granddaughter of Emmeline Pankhurst and granddaughter of Sylvia Pankhurst, leaders of the British suffragette movement, and was involved in the Opening Ceremony of the 2012 London Olympics and the 2015 film *Suffragette*. Helen leads #March4Women events around International Women's Day and convenes the Centenary Action Group and GM4Women 2028.

@HelenPankhurst

HELEN PANKHURST

DEEDS
NOT
WORDS

The Story of
Women's Rights,
Then and Now

S

SCEPTRE

First published in Great Britain in 2018 by Sceptre
An Imprint of Hodder & Stoughton
An Hachette UK company

This paperback edition published in 2019

1

A CIP catalogue record for this title is available from the British Library

Paperback ISBN 978 1 473 64687 2

Typeset in Dante MT by Hewer Text UK Ltd, Edinburgh
Printed and bound in Great Britain by Clays Ltd, Elcograf S.p.A.

Hodder & Stoughton policy is to use papers that are natural, renewable
and recyclable products and made from wood grown in sustainable
forests. The logging and manufacturing processes are expected to
conform to the environmental regulations of the country of origin.

Hodder & Stoughton Ltd
Carmelite House
50 Victoria Embankment
London EC4Y 0DZ

www.sceptrebooks.co.uk

To the Pankhurst spirit, past, present and future

CONTENTS

Figure 1: Scroll of thanks, illuminated address, designed by Sylvia,
signed by Emmeline and given to women released from prison,
from 1908. Source: People's History Museum, Manchester

WHERE DO WE START?

Over the last hundred years, women's opportunities in the UK[1] have improved dramatically. It is now illegal to pay women less for doing the same work as men. We now lead from the top of all professions, have become heads of the most traditional universities, been consecrated as bishops and launched into space. Women have become prime ministers – twice so far. We can have careers in the army, and box at the Olympics. Many of the taboos about our roles have changed, we have gained control over our fertility, and glass ceilings at work have been shattered. Meanwhile, our roles at home – as wives, mothers, daughters – have been transformed, by technical innovations, by the increasing engagement of men in the domestic sphere and by a greater valuation of us – and by us – of what it is to be a woman.

However – and that qualifier is screaming to be let loose – for every step forward there are forces pulling us back. Violence remains a real threat, women are still subordinated socially, politically and economically, and the massive resistance to change remains. Traditional sexist norms endure and often define our lives.

For anyone who wants to understand women's rights or be involved in one of the most exciting and important conversations of our time, basic questions include the following: how far have we really got? where are the areas of gains and regressions? how are these experienced by different categories of women? how relevant is the whole feminist discourse to women's identity today? There are also trickier questions. Why is it taking so long? How can we better understand resistance and engines of change and how can we speed things up? And finally what are our aims for the future?

Deeds Not Words tackles these questions. Published to coincide with the 100th anniversary of the Representation of the People Act – when some women were enfranchised for the first time – it provides an exploration of the changes to women's lives in Britain since then. It is interdisciplinary and eclectic in its approach, and is informed by statistics and a lifetime's work on women's rights in the UK and internationally. Most importantly, interviews and correspondence with women from all walks of life enrich the analysis. Quotations are attributed, sometimes just with a first name to provide anonymity.

The prologue is a personal take on the suffrage backdrop, recognising that as an author and a feminist activist I and many others have been shaped by my family's history. The book follows on with an investigative arc in five thematic chapters covering politics, money, identity, violence and culture. The sixth chapter on power then brings the analysis together by looking at what factors drive women's empowerment, examining case studies of change. After the conclusion, an epilogue takes us forward with the goals from 2018 to 2028 – the anniversary of equal franchise.

A few of the terms used throughout the book need defining, beginning with the concept of 'patriarchy'. This word came to be applied in the 1970s[2] and refers to the system of male dominance over women. It can be reinforced by individuals, collectively by society, and structurally by institutions, including by the government. There is some argument about whether or not patriarchy is a fixed universal phenomenon or whether there are different modes of oppression. For example, the extent to which we have moved from more private expressions of patriarchy to more public ones, and how the experiences of women are shaped by other factors such as age, wealth, ethnicity, religion and education.

Feminism is a recognition of the need to challenge gender-based discrimination. Though women have struggled and campaigned for their rights consistently over the centuries, the history of feminism in the UK and some other parts of the world is often framed in 'waves'.[3] We have had three such waves, and we are now within a fourth one. The first centred on the vote. This was seen to be the foundation – the key – to all other reforms and is associated with the period from the nineteenth century to the 1930s. This wave saw women carving out new roles for themselves in the public sphere and addressing issues such as employment and equal pay, education, prostitution, property rights within marriage, control over fertility, sexuality in marriage, the problem of domestic violence, the right to divorce. They were also involved in philanthropic work that helped lay the foundations for the welfare state. As with subsequent waves, the feminist challenge was for many women entwined with other social movements of the time.

The second wave, identified with the 1960s to late 1980s, was driven by resistance to a resurgence in the 1950s of the primacy of women as homemakers, which itself was a response to the strides towards equality women had made during the Second World War. The emphasis shifted from the political to the economic and personal – including reproductive rights and addressing violence against women. Campaigners used the same tactics as in the first wave but with direct action across a broader spectrum of concerns. New approaches, including consciousness-raising and feminist communities, flourished and we saw a greater institutionalisation within government of services for women.

'Bra-burning' is often associated with the second wave. In 1968, feminists protested at the annual Miss America contest, discarding items symbolic of women into a rubbish bin on the Atlantic City boardwalk in New Jersey. This was not a bra-burning event. A few bras did go into the bin, but so too did cosmetics, mops and other items. After the bra-burning myth had spread, some *were* burned but, in essence, the whole thing was a media creation.[4] Yet, to this day, feminist activism is ridiculed with the false bra-burning image.

The third wave of feminism is associated with the 1990s to 2010s.[5] It focused on women's sexual liberation, an assertive view of their sexual identity and social position, and valuing of their individual choices. This was in contrast to the previous waves of feminism, which tended to have women as victims. At the same time it drew attention to the way society constructed the female image. This third wave gave more attention to social divisions amongst women, particularly those of sexuality, race, colour and class. It involved initiatives at many levels, a wave full of undercurrents.

Then there is the fourth wave – or maybe not. Some reject the idea of a fourth wave and suggest that we are now in a post-feminist world.[6] They argue that feminism is no longer relevant because of the gains already made, or that the male and female essentialist position (i.e. the view that there is something fixed and universally different between men and women) has become irrelevant. Others draw parallels with post-structuralism and post-colonialism, to mean that relationships of power are still around but constructed differently. However, the idea that we are in a fourth wave has gained ground.[7]

This fourth wave is critical of the focus on the individual rather than the structural constraints on women, and it continues to push in all areas, particularly through online feminism. It has seen a return of the age-old tactic of huge demonstrations in many countries, linked to the defeat of Hillary Clinton and the inauguration of President Trump in the United States. The election result in the USA contributed to a sense of the world entering a period of global retrenchment on women's rights and the need to speak up.

The concept of intersectionality, a term coined by Kimberlé Crenshaw in 1989, is central to this wave.[8] It stresses how gender cuts across other forms of privilege and vulnerabilities. Beyond the waves, there are many other categories of feminism that speak to different political or personal starting points: traditional, radical, socialist, conservative, good and bad feminism.[9]

One aspect of the feminist agenda that has rippled through the ages has been what can be summarised as the trinity of objectives. The first is the goal of *equality* – women being equally represented and given the same opportunities. The second is the objective of *difference*, the specific attention to women as women. The third aspect is about *transformation*, the extent to which the feminist objective is not just about policies for women, but the reimagining of what the world could look like for all.[10]

A few other points interlink with those already made, but need to be mentioned explicitly. These are the extent to which feminism is inclusive or not of men and how what it is to be a woman relates to sexual and transgender identities. Generally, the feminist agenda has been focused on women's agency and their voice. However, some feminists have argued that heterosexual women have collaborated in ways that reinforce patriarchy; in other words, men are the problem, but so too are women who have relationships with them. Less radically, many feminists have argued for the importance of women-only safe spaces, particularly for survivors of violence. Others still have reasoned that nothing will change without being as inclusive as possible in our definition of women and involving men in feminism. I will return to all these controversies as we explore the web of influences on women's lives.

This book is about women, our lives, our experiences, what it has meant to be a woman, the continuity and the changes. It is about taking our experiences out of the shadows into the spotlight. Given the unapologetic focus on half the population, even as we increasingly challenge these simple gender binaries, I'm expecting that my readership will be predominantly female. I hope I do their stories and experiences justice but also that men will be willing to put themselves in women's shoes, to read and reflect on how the other half has lived.

The framework I return to at the end – and a constant theme throughout – involves the exploration of how women fight for space and influence in a wider ecosystem. This is most effective when it knits together three elements as tightly as possible: firstly, that of women's agency (i.e. the voice and actions of feminist individuals), secondly of structural or institutional change, and thirdly the more nebulous wider changes in social norms.

Which brings me to my objectives. The first is to pay homage to the women who have got us this far, with their names included wherever possible. The account is necessarily selective rather than exhaustive, a centenary of millions of women's lives squeezed into a few hundred pages. My second aim is to strengthen feminist activism as we move towards 2028 – the centenary of women gaining the parliamentary vote on equal terms with men.

The writing of social history is a political act and this book, with its call for increased vigilance and activism, is no exception. I hope it will amuse and infuriate, inform and promote debate. At the end of each of the five first chapters, I score and encourage others to evaluate the progress, from zero to five, in order to debate the journey to date and actively think about what we want from the future.

For the suffragettes, 'Deeds, Not Words' was a demand for action, not just placating promises of equality in due course. The slogan – which I have appropriated as the title for this book – remains a powerful rallying cry. We need to look back to better understand where we are going – and then we need to keep making waves.

PROLOGUE: 'WOMEN, IMBECILES AND CRIMINALS'[1]

This book takes 1918 as its starting point. The first year some women[2] won the right to vote in national elections. However, I could not launch into the packed centenary from 1918 to 2018, without a reflection on how we got to the vote in 1918. Furthermore, although the suffrage campaign, now identified as the defining element of first-wave feminism, was momentous in its own era, its influence and that of those involved continues to resonate in the ongoing feminist narrative.

The right to vote was symbolically huge – women saw it as the key which would unlock the door to life as full citizens and that this in turn would transform their status and position in society. It had been a very long time coming.

In 1832, as the Great Reform Act extended the vote to property owners for the first time, Mary Smith from Yorkshire became the first woman to petition for the parliamentary vote – and was, inevitably, ridiculed and ignored. However, individual acts aside, the symbolic starting point of organised suffrage activism is the 1866 petition of Barbara Bodichon, Emily Davies and Elizabeth Garrett. They collected 1,521 signatures[3] – a pretty impressive number today, in the age of the internet, and yet this was done in person and by hand, in less than a fortnight. The unsuccessful petition, brought to the House of Commons by the Liberal philosopher and politician John Stuart Mill, was to be the first of more than 16,000 petitions received by Parliament between 1866 and 1918. It then took another ten years before women were granted the vote on the same terms as men.[4]

Meanwhile, in 1881, the Isle of Man (a crown dependency of the UK) became the first country in the world to give some women (propertied single or widowed) the parliamentary vote. The vote followed the visit of two campaigners, Alice Scatcherd and its leader Lydia Becker, from the National Society for Women's Suffrage, which had been formed in 1867, who encouraged the demand for the vote on the island. The organisation's adviser in Manchester was Richard Marsden Pankhurst – my great-grandfather. In allowing women the vote, Tynwald (the legislature of the Isle of Man) was exerting its independence from Westminster, one politician saying: 'Why should we always wait to follow the footsteps of England?' Another: 'Matters of legislation here are chiefly, if not entirely, confined to home affairs and are not these the objects of peculiar interest to women?'[5]

Elsewhere in the Commonwealth – then the Empire – women in Australia (not including Aborigines) and in New Zealand (including Maoris) also obtained the vote. Women's suffrage was becoming a global if still far from inclusive concern, with feminist campaigners travelling across continents, exchanging letters and sharing debates, ideas and strategies. In 1911, three eminent women – Mrs Margaret Fisher, the wife of the Australian prime minister, Mrs Emily McGowen, the wife of the New South Wales premier, and Australia's leading feminist and suffragist Vida Goldstein – marched in London under a Commonwealth of Australia banner stating: 'Trust the Women Mother as I Have Done'. An Australian visitor to the UK wrote of a fellow visitor:

Being in London, she called at the office of the Anti-Suffrage League curious to know something of their views and methods. Ignorant of her nationality they talked to her kindly, but firmly, on the evils of the woman's vote and ended thus: – 'My dear, if you had the vote you would be quite changed. You would be unsexed.' 'Do you think so?' said the Australian. 'Then, perhaps it will interest you to know that I have had the vote for 15 years.'[6]

Muriel Matters, an Australian who joined the fight in Britain, commented a couple of years later:

> It is a hackneyed phrase – 'England is Conservative' – yet coming from a younger country, where the tides of life run high and pulses beat more strenuously, one can testify to the profundity of such a statement. Into the very bones and marrow of its sea-girt people has entered that insularity . . . Every fresh idea . . . is met with a resistance worthy of their best naval traditions.[7]

In the UK, two main wings of the women's suffrage campaign emerged. Firstly, the constitutional suffragists, united in 1897 as the National Union of Women's Suffrage Societies (NUWSS), which came to be led by Millicent Fawcett. They held meetings, lobbied, issued petitions and distributed leaflets. Then, in 1903, the Women's Social and Political Union (WSPU), dismissively nicknamed the 'suffragettes' by the *Daily Mail*, was established in Manchester by Emmeline Pankhurst, her daughters and a few friends. Emmeline loved the nickname and adopted it with pride. The WSPU started off closely linked to, though not affiliated with, the Independent Labour Party; and then embarked on a policy of independence, keeping the pressure on all parties but particularly on the Liberal government, targeting ministers who theoretically supported suffrage but did nothing to advance it.

The differences between the suffragists and the suffragettes have sometimes been overstated. Ultimately the women's organisations had the same goal – for women to vote on the same terms as men. Many women joined both constitutional and militant organisations – including offshoots such as the Women's Freedom League and the East London Federation of Suffragettes. These and many other groups often collaborated, particularly at a local level. The historian Krista Cowman reflected:

> The extraordinary diversity of organisations – over 50 listed in the suffrage paper *Votes for Women* by 1914 – shows just how many

women from different regions, occupations, religious and political groups wanted the vote. The need of many women to join a suffrage society that allowed them to retain another identity – as a Conservative, a Catholic, a teacher or an actress – also serves to remind us that the suffrage campaign was always about much more than just getting the vote.[8]

Over time, this diversity and complexity has been forgotten. In its place has developed a one-dimensional caricature of a suffragette. For much of the twentieth century, they were mocked and derided – the 1964 Disney classic *Mary Poppins*, for example, was part of a well-established pattern that ridiculed them. Yet it is suffragettes who continue to be remembered, not least because they had such a strong image and brand. The purple, white and green colours of the WSPU have become ubiquitous symbols of feminism. Increasingly, popular culture has embraced the activists, and treated them with much more respect than they had in their lifetime. At the same time, there is a tendency to gloss over their militancy – especially the most violent acts – in a way which diminishes and 'domesticates' them.

There has also been confusion about the different Emmelines and Emilys,[9] who have become merged in the public imagination into a single image of a woman marching, being chained to the railings in Westminster, before being knocked down by a horse at the Derby. Somehow it seems too much to remember more than one famous suffrage campaigner!

Thankfully, the movement has been well documented and continues to be researched. In this, a number of initiatives have been pivotal. Firstly, in 1926, a converted pub in Marsham Street, not far from the Houses of Parliament, became home to the library of the London Society for Women's Service. The society aimed to preserve the history of the vote and provide a resource for women in public life. Between 1953 and 2002 the library was known as the Fawcett Library. The collection consisted of books, personal memorabilia and archives, press cuttings and banners. Thanks to my mother, Rita

Pankhurst, it was found space in the City of London Polytechnic, later renamed London Metropolitan University, where she was the head librarian. Additional materials such as the Emily Wilding Davison archive were added and in 2002 the expanded library opened as the Women's Library. In 2013, the London School of Economics became the latest custodian of the collection.

Another initiative was that of the Suffragette Fellowship, formed in 1926 to keep alive the suffrage spirit, under the leadership of Edith How-Martyn. It organised annual programmes of events, published a newspaper, commissioned different commemorations, encouraged suffragettes to maintain their archives and publish auto-biographies.[10] Rose Lamartine Yates and her family safeguarded the growing collection, including from bomb damage. In 1950, it was taken over by what became the Museum of London. Beverley Cook, curator of Social and Working History at the Museum of London, explains: 'The Fellowship collection, which provides a unique insight into the women who dedicated their lives to the cause, has been regarded by the Museum as one of its most significant and inspirational collections.'[11]

Emmeline's old home in Nelson Street, Manchester, where the suffragette movement was born, for a long time remained abandoned but was then rescued and turned into the Pankhurst Centre. In 1987, I had the privilege of opening it with Barbara Castle. It has a small parlour, furnished to evoke the Pankhurst home, and hosts a number of women's organisations including Manchester Women's Aid.[12]

A suffrage legacy and continuing to work on the feminist agenda are also at the heart of the Fawcett Society, formed in 1953, which remains an influential feminist charity campaigning for women's rights and gender equality.[13] Its chief executive, Sam Smethers, reflected:

We know from our suffrage history that the road to equality and rights for women can be long and will face many obstacles. Sometimes it feels as if we are going backwards. But at its heart our cause is about justice and freedom. Our history gives us the strength to carry on the fight to face the challenges of today.[14]

Regarding representation of the suffragettes in popular culture, the 1975 BBC series *Shoulder to Shoulder* is fondly remembered by many women on whom it had a lasting influence, and the 2016 film *Suffragette* is having a similar effect on a younger generation.

There are four interlocking reasons for a cultural resurgence of interest in the suffragette campaigners. Firstly, their cause was just and most people now agree with women's suffrage, which has been granted on the same terms as men, almost universally. Women were finally given the right to vote and stand in municipal elections in Saudi Arabia in 2015, and the Vatican remains the only state where women do not have voting rights. In the preface to my grandmother Sylvia Pankhurst's first book, *The Suffragette*, published in 1911, her mother, Emmeline, wrote: 'When the long struggle for the enfranchisement of women is over, those who read the history of the movement will wonder at the blindness that led the Government of the day to obstinately resist so simple and obvious a measure of justice.'[15]

And wonder we do. The absurdity of the government's long-drawn-out opposition to women voting is expressed in a letter of 20 March 1912 by Myra Sadd Brown while serving a sentence of two months' hard labour for window-breaking at the War Office. She comments: 'Mrs Pankhurst and Ethel Smyth came back to this wing yesterday . . . Oh just fancy these two great women sitting sewing all afternoon on garments for prisoners – can you imagine anything more ironic, it certainly does seem that the world is topsy-turvy. Why not put Asquith and Sir E. Grey to blacking boots?'[16] The topsy-turvyness has, to some extent, been rectified.

Years later, reflecting on the struggle, another suffragette, Audrey Rees Webbe, remained both proud and incredulous. 'I wouldn't have missed it . . . Oh it was marvellous! Just marvellous a cloud had been lifted off you . . . Big celebration oh yes I mean it was so ludicrous because you were a woman, ridiculous, ridiculous, that everybody could vote except women, imbeciles and criminals.'[17]

The second reason for the interest in the suffragettes more especially is an appreciation of the unstinting courage and incredible physical and emotional strength the women showed. They faced private and public ridicule and years of setbacks from a brutal and repressive state. The campaign became 'for freedom or death' and the ultimate cost was paid by a few, including Mary Clarke, Emmeline Pankhurst's sister, who died in 1910 two days after being released from Holloway Prison, having been on hunger strike and force-fed. Then there was the momentous death of Emily Wilding Davison. She had been force-fed forty-nine times and following many other forms of defiance her dramatic act of resistance was at the Derby in 1913 when she was knocked over by the horse ridden by the king's jockey. She died soon after. Captured on Ciné film and replayed ever since, her martyrdom became an iconic image of the struggle.

What is striking is the contrast between the suffragettes' femininity, purposely reinforced by particularly feminine attire, with the brutality they faced. The tragedy of the sacrifices continues to be deeply moving. June Purvis, one of the foremost scholars of suffrage, commented:

> I can remember when I was filming for a TV programme about Emily Wilding Davison, being allowed to hold in my hand the small, brown leather purse that was on her person that day. It was a poignant moment. There is something about the physicality of suffragette ephemera that is deeply moving – the letter of a suffragette prisoner written on toilet paper with a blunted pencil because writing materials had been denied her, the small purse of a suffragette who died as she was making her protest.[18]

Modern-day feminists are often asked if they would have been suffragettes. Most respond they hope so, but they fear that they might not have had the courage to speak up and engage in direct action. Yet women still give thanks to the suffrage campaigners for their bravery and feel inspired to make something of their lives as a consequence. Dee, Annie, Alexandra and Noor provide examples of such testimonies:

It is through the acts of such women that I'm able to do my job today. (Dee Collins, chief constable, West Yorkshire Police)[19]

Just as I inherited my rights through the noble and dedicated effort of the Suffragette Movement, I feel it's incumbent upon me to engage and make a contribution towards global justice, protection and rights for women and girls around the world. (Annie Lennox, singer and campaigner)[20]

The Pankhurst legacy shows it's possible to make a revolutionary step for women, that equality and empowerment doesn't just make an impact in your lifetime, but affects generations of women to come. (Alexandra Thacker – aged seventeen)[21]

The Pankhurst legacy means I'm not afraid to have ambitions, not stupid to dream, not deluded for wanting to transform the world in which we live; they taught me if they can make it possible, I can make it possible. (Noor Al-Saffar – aged fourteen)[22]

The third reason for the embracing of the suffrage activists is that they appeal to people from all backgrounds and across the party-political spectrum. The campaigners themselves came from different walks of life, from factory workers to aristocrats, and they provide role models for women from the far left to the far right, and anywhere in between.

A final reason is that, in the sometimes colourless and drab roll call of history, the suffragettes showed panache and humour, using symbolism and merchandising – everything from cups and saucers, to games, jewellery and clothes. They took politics from the tea room, to the street, to the hustings, to wherever they could. They protested at theatres and cinemas. Holiday campaigns took place from the Isle of Man to the Kent coast; women interrupted church services to pray for hunger strikers and were violently ejected for their daring. Other tactics included a boycott of the 1911 census,[23] with women hiding or partying away from home. Many refused to fill in the census or commented on the form: 'No vote no census', 'If I am intelligent enough to fill in this census form, I can surely make an x on a ballot form' or 'Dumb Politically, Blind to the Census, Deaf to the Enumerator'. At least one respondent scribbled 'not enfranchised' under the disability column. Emily Wilding Davison hid in a broom cupboard in a crypt in the Palace of Westminster, recording the House of Commons as her location. Her protest managed to combine the imagery of the broom cupboard – a domestic feminine preserve – the religious associations of a crypt, especially important to many suffragettes, and the goal of residence in the Houses of Parliament.

There was also the sheer scale of the movement; around 30,000 marched in a procession to Hyde Park in 1907 and in 1908 it was estimated that 300,000 to 500,000 attended the mass rally – an extraordinary number even from today's perspective. And for each of those women, there were many more who could not participate – because of distance and cost, work or family commitments – yet who nevertheless supported the cause.

In general, male bastions of privilege were favoured targets for militant action. An official at the Tunbridge Wells cricket pavilion unwisely quipped: 'It is not true that women are banned from the pavilion. Who do you think makes the teas?' The suffragettes responded by burning it down.

That sense of empowerment, of women rising up, making friends with common interests, planning, fundraising, campaigning . . . and then starting all over again defines the movement. This was done patiently until the law, and more critically, social norms changed. As Lady Rhondda put it:

The vote was really a symbol. And the militant fight itself did more to change the status of women – because it did more to alter our own opinion of ourselves – than ever the vote did. In actual fact, in those years we were changing the attitude of a country – nay, of the world . . . That was infinitely worth the doing . . . Alter a nation's habit of mind, and the laws will alter of themselves.[24]

What is not so well known now is how much the campaigners continued to make their mark after women got the vote in 1918. In fact, the 1920s have often been portrayed as a period of stagnation. Yet nothing could be further from the truth. Women became organisers for social, economic, political and religious reform; they became trade unionists, journalists, writers, teachers and doctors. They sustained their radicalism, taking it into their homes, relationships and families. Reflecting the many differences between women beyond the commonality of the vote, some became advocates of the British Empire and powerful allies of the government, others worked across national boundaries for peace, internationalism and humanitarian causes. There was also a proliferation of voluntary groups and societies working for improved welfare and living conditions led and sustained by women who had been politicised by the suffrage movement.

As for the Pankhursts, in the history of social change it is almost unheard of to have a mother and her daughters lead a movement. The Pankhursts were brought together by their feminist beliefs, but they were, over time, torn apart: by arguments such as how far to extend women's franchise, whether leadership should be democratic or authoritarian; whether to campaign only on the vote, or bring in wider women's rights considerations; how closely to link with other social reform agendas; whether to have a political affiliation or stay neutral. They were also split by how to respond to other events, including the world wars. These schisms within a single family and despite a common feminist agenda are telling. Their story highlights the complexity of the intersection between gender, party and global politics, religion, sexual rights and family structure. Emigration is also important to their story since they all ended up living in different countries and continents: Emmeline in Canada; Christabel in the United States; Adela in Australia and Sylvia in Ethiopia.

Once the First World War was declared, Emmeline and Christabel stopped overtly campaigning for the vote, believing they could further the cause by supporting the war effort. They became staunch nationalists, making friends of old political foes including Lloyd George, and campaigned for women to play a full part in waging war – not on the front line, but in the factories and on the land, sustaining the nation through the war effort. They were involved in shaming men into enlisting to prove their masculinity and commitment to king and country, partly by giving out white feathers and ostracising men who had not signed up.[25] As part of the war effort, for a while Emmeline also adopted four orphaned 'war babies' and campaigned for other families to do the same. At the end of 1917, Emmeline and Christabel formed the Women's Party, the first attempt at an independent women's parliamentary party. It espoused patriotism, practical solutions to the war such as reducing food wastage, introducing food kitchens and cooperative housing, abolishing trade unions, and adopting progressive feminist policies. These included equal pay for equal work, equal marriage and divorce laws, maternity benefits, equal rights for parents and equality in public service.[26] Christabel stood and lost in the Smethwick constituency in Staffordshire in 1918 as a Women's Party candidate, gaining 48 per cent of the vote but losing by 778 votes. Soon after, the party disintegrated and both women embarked on new phases in their lives.

Emmeline went on to travel extensively in the United States and became a Canadian citizen. She came back to England and joined the Conservative Party, planning to stand for elections. However, she fell ill and died on 14 June 1928, the final stage for the Equal Franchise Bill of 1928 taking place on the day of her funeral.[27]

Emmeline is regularly named in lists of the most influential people of the twentieth century.[28] On 14 July each year, her official birthday,[29] the Suffragette Fellowship – which had raised funds for and overseen the building of a statue of her in Victoria Tower Gardens beside the Houses of Parliament – started the tradition of putting purple, green and white flowers by her statue. The tradition is now continued by the Conservative Women's Association, which annually lays a wreath there. In 1968, Emmeline was the first non-royal female to be commemorated on a stamp, as part of the fifty-year anniversary of 1918. In 2015 people voted overwhelmingly for Emmeline in a competition spearheaded by Councillor Andrew Simcock to celebrate Mancunian women. A statue of her made by the sculptor Hazel Reeves was unveiled in St Peter's Square on 14 December 2018.[30]

Christabel, Emmeline's oldest daughter, was the strategist and the family member most committed to militancy. In 1912, she escaped imprisonment for suffragette activities, fleeing to France. She also campaigned on 'purity for men', i.e. chastity outside marriage given the dangers from sexually transmitted diseases, which would be blamed on women. After her failure to get into Parliament, she moved to California in 1921 and became a prominent member of the Protestant Second Adventist movement. She returned to the UK in the 1930s and, in a complete reversal of fortune, was honoured by King George V as a 'Dame Commander of the Order of the British Empire' before returning to the United States where she died on 13 February 1958. The University of Manchester is opening a research institute, the Christabel Pankhurst Institute for Research in Health, Technology and Innovation, in her honour.

Adela, Emmeline's youngest daughter, had been a tireless northern activist of the WSPU. She was shipped off to Australia by Emmeline in 1914 for health reasons and because Emmeline was fearful of emerging political differences between them. There she married and with her husband, Tom Walsh, was active in the militant Seamen's Union and, in 1920, became a founding member of the Australian Communist Party. Although she remained a lifelong pacifist, her political views moved from the far left to the far right. She became involved in the Australian Women's Guild of Empire in 1927 to campaign against Communism, safeguard family and Christian values, and provide support to working-class women in the face of the economic depression. Subsequently she was involved in the anti-British Australia First Movement and in 1942 was the only Australian woman to be interned by a government fearful of her and her husband's Japanese sympathies, although these were based on their pacifism. Adela died in Sydney on 23 May 1961. Her granddaughter Susan Hogan shared:

> Because Adela alienated both sides of politics she has a lot of critics, but her optimism about the inherent goodness of human nature, her trusting nature and generosity inspired a protective love in everyone who was not ideologically driven to oppose her. People still living who knew her remember her with affection and respect. One small maybe trivial example of her influence that I was reminded of as I stooped to pick up a discarded glass bottle on my walk before writing to you this morning. I always collect trash as I walk especially in community space: a habit started when Adela told the unwilling eight-year-old me that it didn't matter that I didn't drop the trash, our responsibility to the public benefit was more important than how I felt.[31]

My grandmother Sylvia was Emmeline's middle daughter. She was the artist behind many suffragette designs and campaigned in the East End of London, including by editing a series of newspapers, and at the same time looked for solutions to the practical needs of impoverished women. Like a number of others, she was expelled from the WSPU by Christabel and Emmeline but continued the work regardless, under the new name of the East London Federation of Suffragettes. She was a pacifist in the First World War, sympathetic to the Easter Rising in Ireland, and was quick to speak out about the danger of fascism prior to the Second World War. By then, Sylvia had become increasingly involved in domestic and international left-wing politics. Mary Davis, who wrote about her radical politics, explains:

> Sylvia Pankhurst made a substantial contribution as one of the first propagandists for Bolshevism in Britain, founding the People's

Russian Information Bureau. Her group, the Workers' Socialist Federation (WSF), was the first in Britain to affiliate to the Third International (Comintern) and Sylvia herself attended its 2nd congress in 1920. Lenin makes no less than 10 major references to Sylvia Pankhurst – more than any other British revolutionary socialist. She and her group were part of the unity talks to form the Communist Party of Great Britain which she joined briefly in 1921.[32]

Sylvia had a son, with her partner, the anarchist Italian refugee Silvio Corio, 'out of wedlock' partly because, like other radical feminists, she felt marriage epitomised gender inequality. Following her experience of childbirth, she became concerned about improving maternity provision for the poor. She lived and worked with Silvio, a typographer and journalist, until his death in 1954. Their son was my father, Richard Keir Pethick Pankhurst. The author Shirley Harrison remembered:

> I grew up in Winston Churchill's constituency of Woodford Green when, to my parents' dismay, Sylvia was living four roads away from my home. On the way to Sainsbury's I had to pass the house and was warned by my mother to walk past quickly on the far side of the road 'just in case *she* appears'.[33]

Harrison ended up writing her neighbour's biography many years later, 'in admiration'.

Sylvia was the first British editor to employ a black journalist, Claude McKay, a Jamaican writer and poet, and was involved in numerous international initiatives including the pan-African movement. When Ethiopia was invaded by Italy in 1935 and the League of Nations failed to act, she took up the cause, becoming an ally of the Ethiopian Emperor, Haile Selassie, who was exiled in Bath. In 1936 she had a stone anti-war monument erected in front of her home, to highlight the horrors of bombing on civilians. At the age of seventy-four, Sylvia went to live in Addis Ababa. There, together with her son Richard, she continued to write and edit, for a cultural magazine this time – the *Ethiopia Observer*. She also fundraised for Ethiopia's first teaching hospital, and was involved in establishing the Social Service Society. She died in Ethiopia on 27 September 1960 and was given a state funeral and buried in front of the Holy Trinity Cathedral in Addis Ababa, the first foreigner given this honour and laid in the area reserved for Ethiopian patriots.

Remembrances of Sylvia Pankhurst in the UK include an annual lecture in her name in Sheffield and a Memorial Hall and Green in Woodford, East London. In Tower Hamlets, at Mile End Hospital, a Sylvia Pankhurst Centre provides contraception and sexual health services. Her paintings of women at work and some of the suffragette materials she designed were exhibited at Tate Britain in 2013, with four paintings being acquired in 2018 for their permanent collection thanks to a donation from the Denise Coates Foundation. The collection was also shown at the Manchester Museum of Art and other locations during the centenary year. A dance, hip hop, soul and funk piece called *Sylvia* has also been co-written by Kate Prince and Priya Parmar for the centenary. A statue of Sylvia is due to be erected on Clerkenwell Green in Islington and Manchester Metropolitan University has inaugurated a Gender Research Centre in her name. Kate Cook and Julia Rouse, at the Centre, reflected:

Sylvia's legacy and spirit act as a strong rallying point for our research and activism and we are hugely proud to be associated with her legacy.[34]

The Pankhurst family name and legacy continue. My father, Richard, was a scholar and campaigner for Ethiopia's cultural heritage. In 2017, he joined his mother, Sylvia, at her final resting place, following a state funeral honouring him for his outstanding work for Ethiopia. My mother, Rita Pankhurst, as mentioned above, was involved in ensuring the existence of the Women's Library and has written about Ethiopian women in history. My brother is an anthropologist living in and writing about Ethiopia.

I have been shaped by my Pankhurst background and the British and Ethiopian connections. My personal life, academic background and career have had international feminism at their core. Within this theme, two events brought me even closer to my forebears. The first was an invitation to meet Danny Boyle, which resulted in my and my daughter's involvement in the Opening Ceremony of the 2012 London Olympics. We joined others selected to represent the suffragettes, stayed in touch through a Facebook group, and continued to campaign and march together as the Olympic Suffragettes. Aceil and Lesley, two members of the group, shared their experience as follows:

> I had never identified myself as a feminist; to me, it was a niche group of women who represented something that I felt alienated from, especially as I have never seen my gender hold me back – thank you mum and dad. But joining the suffragettes at the London Olympics, and indeed on our ventures since, I have learnt that my privilege stems from others fighting for my rights and saying this is not right. I wear the feminist badge with honour now and I would encourage others to do the same.[35]

> There was much talk around the Olympics about legacy and for me this legacy – our legacy – has been most unexpected. It's been about new and continuing friendships and an awareness of the issues that still affect women today and knowing that collectively – continuing the work of the suffragettes – change can happen.[36]

A couple of years later, I was contacted by Sarah Gavron, who was directing the film *Suffragette*. I provided approval, support and advice, and my daughter and I had small cameo parts in the film. There followed a few years of its promotion across five continents.

Throughout my life, I have been asked what the suffragettes would make of how far we have come and what I thought. Based on the increasing interest and my own feminist journey it felt like time to answer these questions. The result is this book with its long lens looking back, but also one holding a magnifying glass to the present – and with expectations of the future. It is a personal – but also a collaborative – account.

Figure 2: Olympic suffragettes in front of Parliament during UK Feminista's feminist lobby of Parliament 2012. Photographer: Guy Bell

POLITICS

'If we allow women in the House where will this emancipation
end?' (Earl Ferrers, House of Lords Debates)[1]

Caring for children and other members of the family has traditionally been thought of as the woman's role, while men as well as being
head of the household have also claimed the public world. There
are exceptions to the pattern: matriarchal societies such as the
Mosuo in China, the Akan of Ghana, the Bribri of Costa Rica and
the legendary Amazons of central Eurasia. Even in patriarchal societies, some queens have ruled, such as the female pharaohs in Egypt,
Maria Theresa in Austria, Catherine the Great in Russia, Empress
Dowager Cixi in China and in Ethiopia, Makeda, the legendary
Queen of Sheba. In the UK, Boudicca reigned around 60 AD and
became an icon of British defiance as the Celtic queen who fought
the Romans.

Queen Elizabeth I was portrayed as 'Gloriana' and the 'Virgin
Queen'. During the approach of the Spanish Armada in 1588 she
is said to have declared: 'I know I have the body of a weak and
feeble woman, but I have the heart and stomach of a king, and of
a king of England too; and think foul scorn that Parma or Spain,
or any prince of Europe, should dare to invade the borders of my
realm.'[2]

On the other hand, Queen Victoria, despite her position as Queen
of the British Empire, wrote in 1870: 'Let women be what God
intended, a helpmate for man, but with totally different duties and
vocations.'[3] The same year she commented in a private letter: 'Lady

Amberley [a suffragist] ought to get a good whipping. Were women to unsex themselves by claiming equality with men, they would become the most hateful, heathen and disgusting of beings and would surely perish without male protection.'[4]

Notwithstanding their success as monarchs, both Queen Elizabeth I and Queen Victoria were uncomfortable with challenges to the social order.

Times are a changing, however. Since the accession of Queen Elizabeth II in 1952, the idea that a queen needs to portray herself as a surrogate male has become unconscionable. Elizabeth is the world's longest-serving monarch, male or female, the sovereign figurehead in more than thirty countries. Thirteen British prime ministers have had regular meetings with her and she has exercised her right to advise and be consulted. As with her predecessors, the Queen has not been overtly associated with promoting women's rights. Nevertheless, notable symbolic acts have demonstrated her willingness to make a point, witness her decision to drive King Abdullah of Saudi Arabia in her Land Rover on her estate, knowing that women were prohibited from driving in his country. Journalist Emma Barnett writes: 'In a world still dominated by men at the upper echelons of society, there has been something comforting and bloody brilliant about having a female monarch at the helm of our country – year in, year out.'[5]

The Right to Vote

The 1918 Act giving some women the right to vote was passed, resoundingly, by 385 votes to 55 in the House of Commons then led by a coalition (Conservative and Liberal) government, and by 134 to 71 in the Lords. The years of conflict over the matter had exhausted all parties and, according to some historians, a resolution had begun to look likely when war broke out.[6] This cataclysmic event changed society in many ways: old hierarchies of gender, class and age waned. Women took on men's work as well as looking after families. A number of women's groups had been actively campaigning to support the war effort; at the same time, the demand for women's franchise had not gone away.[7] Some campaigners allied themselves to Liberal and independent-minded Conservative MPs, while others worked with those Labour MPs who advocated the inclusion of women in future reform bills.[8] By 1918, even the 'dinosaurs' in Parliament had changed their minds, and given that women were enfranchised in an increasing number of countries around the world it was embarrassing to be left behind.

Only those aged over thirty who were householders, wives of householders, occupiers of property with an annual rent of £5 or more, or graduates of British universities were given the vote in 1918. The Act also ensured that men were the majority of the electorate since all men aged over twenty-one and those who had turned nineteen and were serving during the war were also given the vote. Fearing the nation could be overly influenced by women given the losses from the war and because women generally live longer than men, the Conservative government only enfranchised wealthier and older women. Their assumption was that this group were more likely to vote Conservative. Self-interest as the driving motive behind policy change or policy obstruction resurfaces time and again. The exclusion of younger and poorer women – those who had done most of the war work – is at odds with the standard argument that the vote was a 'reward' for their service. That same year, with little fuss, the Parliament (Qualification of Women) Act allowed women over twenty-one to stand for Parliament. The result was the anomaly that a woman could be too young to vote and yet stand to be a Member of Parliament.

Suffrage organisations continued to lobby, and held protest meetings and parades to highlight this absurdity and demand equal franchise, joined now by the women MPs already in Parliament, and across party lines. The illogical age difference could not be sustained and despite opposition from diehards such as Winston Churchill – and the *Daily Mail* – equal voting rights were eventually granted by the Conservative government in 1928.[9]

In the meantime, once it was clear that women would make up part of the electorate, Parliament started to take women's interests more seriously. Between 1918 and full franchise in 1928, more than twenty Acts that concerned women and children were drawn up. These included ones addressing maternity and child welfare; making it unlawful to bar women from public office or certain civil and judicial positions; equal grounds for divorce; strengthening mothers' rights and claims over their children; and pensions to widows.[10]

In 1918, 8.5 million women in the UK, just under 40 per cent of the electorate, were added to the 13 million male electorate; then in 1929, the first election where all women over twenty-one could vote, for the first time there were more women voters, 15 million, compared with 13.5 million men.

Frustratingly, the national turnout data was not initially gender disaggregated.[11] However, from when we have the breakdown to the present, there seems to be little overall gender difference to turnout figures. For example, in 1992 78 per cent of women and 77 per cent of men voted, and in the 2015 election the 1 per cent difference was reversed with 67 per cent of men and 66 per cent of women.[12] Historically much more relevant than gender have been other socio-economic factors: with, for instance, the older electorate voting consistently more than the younger ones.[13] Even in 2017, declared as one in which the young were 'switched onto' politics, while 57 per cent of eighteen- and nineteen-year-olds voted, for those aged seventy-plus the figure was 84 per cent.[14]

Despite women gaining the right to vote, attitudes persisted that women did not, or should not, have their own political opinion. For example, Ann Goulden, a descendant of one of Emmeline's brothers, shared: 'Soon after I was first married, there was an election. I was studying the various parties' pamphlets, when [my husband] informed me not to bother reading them as I would be voting as he did. Needless to say, I voted as I wanted, after all he couldn't follow me into the booth. This was 1958.'[15]

There is still a perception that women's political views may be more malleable than men's.[16] In 2015 at least twice as many women as men were estimated to be swing voters.[17] Why? Is it because they are uninterested? Or because the political system does not seem to represent women's interests? Conversely, why do men have greater certainty? Are their identities more linked to a particular party through work and social circles? Or do they place a higher priority on reaching a viewpoint and then not revisiting it?

I am regularly asked what my great-grandmother Emmeline and the other suffragettes would make of the fact that millions of women who could vote still fail to do so. My response is that it is surprising that around the same proportion of women as men are voting, given how little Parliament looks like them and reflects their interest. There is also a catch-22 situation, with those who feel least represented and least valued being the least likely to vote. Historically this has included the young and the poor abdicating the little power that they have. For ourselves and for the sake of those who came before us we must all take responsibility, grab opportunities and create new ones for the generations to come.[18]

What party did women vote for and how has this changed? Overall, the pattern in the UK is that more women than men have voted Conservative.[19] The Conservative–Labour gender gap has been mostly less than 10 per cent, with variations along the way. The difference decreased over time; however, it has been unusual.[20] In other countries, even where conservative parties initially gave women the vote, women have tended to vote for the left – the explanation being that women's unequal role in society makes them more progressive.[21] The UK follows this trend in the smaller parties, as more women support the left-leaning Greens, and fewer support UKIP, which has appealed mostly to older, male, working-class, white and less educated voters.[22] However, lest we fall into simple stereotyping, it was a woman, Rotha Lintorn-Orman, who set up the first fascist movement in the UK, the British Fascisti in 1923.[23]

As well as the older regional parties, a newcomer to the wider political scene is the Women's Equality Party (WEP) formed by journalist Catherine Mayer and broadcaster/comedian Sandi

Toksvig. As Sandi explained: 'I was giving a talk in 2015 about the suffragettes . . . those magnificent women who fought so hard for the right for women in Britain to vote . . . and as I'm talking, what I realised was, this was not a history I was giving, this was not something where the job was done, this was something where there is so much still to do.'[24]

The party aims to be a cross-party pressure group and women and men are encouraged to belong to WEP without abandoning other party affiliations. In 2018, it had 45,000 members. This contrasted with 8,000 Welsh Plaid Cymru members, 23,600 UKIP, 99,200 Liberal Democrat, 124,000 Conservative, 125,500 SNP, and 540,000 Labour.[25]

As for standing to be a Member of Parliament, it was not until a few weeks before the general election of 1918 that women knew they could be candidates. Out of the 1,623 candidates, 17 women stood, and only one succeeded: the suffragette and socialist Countess Constance Markievicz, as a member of Sinn Féin. She did not take her seat because Sinn Féin were boycotting Parliament. Markievicz had taken part in the Easter Rising as a member of the Irish Citizen Army, a revolutionary socialist militia, and was the most senior woman to have done so. She was sentenced to death for her part in it, though this was commuted to a life sentence. Released under a general amnesty, she was then re-imprisoned for sedition and fought her Westminster campaign from prison. Women effectively ran her campaign in her absence, and Markievicz herself hoped that her constituency could be made into 'a rallying ground for women and a splendid centre for constructive work by women'.[26]

There are a number of ironies here. First, because she did not take her seat, symbolising the problem of women's invisibility even when they are elected. Second, with the Irish question, the first woman to be elected to Westminster represented those who challenged Westminster's authority. Third, she may not have been able to take her seat anyway because, as a woman, she had lost her British nationality on marrying a foreigner – even ignoring the fact that she had been convicted of treason. After Irish independence, she was elected to the revolutionary Dáil and served as Minister for Labour 1919–22 – the first female Cabinet minister in Europe. It would be another sixty years before another woman would serve in a Cabinet in the Irish Free State or Republic.[27]

The irony continues: in 1919, the first woman MP to take her seat was an American, Lady Nancy Astor, married to an American-born British politician. She had not been involved in the suffrage campaign. In her maiden speech she commented: 'I know that it was very difficult for some hon. Members, to receive the first lady MP into the House. It was almost as difficult for some of them as it was for the lady MP herself to come in. Hon. Members, however, should not be frightened of what Plymouth sends out into the world. After all, I suppose when Drake and Raleigh wanted to set out on their venturesome careers, some cautious person said, "Do not do it; it has never been tried before. You stay at home, my sons, cruising around in home waters".'[28] Amongst other influences, she successfully introduced a bill raising the legal age of drinking from fourteen to eighteen. She would receive 2,000 letters a week from women, and worked on building a women's voice within Parliament.[29]

Her experience was repeated in the election of 1923, when the anti-suffragist Scottish Unionist Party MP Katharine Stewart-Murray, the Duchess of Atholl, became the first woman MP in Scotland and the first to serve in a Conservative and Unionist government. She explained the problem that: 'The women of this country have a charming habit of thinking that it is they who have sent you there and that you are only responsible to them.'[30] Another political maverick, she was nicknamed the Red Duchess because of her international policies, including the evacuation to the UK of 3,840 Basque children in 1936 at the start of the Spanish Civil War. Her stand against appeasement forced a by-election in 1938, which she narrowly lost.[31]

The first female in Cabinet was Margaret Bondfield, elected in 1923 and Minister of Labour in 1929. She also became the first woman privy counsellor. After losing her post at the next general election, Bondfield continued as a trade unionist and a social reformer, working on urban poverty.[32]

Ellen Wilkinson, a suffragist, became the Labour MP for Middlesbrough East in 1924 and then for Jarrow. She is remembered most for initiating the 1936 Jarrow March against unemployment and poverty. She ensured that interest rates on loans and repossessions were curbed in the Hire Purchase Act of 1938. She was nicknamed 'The Shelter Queen', having overseen the provision of indoor 'Morrison shelters' against bombing during the war. In 1945, she became the first woman Minister for Education, raising the school leaving age to fifteen and bringing in free school milk and school meals.[33]

With some exceptions, the first women politicians served for less than three years. Until the end of the Second World War there were no more than fifteen at any one time. Women's representation improved very, very slowly over the decades until the 1997 election with a doubling of women MPs from 60 to 120, an increase from 9 to 18 per cent of the total. The euphoria was only slightly dented by the fact that this was still a long way from 50 per cent, and by the *Daily Mail* photo caption of the women Labour MPs as 'Blair's Babes'.

In the 2010 election, 73 new women MPs were elected. True to form, the *Daily Mail* called them the 'Cameron Cuties'. In 2015, only a total of 456 women had joined the Commons, just surpassing the number of men sitting in Parliament at that point.[34] By June 2017, the proportion of women had risen to 32 per cent and the Cabinet had 26 per cent women.[35] Compared with other countries in the world, the UK was still ranked a lowly 43rd out of 192 in terms of female representation in the lower chamber.[36] Meanwhile, in 2017, female representation in the Lords – of which more later on – was also only 26 per cent,[37] not much more than the global average, which was 23 per cent.[38] The lack of diversity in both houses also applies to all other socio-economic characteristics.[39]

In the last twenty-five years or so, with some fits and starts, the different parties have gradually moved towards the use of quotas to counter the over-representation of men in Parliament. Labour implemented a range of different policies from the 1992 elections, the most effective being to have all-women shortlists for half the winnable seats. This resulted in an increase from 37 to 101 women

Labour MPs.[40] However, the strategy was successfully challenged under the 1975 Sex Discrimination Act, the result being that fewer women MPs were elected in 2001. After internal lobbying the Sex Discrimination (Election Candidates) Act 2002 was introduced allowing positive discrimination until 2030. At the 2017 elections 45 per cent of Labour MPs elected were women and a target was set for 50 per cent by the next election.

Meanwhile, in 2001, the Liberal Democrats – with only 3 women among its 52 MPs – rejected quotas. Shirley Williams accused her party of being 'backward and old fashioned'.[41] They subsequently adopted a target of 40 per cent women in winnable seats, but did not devise any mechanism to make this happen.[42] In 2017, in its much diminished party, 4 women, representing 33 per cent of the Liberal Democrats, were elected. In the meantime the SNP, which was implementing quotas, had overtaken the Lib Dems as the third party in Parliament. In 2017, there were 12 women SNP MPs, 34 per cent of their party.[43]

There were only 17 female Conservative MPs in 2005, representing 9 per cent. David Cameron started to introduce so-called 'A-lists' in 2009 to increase diversity despite opposition including from some female MPs.[44] In 2010, the number increased to 49 and then to 67 in 2017, representing 21 per cent, the highest percentage to date in that party.[45]

In 2017, a Women and Equality Committee report recommended that political parties in Britain should legislate for at least 45 per cent female candidates. The recommendation was rejected. In frustration, the Conservative MP and Chair of the Committee Maria Miller commented:

> It's very disappointing the Government rejected all of the Committee recommendations for getting more women in Parliament. Political parties are not the only agent of change – Parliament itself and Government itself have crucial roles to play. They can't bury their heads in the sand![46]

Despite the obstacles, across parties, the view has gained ground that whether you like it or not, quotas work.[47] This is especially the case with a 'quota-plus' system in which parties also recruit, train, mentor and support those who come forward.[48] Greater transparency in the candidate selection process including the need to publish the gender and ethnicity of candidates in political parties would also shine a light on where problems persist. The voting system itself also has a significant influence, with proportional representation (PR) tending to increase women's presence. Despite suggestions from 1917 onwards, Westminster continues to operate a 'first past the post' scheme.[49]

Comparing the main parties, can an assessment be made of which has been the more beneficial for most women over the last hundred years? For the Conservatives, the ideological link to gender has often been with the image of the sensible housewife looking after a household budget, and as a party that is fiscally responsible, in favour of free trade, 'choice' and people being left to get on with fulfilling their economic potential. The Conservatives have given the nation not just its first female prime minister but also its second one. We have had progressive Conservative governments, for example in the 1920s – with numerous policies aimed at women – and regressive ones, as with the public-sector cuts of the 1980s and from 2010.

The Liberals, operating within a less materialist explanation of gender inequality, were the first to develop a women's wing and it was the Social Democratic Party that first considered but did not implement a quota system. They have been socially progressive in policies addressing gender-based discrimination and have pushed for proportional representation.

The Labour years 1997–2010 were arguably the closest so far to a feminist government, with the introduction of a Cabinet minister for women and initiatives addressing violence against women – including the Sexual Offences Act and the Equality Act. Overall, the left has tended to see class inequality in material terms. The assumption has always been that strengthening workers' rights and combating poverty would address women's concerns since they are overly represented among the poor. But this position has ignored how women can be oppressed within their own class. The Labour Party's historic close ties to trade unions and a male-dominated group-think has alienated many women.

Trade Unions

The story of women in trade unions mirrors that of their struggle for inclusion, voice and power within other parts of our democracy, and most trade unions fought against women's interests, in order to safeguard men's jobs. There were exceptions, with women significantly involved in the textile industry in the North of England, and a small number of women's unions, including the National Association of Women Civil Servants, which disbanded in 1959, and the National Union of Women Teachers, disbanded in 1961.

Unions started to take women's interests more seriously from the 1970s. However, by that time the power of the unions was curtailed and their very survival under threat because of government policies including rules limiting secondary strike action.[50] Numerically, the figures for trade union membership by 2015 were very similar to those a hundred years before, at 6.5 million. Given the growth of the workforce during the intervening century, this represents a shrinking percentage of workers. Now only 28 per cent of female employees and 22 per cent of male employees belong to trade unions, the greater percentage of women in stark contrast to the early years.[51]

As leaders, women trade unionists remain the exception, though sometimes particularly powerful ones. The TUC appointed its first woman General Secretary in 144 years: Frances O'Grady in 2013. She rose through the ranks, working and raising a family as a single mother, and championed the rights of part-time workers and the low-paid. Even where the overall power and structure of unions have not shifted, they often have a kernel of activist women in feminist sections.

In the Labour Party, possibly because of the valuing of those who are part of the collective and a dislike of individualism, women – who by definition are in some senses different – have not been able to belong enough to get the top job.[52] Even in the recent past the party has had to fend off accusations of misogyny.[53] Nevertheless, Labour remains a party of social reform in ways that have benefited the vast majority of women and they have had a greater percentage of female MPs than the other major parties. Regional parties have tended to be similar to Labour in their left-wing leanings.

The welfare state, introduced from 1945, generated many benefits for women, but it operated within a framework where heads of households were assumed to be male. And it is not necessarily the party in power when a particular law is passed that should be thanked for beneficial changes. The 1975 Sex Discrimination Act was implemented by the Labour Party, but was based on reports from select committee work under the previous Conservative government. To some extent, policy paths continue and are extended by different parties once a precedent is set. For instance, the Labour government introduced the Civil Partnership Act in 2004 and then the Conservative–Liberal Democrat coalition went one step further, changing this to equal marriage under the Marriage (Same Sex Couples) Act in 2013.

Over the years party manifestos show differences in targeting the female voter. In 1918, when there was a fear that women would vote as a bloc, policies were geared to women's interests. Once it became clear their voting patterns were not so different from men's, the policies 'dried up', although external events including the financial crash in 1929 and the rise of fascism in Europe contributed to the crowding out of women's concerns. The parties have, however, continued to woo women voters. Labour in 1997 commenced a national 'Listening to Women' campaign, which led to some of their key policies including flexible working regulations, enhanced childcare provision and strategies to deal with teenage pregnancy. In 2005, they introduced a women MPs' battle bus that toured the country; and did so again in 2015 – this time the bus was pink to gain more attention. The mainstream media was happy to oblige, denouncing it as 'sexist twaddle'.[54]

The record of any one government is the result of different influences at play. As a positive example, the 2010–15 Conservative–Liberal Democrat coalition introduced greater flexibility in parental leave, the right to request flexible working for all, greater support with childcare and a number of Acts addressing violence against women. On the negative side, most notable was the attempted inclusion of rape anonymity for the accused, which created a huge backlash and was dropped, and the decision to cut public services rather than increase taxes, a choice with gendered ramifications. There was also the episode of David Cameron's exchange with Angela Eagle when he told her to 'Calm down, dear', then batted it away as a joke, rather than apologising.[55]

If there is a dominant theme, it is that a male-dominated Parliament has been slow to take seriously the concerns of women MPs. The protracted process of getting equal pay legislation, of which more in the next chapter, is evidence of how sluggish the law has been. Arguably without exception – both in presentation and content – the gender agenda has been an add-on rather than embedded in policymaking.

Women's Support from Their Parties?

Even before women entered Parliament, they were involved in party-political organisations. Women's branches provided essential support to parties in canvassing, fundraising and generally fuelling the workings of the political machinery. The women's wings were sometimes also able to hold the parties to account on gender concerns. They were less successful at forming gender-based alliances across parties.

The Women's Liberal Federation set up in 1877 was, in the years leading up to 1918, at odds with its party's leadership, which opposed the women's franchise. Nevertheless, it had influence on the party before and after, and particularly towards the end of the 1920s when it had around 100,000 members. In more recent years it supported equal pay, family allowances and divorce law reform, with some individual male politicians – such as David Owen MP and Lord Lester – important allies at key moments.

By 1929, the Women's Labour League had 250,000 members in over 1,800 sections. This was a Labour pressure organisation founded in 1906. Women were over half the members of the League and feminist concerns were regularly presented at Labour Women's Conferences.[56] How they were received within the national policy-making body varied. Successes included the establishment in the 1980s of the Labour Women's Action Committee, the Parliamentary Labour Party Women's Committee and the Labour Women's Network, which helped to create the influential position of Minister for Women. In 1993, the 'Assisted Places Scheme' failed with its attempt to require ballot papers to include women. Tellingly, it became labelled 'the tarts' charter'.[57] More successful was Emily's list UK, launched by the MP Barbara Follett to provide financial support to female Labour candidates, on the 75th anniversary of the first right to vote. A recent initiative has been the 2016 launch of the Jo Cox Women in Leadership programme, which aims to encourage and support Labour women through a training scheme.

In the Conservative Party, what is now called the Conservative Women's Organisation had 4,000 branches by 1924 and is said to have had a million members by 1928.[58] It continues as a separate body and has pushed for policies relating to women's concerns such as low-cost housing, equal pay and an end to post-Second World War austerity. A Women's Policy Group was also established within the party in 1962 and in 1968 the party set up a committee to explore gender equality. Its rather patronisingly titled report 'Fair Share for the Fair Sex' became the basis for legislation concerning women's rights after the party came to office in 1970.[59] Something similar happened prior to the 2010 election, when a substantial policy review from the women's section fed into the party's manifesto.[60] In 2005, the campaigning organisation Women2Win was founded by Theresa May and Baroness Jenkin, which aimed to strengthen the

Conservative Party's commitment to selecting women for winnable seats.

So, again, the record is mixed: despite assisting the party machinery in great numbers, and sometimes being powerful, women's sections have more often than not been sidestepped.[61] Nevertheless, some training and peer-support has been available through the years. Moreover, good practice could also be infectious between parties. As the Conservative MP Nicky Morgan put it:

[In] 2010 the number of female Conservative MPs was boosted. After watching how the Labour women supported each other we began organising meetings to which Ministers were invited and asked to explain how their policies related to women. We also ensured we had female MPs in the Chamber for relevant debates and questions so that the Labour Party didn't have a monopoly in talking about women's views.[62]

Parliament and Women

'Enemy territory' was what the House of Commons felt like for women a hundred years ago. The vast majority of members initially treated women as 'space invaders'.[63] Parliament operated like an old white gentlemen's club with a shared sense of entitlement. Many members had gone to the same set of schools and networks and had similar interests. To lessen the shock and inevitable comments, the first female MP, Nancy Astor, avoided colour and always wore a white blouse, black skirt, a jacket with a white flower and a hat.

The early female politicians faced numerous humiliations including a lack of toilets and restrictions on the use of the Smoking Room and the Commons Dining Room. The 'Ladies' Members Room was mockingly nicknamed 'The Boudoir',[64] or by Ellen Wilkinson, the 'Tomb', which more accurately described it.[65] Women addressing the House were jeered, with male MPs shouting 'melons' and jiggling imaginary breasts.[66] Until televising of the

debates began in 1989, the culture of heavy drinking also contributed to unacceptable behaviour.[67]

Black women MPs, those from working-class backgrounds, and
gay or bisexual women faced additional discrimination and found it
difficult to shift Parliament's make-up. For example, Diane Abbott,
the first black woman elected to Parliament in 1987, explained:

> I became active in politics in the 1980s, at a time of enormous
> turmoil – there were riots in Brixton, Liverpool and Bristol,
> 'Scrap sus' was a huge issue and young black men were seen as
> the enemy within, just as young Muslim men are today . . . It is
> easy to stand up for the civil liberties of our friends or of people
> in our trade union, but it is not easy to stand up for the civil liber-
> ties of people who are unpopular, suspect and look suspicious.[68]

Women MPs who were older found that they faced double standards around attitudes to ageing and younger ones found that they
tended to be taken less seriously.[69] Even in 2016, Mhairi Black was
referring to Westminster as: 'Still a complete boys club . . . patronising, sexist, arrogant . . . a totally defunct institution that allows
tradition to rule over reason.'[70] One of the traditions is entitlement
based on seniority, for example as chairs of select committees. This
results in different rights to speak first, and to how much you can
speak, with the consequence that women are less likely to have a
voice.[71] To compound this, a study in 2014 showed that only 24 per
cent of witnesses and only 17 per cent of experts called to Commons
committees were women.[72]

Another study in 2014 found that 28 per cent of men in Parliament
had no children, compared with 45 per cent of women – and this
compared with 20 per cent of women with no children in the same
age bracket nationally.[73] For women MPs who had children, the age
of their eldest when they first entered Parliament was sixteen
compared with twelve for men. Having or not having children was
political: if you had children, what were you doing entering
Parliament? If you did not you were considered unfit for the job,

something Betty Boothroyd, who went on to become Speaker of the House between 1992 and 2000, was accused of.[74]

Women MPs also faced problems with access to childcare and breastfeeding facilities. After years of campaigning, in 2010 a nursery was opened for the Parliamentary Estate; the Speaker John Bercow being one of its strongest advocates. Late-night sittings introduced in 1945 were another problem for those who could not get back to see their children after work. Following sustained pressure, these were reduced and by 2014–15, sitting after 10 p.m. took place only on sixteen occasions, compared with more than 70 per cent of the time between 1979 and 2002.[75] Conservative MP Nicky Morgan explained: 'A cross party group of women worked together to secure changes to the sitting hours of the House in the 2010–2015 Parliament. Many of us felt it was more important than ever to follow a more normal working week and we were supported in this by many of our male colleagues.'[76]

Following the campaigning by Lib Dem Jo Swinson and Labour's Lucy Powell, successes also include the lifting of the ban on babies in the lobby, allowing parents to be 'nodded through' during the voting process – an already established system by which an MP's vote can be counted as long as they are on the premises. On the down side, family travel expenses between home and work were cut.

Although the procedures within Westminster have created barriers for women, there have always been influential men championing women's interests, such as the Speaker John Bercow as just mentioned. He also commissioned 'The Good Parliament', a report by Professor Sarah Childs, which in 2016 made forty-three recommendations, each attached to a named responsible decision-maker. These covered equality of participation, parliamentary infrastructure and the culture of the Commons.[77]

Despite progress, there have also been tragic setbacks. On 16 June 2016, the Labour MP Jo Cox, who had previously been subjected to internet harassment, was shot and stabbed to death while doing her constituency work. A week later, on what would have been her 42nd birthday, her life was commemorated at a rally in London using the words from her maiden speech, 'we have far more in common than that which divides us'. Among the crowd stood a hundred women activists, wearing black and sashes in suffragette colours.

Jo Cox had been a great enthusiast of the suffragettes. As her friend Jess Phillips MP shared: 'I attended the brilliant celebration of the interment of Jo Cox's ashes with her family this week, danced and sang suffragette songs as Jo and I certainly walked shoulder to shoulder into the fray.'[78]

Sarah Champion wrote: 'I will continue to do my part to get better representation but also to challenge the increasing violence against women and girls in this country and internationally.'[79] And Anna Turley: 'With all the noise and anger and aggression it is easy to forget why we are here and what we are here to do and how we can make it better for those who come after us.'[80]

Putting violence aside, how have women MPs fared in the House? Have they been any different than male MPs? At the beginning, they had to swim with the tide and behave like men, or they would sink.[81] Yet gendered patterns have also emerged regarding how they relate to different aspects of the job. This includes a preference for the deliberative debates of committees and cross-party groups compared to the House's more gladiatorial debates or the weekly Prime Minister's Questions, PMQs.[82] Although PMQs is the best-attended event, some women MPs dislike these so much they avoid them.[83]

PMQs is a ritual that the public also seems to dislike. Yet, as Emma Crewe explains: 'In some ways, it is the reporting by the journalists and twitterers that is more problematic than the actual event. But when the noise of the backbenchers increases, and insults become personally offensive, then they sound ridiculous even to themselves. Although many women are not comfortable speaking at PMQs at the despatch box, they don't seem to mind asking questions or heckling.'[84]

A study of early women MPs showed that a few who rarely spoke in the Chamber played a much larger role in select committee work, for example Mary Pickford on India in the 1930s and Joan Davidson on national expenditure during the Second World War.[85] More recent examples include the committee work of the Conservative Dr Sarah Wollaston and Labour's Louise Ellman and Kate Green.

The constituency aspect of the work has been growing in importance. MPs now tend to spend two days a week in their wards when Parliament is sitting, and significantly more of the rest of the time providing advice and support to their constituents. A pattern has emerged with women MPs tending to value and be more comfortable with this work, whereas men are more likely to delegate it. Some describe it as 'glorified social work'. However, the visibility and value of constituency work seems to have increased over time, particularly following the 2009 expenses scandal, when Parliament's reputation was salvaged by the visibility and direct impact of MPs' constituency work.

Because of gendered social norms, many women MPs have felt they needed to be likeable, yet some have also thrived by rejecting the label. For her unwillingness to play to type, Edith Summerskill, a Labour MP from 1938, was called a 'cantankerous bitch' by a fellow male MP.[86] Labour's Gwyneth Dunwoody, whose grandmothers were both suffragettes, came into Parliament in 1966, and stayed there for over thirty-seven years, one of the longest careers in Parliament. She had a reputation for speaking her mind and is quoted as saying: 'I have no problem being called the battle-axe – very well made, very sharp and very efficient at what it does.'[87] Margaret Hodge, chair of the Public Accounts Committee 2010–15, is renowned, and also widely respected, for speaking directly and with no holds barred.[88] And, during the 2017 election, Theresa May briefly turned to her advantage the derogatory label 'a bloody difficult woman' coined by her fellow MP Kenneth Clarke – claiming she would not be a 'pushover' in Brexit negotiations with the President of the European Commission Jean-Claude Juncker.[89]

Women MPs are talked about – with some hedging – as being more collaborative and supportive of each other than men are. Catherine Mayer, journalist and co-founder of the Women's

Equality Party, wrote: 'My own experience encouraged me to believe women might be less inclined to party tribalism. I had seen Westminster women from different parties not only forming alliances in recognition of common goals, but bonding and swapping tips about how to avoid being slapped down or touched up.'[90] Nicky Morgan MP similarly reflected: 'Women MPs do look at issues in different ways from men – we also talk about them differently and work collaboratively. I've never believed there are "women's issues" but there is a woman's perspective which it is vital to have on all issues of policy.'[91]

Some women have also had an impact on the workings of Parliament. For example, Natascha Engel as the first chair of the Backbench Business Committee in 2010–15. First, she made sure its proceedings were in public so that everyone could hear backbenchers make their pitches. Second, she insisted that they must have supporters from all parties and enough disagreement to ensure a debate. This approach made backbench debates particularly significant.[92]

Eleanor Rathbone entered Parliament in 1929, and became one of the most influential backbenchers of her time. As the first Independent woman MP, she had the advantage of not having to conform to party positions. Many of the causes she took up are as pertinent in 2018 as they were in her time: the plight of refugees, domestic slavery, female genital mutilation (FGM), child marriage, family poverty and housing. She also campaigned doggedly for a family allowance to go directly to mothers, a policy she finally achieved in 1945. According to her biographer Susan Pedersen:

> In her insistence that feminists pursue not only equal opportunities within that gendered system but equally the reconditioning of those structures to eradicate their masculine bias, Rathbone anticipated much later feminist thinking and politics. Few have thought so creatively and at the same time so practically about what it would take to bring about a genuinely equal citizenship for women.[93]

More recently, the Green MP Caroline Lucas has likewise proved successful at keeping green issues on the agenda of mainstream politics, despite being her party's only member. She is also a vocal feminist and throughout her years in office has managed to command respect across the House. She shared the role of leader with Jonathan Bartley – the first job share for a party leader.

The extent to which female MPs have wanted to be associated with women's concerns is another interesting question. In 1920 Margaret Bondfield MP campaigned on class, with hardly any reference to the seismic shift regarding women's entry into Parliament.[94] Others such as Barbara Castle stuck tightly to their feminism. She held a variety of key positions at Westminster for more than twenty years, and was one of the most influential MPs of the century, becoming an MEP and then a peer in the Lords. She is best known for reforming Britain's industrial relations and sponsoring the Equal Pay Act but also supported welfare reforms, brought in the 70 mph speed limit, breathalyser legislation and compulsory wearing of seat belts in the front seat of cars. Her energy, the breadth of the different portfolios she held, and the length of her service remain exceptional to this day.

By contrast, Margaret Thatcher, one of the most dominant and divisive political figures of the twentieth century, was no feminist. Her leadership saw a reduction in abortion terms, in maternity rights and public services, and she failed to promote other women in Parliament. However, she oversaw the introduction of some progressive policies for women, such as independent taxation and she remains a role model for feminists on the right, having got to the top in a man's world and putting her imprint on it during three terms in office.

She used her femininity as a counterpoint to the image of 'The Iron Lady' and did on occasion refer to attributes she associated with her gender. Her sayings include:

In politics, if you want anything said ask a man, if you want anything done ask a woman.[95]

I've got a woman's ability to stick to a job and get on with it when everyone else walks off and leaves it.[96]

Any woman who understands the problems of running a home will be nearer to understanding the problems of running a country.[97]

Theresa May, Britain's second female prime minister, coming to the post in 2016, having been Minister for Women and Home Secretary, is very different in being a self-identified feminist. She campaigned to get more Conservative women into Parliament and has a record of addressing violence against women. In 2017, she wrote that she was proud to serve as the country's second female Prime Minister, that she recognised the potential in all young girls and women, and that more needed to be done to achieve gender equality. Referring to the 2018 centenary, she asked that we 'reflect on the dedication and sacrifice of those who fought so hard to allow us the opportunities we have today'.[98]

The transformation in the House of Commons has been slow but cumulative, with some giants in the field pushing things forward. These include Shirley Williams, elected in 1964 first as a Labour MP, and then as one of the four founders of the Social Democratic Party in 1981, and then serving in the Liberal Party. From 1982, Labour's Harriet Harman has played an even more critical role as one of the longest-serving and most prominent female MPs, taking up roles such as the first Minister for Women and leader of the Opposition. She was one of the first women MPs to give birth to children during her parliamentary career.

Overall, women in politics have tended to support policies to increase gender equality, tackle gender-based discrimination and improve the domestic environment.[99] Furthermore, as the number of women in Parliament has increased, their influence has grown and these policies have become mainstreamed.[100] As the Conservative MP Margot James put it: 'We've seen an important shift so that it's now far broader than when politics was dominated by men. Issues like education, the work environment and the gender pay gap are all in mainstream political debate and that is because of women's influence.'[101] However, as Labour MP Emily Thornberry has said: 'I think many women MPs are still self-conscious as women and fear being labelled as feminists because Parliament, political parties and the wider culture still don't like seeing women rocking the boat. It is getting better but we are not there yet.'[102]

Institutional attention has come through a number of different mechanisms. As well as legislative change, commissions, such as the one on equal opportunities, established in 1975 and replaced by the Equality and Human Rights Commission in 2007, have played a key role. In 1997, the introduction of a Minister for Women was also symbolically critical. However, the post has always been held by a minister who has another Cabinet position, so the women's portfolio has always been secondary. In 2017 Justine Greening commented:

> Less than 100 years ago women were absent from our polling stations. A century later, as a woman working in politics and as Minister for Women and Equalities, I couldn't be prouder to see more women than ever before elected to Parliament. This progress is to be applauded – and we are going in the right direction, but this is no time to let up the pressure.

A Women and Equalities Select Committee was created in 2015 and holds the Minister for Women and Equalities to account. As the Conservative MP Maria Miller explained:

> The best Select Committees are the grit in an oyster, they challenge Government and Civil Service thinking and disregard the artificial boundaries created by Government departments. There was significant resistance to establishing the new Women and Equalities Select Committee in 2015 and initially it was only a temporary committee. The work of the committee and tenacity

of our members has however led to the committee being made permanent following the 2017 election.

It was a tremendous privilege to be elected as the first Chair of the Women & Equalities Select Committee and slightly daunting too. How was I going to get Conservative, Labour and SNP Members of Parliament to agree on issues of equality? On women's rights and to use Jo Cox's words, we have found that there is far more that unites us than divides us.[103]

The Select Committee has undertaken inquiries into the gender pay gap, employment opportunities for Muslims in the UK, sexual harassment and sexual violence in schools, and transgender equality. Another important mechanism has been the all-party parliamentary groups (APPGs). These are informal and have the remit of focusing on single issues. They are run by and for Members of the Commons and Lords, and often involve individuals and organisations from outside Parliament. The number of groups and their influence has grown since 1995: in 2016, for example, there were APPGs on 'Women in Parliament', 'Women, Peace and Security' and 'Women's Sport and Fitness'.

Policy is also developed and expenditure delivered through arm's-length public appointments. These cover everything from the Land Registry, the Gambling Commission, Equality and Human Commission to the Homes and Communities Agency. In 2010, a commitment was made to ensure that there are 50 per cent women on these boards and progress is being made. However, departmental performance varies wildly. Looking at the records for 2015, for example, 56 per cent of new appointments went to women in the Cabinet Office and only 20 per cent in the Department for International Development (DFID).[104]

A few moments in the political landscape are worth noting in that they have contributed to a sense of women's emerging visibility. An example was the spontaneous group hug of Nicola Sturgeon (SNP), Leanne Wood (Plaid Cymru) and Natalie Bennett (Green) at the last televised debate prior to the 2015 election, with the two male party leaders (Ed Miliband and Nigel Farage) looking on. Another was the photo of Theresa May and Nicola Sturgeon meeting on 15 July 2016. Nicola Sturgeon tweeted the photo with: 'Politics aside – I hope girls everywhere look at this photograph and believe nothing should be off limits for them.' Then in the 2017 election campaign, women were in predominant positions; for the first time, being a woman became a common factor not a defining one.

The House of Lords

So much for women's experiences in the Commons. How have they fared in the Lords?

The suffragette Margaret Haig Thomas, Lady Rhondda, was the first woman to try to succeed her father in the House of Lords, as he had no sons. She was a feminist campaigner, founding the journal *Time and Tide* in 1920 and, together with eminent feminists including the writers Winifred Holtby and Vera Brittain, formed the Six Point Group in 1921, an influential organisation that campaigned for gender equality in political and social spheres.[105] Lady Rhondda was barred from the Lords, despite the Sex Disqualification (Removal) Act 1919, which stated 'a woman shall not be disqualified by sex or marriage from the exercise of any public function'.

The attitude in the Lords was if anything more hostile than in the other chamber. As recently as 1957, Earl Ferrers commented: 'Why should we encourage women to eat their way, like acid into metal, into positions of trust and responsibility . . . If we allow women in the House where will this emancipation end?'[106] It didn't end. Legislation allowing women entry as life peers was passed in 1958 and as hereditary peers in 1963.

The sociologist Barbara Wootton was the first female life peer and the Lords' first female Deputy Speaker. She later sponsored the bill for the abolition of the death penalty. Stella Isaacs, Marchioness of Reading, was the first woman hereditary peer to take her seat, as

Baroness Swanborough, having founded the Women's Voluntary Service in 1938. Her motto was 'Not why we can't but how we can'.

Now, compared to the other House, women thrive in the Lords. This is for a number of reasons. Peers have generally proved themselves in previous careers, often having fought their way up in organisations hostile to women's leadership. Their voices and experiences are recognised. Furthermore, they do not have the pressure of the election cycle and there is more debate. Verbal attacks are not considered appropriate. Also, the work/life balance is easier, as peers do not have to maintain a physical presence in a constituency.[107] Cross-party peers in particular flourish in the House of Lords. In 2017, they represented the third-largest group, 22 per cent of the Chamber. Baroness Deech, who joined in 2005, explained:

> We are free to follow our consciences and we are wooed, not whipped . . . to be in the company of other equally committed women is invigorating, and I have found the Lords to be the most egalitarian place I have ever worked in; save only on my first venturing to the Long Table for lunch where an elderly peer asked me for more cabbage, assuming I must be the waitress.[108]

Baroness Jane Campbell, who has long worked on disability rights and who was influenced by Sylvia Pankhurst into a radical reframing of disability politics, also became a cross-bench peer in 2007. She uses an electrically powered wheelchair and commented on how difficult it was for Parliament to adapt to her severe disability (spinal muscular atrophy): 'It took me two years to overturn a 300-year-old Standing Order in the House of Lords to allow a personal assistant to accompany me in the Debating Chamber and to speak for me, when necessary.'[109]

Baroness Bakewell of Hardington Mandeville became a Liberal Democratic peer in 2013. She reflected: 'I was offered the opportunity to come to the House of Lords. I accepted on the basis that the House would be moving to an elected Chamber within 5 years, I would assist in this and could cope with that timeframe. How wrong I was. By the time I took the oath, Reform was dead in the water.'[110]

Although there is still a way to go, women peers have found themselves increasingly at ease, attending and contributing with fewer constraints. This contrasts with more sluggish change when we look at the judiciary.

The Judiciary

My great-aunt Christabel Pankhurst, having been Manchester University's first female law graduate in 1906, was legally barred from following in the footsteps of her barrister father. She was not the only one trying to enter the legal establishment. In 1913 Gwyneth Bebb and Maud Ingram (later Crofts) started a legal action against the Law Society to be allowed to take the law exams and become solicitors. Despite the Court of Appeal's rejection, their campaign contributed to the passage of the Sex Disqualification (Removal) Act 1919, paving the way for women to become lawyers, magistrates and members of a jury.

In 1920, six women became the first female jurors in the Bristol quarter sessions. This was the first time the words 'Ladies and gentlemen of the jury . . .' were used, greeted by a murmur in the court. According to the *New York Times*, the women gave their judgement during the day and then two of them asked, and were excused, to look after their children, with two other women taking their places. The prosecuting counsel congratulated the women for 'at last taking their proper place in the administration of justice in England'.[111]

An analysis comparing verdicts before and after women were included in juries found little effect on conviction rates, but a few other trends. Firstly, an increase in the time taken to reach a verdict; secondly, a greater number of convictions for sex offences.[112]

The first women to sit the solicitor exams were Carrie Morrison, Mary Sykes, Mary Pickup and Maud Ingram in 1922. Ten years after a legal challenge to allow her to practise, Maud Ingram became the first woman solicitor.

Gwyneth Bebb, who petitioned Lincoln's Inn for admittance as a barrister, died in childbirth before she could be called.[113] Ivy Williams, the first woman to graduate as Doctor of Civil Law and the first woman to teach law in a university then became the first woman called to the Bar in 1922. That same year the suffragette Helena Normanton was finally admitted as a student of the Middle Temple, having in 1918, been 'rebuffed in the curtest fashion, with no reason given for the refusal'.[114] She had then campaigned for a change in the law, and when it did change, she handed in her application within two days of the event. She also became the first female counsel in the High Court of Justice, the first female counsel at the Old Bailey and, in 1949, the first woman, together with Rose Heilbron, to be appointed a KC. When she got married she kept her maiden name even though the legal profession disapproved; the Foreign Office eventually agreed to issue a passport in her maiden name, the law being changed as a consequence.

Subsequently, more and more women entered the legal profession. Even so, as recently as 2012, more than 70 per cent of the top hundred firms still had less than 30 per cent women partners and women remained under-represented at partnership level at the top firms known as the 'Magic Circle'.[115] While 36 per cent of barristers were women, only 13.7 per cent of QCs and only 28 per cent of judges were women. Regarding women's representation in national courts in general – and the supreme court in particular – the UK has been lagging behind other Western democracies, and is worse than Eastern Europe.[116] According to a study in 2009 the UK ranked 32nd out of 35.[117]

By 2014, in spite of there being more women than men taking law degrees, doing particularly well in their exams, and getting a higher percentage of training contracts as solicitors, at senior levels they continued to vanish. The gap remains greatest between solicitor and associate level, the point at which many women take time out to have children. They also tend to become partners later than men.[118]

Jayne, a solicitor shared:

When I first started here, I had a real feeling of being an imposter. I laugh about it now, but at the time I literally used to die a little inside every time someone spoke to me, and it does come back every now and again, for example if I go to a meeting and there are very few women but all the men seem to know each other. I have to tell myself that I am supposed to be there and that people aren't looking at me wondering if I've walked into the wrong room by mistake.[119]

Women in the judiciary have had to break through barriers similar to those in Westminster and the system has had to adjust to their presence. New language was needed for the different legal roles, the ceremonial robes were adapted; the informal spaces that are part of the culture all had to open up. This happened but very slowly and begrudgingly. Margaret Owen, called to the Bar, in 1954 shared:

It was a difficult time, as it is now, for women to get pupillages, and even more difficult to obtain tenancies, since chambers were full of young men, older than us, who had done military service, followed by Oxbridge. They were very much favoured by the clerks. I was the only woman pupil and the clerk was initially reluctant to take me on due to the lack of a ladies' loo. That was neatly resolved by an invitation to use the facilities next door. Also, he confided in me that solicitors were not that keen to brief women barristers, and he did not work that hard to get these for me.[120]

In 1955, twenty-five years after the first women were admitted to the Inns of Court, girls were still being advised against a career at the Bar.[121] Yet they continued to try . . . and to succeed. In 1962,

Dame Elizabeth Lane became the first female county court judge and, in 1965, the first woman appointed to the high court. Number 4 Brick Court chambers, otherwise known then as 'the Monstrous Regiment of Women', was set up in 1974 by Barbara Calvert and three other women barristers. Calvert became the first female QC to take a case to the European Court of Human Rights. She won the case in 1987, which led to a change in the law, giving parents whose children were in the care of the local authority the right to contact them. Dame Elizabeth Butler-Sloss became the first female Lord Justice of Appeal in 1988, and in 1999 the first president of the Family Division of the High Court of Justice, and a life peer. Among other notable cases, she chaired the Cleveland child abuse inquiry.

In 1991 Patricia Scotland became the first black woman QC. Having specialised in family and children's law and served as a member of the Commission for Racial Equality, she received a life peerage in 1997, became the first woman attorney general in 2007, and then the first Secretary General of the Commonwealth in 2015.

A woman who made her mark as the youngest person ever to be appointed to the Law Commission was Lady Brenda Hale, in 1984. She co-wrote the first wide-ranging survey of women's rights at work, in the family and within the state, and was instrumental in introducing the Children's Act in 1989. In 1999, she became the first woman law lord in the House of Lords, then in 2009 the first woman justice of the supreme court, before becoming its president in 2017.

The narrow background of those at the top of the legislature matters. As Lady Hale put it:

> Diversity of background and experience enriches the law. Women lead different lives from men, largely because we have visibly different bodies from men ... by and large the interaction between our own internal sense of being a woman and the outside world's perception of us as women leads to a different set of everyday and lifetime experiences ... They will not always make a difference but sometimes they will and should.[122]

As with all forms of political power, a truly representative judiciary is important because different segments of society can have different perspectives and approaches. For a profession that represents fairness and justice this seems particularly pertinent. Anybody with the right skills should be able to succeed and diversity of representation is important; the law would be richer for understanding the whole – in essence it could be reimagined.[123]

Local and International Governance

For decades before 1918, many women were involved in local government as poor law guardians, on education boards and at parish council level. However, they were only allowed to be county and borough councillors from 1907, and even then, few were elected. Labour councillor Ada Salter was a Quaker, a supporter of the Women's Freedom League and campaigned for social housing and greening of the urban environment. In 1922, she became Mayor of Bermondsey, the first woman mayor of a London borough.

Many women were interested in local government because they wanted to make a difference in their communities and this turned out to be a training ground for Parliament. In 1976 Shreela Flather, having arrived from India less than a decade earlier, became the first woman councillor from an ethnic minority. In 1986, she became the Mayor for Windsor and Maidenhead and subsequently the first Asian woman peer.

Although things are changing, thanks to increased childcare provision, greater flexibility within councils and evolving roles within the home, a lack of women and diversity prevails.[124] In 2013, 67 per cent of councillors were male, 96 per cent were of white ethnic origin with an average age of sixty.[125] Baroness Cathy Bakewell, the former leader of Somerset County Council shared: 'When elected in 1993 there were half a dozen of us women. However, no younger women (or men for that matter) were elected during subsequent elections. Perhaps local government needs to consider how it can attract younger women (and men) – or are essential services only to be delivered by the retired or the well-off?'[126]

In Manchester city council, in 2016, there was for the first time a small majority of women elected members. Councillor Sarah Judge reflected:

> I question whether this means we have gender equality. Across many areas of politics women who are confident, powerful and independent are still described as arrogant and bossy. I often see female politicians changing their behaviour to become more masculine to compete with their male colleagues. This is a real shame as women often bring a totally different set of skills that should be welcomed and celebrated. Women need to feel confident enough to embrace their qualities rather than just mirror men.[127]

Women have fared best in the devolved structures. In 2003, the Welsh Assembly became the first legislative body in the world with equal numbers of men and women, and in 2014 the Scottish Assembly put forward a gender-balanced Cabinet.[128] In 2015, 40 per cent of the London Assembly, 42 per cent of the National Assembly for Wales and 35 per cent of the Scottish Assembly were women. The London Assembly has also showed leadership in other aspects of diversity, with for instance 30 per cent of the women members being of Black, Asian Minority Ethnic (BAME) background.[129]

In the last few years, women have reached the top in the regional Assemblies. Nicola Sturgeon, a proud feminist, became leader of the Scottish National Party and was given the title of 'the most dangerous woman in Britain' by the *Daily Mail* in 2015. She explained: 'Thatcher was the motivation for my entire political career . . . I hated everything she stood for. This was the genesis of my nationalism. I hated the fact that she was able to do what she was doing and yet no one I knew in my entire life had voted for her.'[130] Ruth Davidson also rose to the top, becoming a Member of the Scottish Parliament, then, in 2011, leader of the Scottish

Conservatives and in 2015 leader of the Opposition in Scotland. She recalled being a young child during Margaret Thatcher's time and asking her mother whether a man could ever be a prime minister.[131] She and Kezia Dugdale, who became leader of the Scottish Labour Party between 2015 and 2017, also contributed to a sea change in attitudes about sexual orientation. In 2012, Leanne Wood became the first leader of Plaid Cymru – the Welsh Party – and from 2015 Arlene Foster was the First Minister of Northern Ireland. Suddenly women were at the top, almost everywhere.

Northern Ireland had lagged behind other parts of the UK in female representation. Previously torn by sectarianism and violence, it had seen the emergence in 1996 of the cross-community Women's Coalition, which played a vital role in the peace process. Yet at Stormont, women were initially mooed (i.e. with the sound of a cow) by the men when they first joined the talks.[132]

In the period 1998–2015, 58 per cent of women served only one term, compared with 42 per cent of men. A group of cross-party women and Speaker Mitchel McLaughlin looked at ways to address the democratic deficit. They commissioned a report, established a Speaker's Reference Group on a Gender Sensitive Assembly, developed a Gender Action Plan, created an Assembly Women's Caucus and undertook many formal and informal activities, including a field trip to Sweden to look at best practice.

In 2016, the Assembly doubled its female representation to 28 per cent. Then, amid all the uncertainty following the dissolution of the Assembly and the fresh elections in 2017, the proportion of women increased to 30 per cent. Women also came to lead three parties. As well as Arlene Foster for the Democratic Unionist Party (DUP), there were Naomi Long of the Alliance Party, the Green Party's MLA Clare Bailey and Sinn Féin's Michelle O'Neill. In the June 2017 national elections, 33 per cent of Northern Ireland's candidates were women, however, under the 'first past the post' scheme only 22 per cent were elected.

Beyond our shores, the League of Nations from 1937,[133] replaced by the United Nations in 1945, has provided a political framework for women's interests. Pivotal from 1946 has been the Commission of the Status on Women, the intergovernmental institution promoting gender equality. Four world conferences – Mexico City 1975, Copenhagen 1980, Nairobi 1985 and Beijing 1995 – also focused attention on women's rights. At Beijing, a relatively comprehensive declaration and platform for action was agreed. Hillary Clinton, then First Lady of the United States, made what was arguably one of the most influential speeches. She declared: 'If there is one message that echoes forth from this conference, let it be that human rights are women's rights and women's rights are human rights, once and for all.'[134] Recognition was given to thousands of feminists from all corners of the world, challenging the marginalisation of women's concerns, showing the potential of collective action, and generating the beginnings of an international language and associated mechanisms with which to address women's rights. For example, in 1981 the Convention on the Elimination of all Forms of Discrimination Against Women (CEDAW) was ratified by most states.[135] One of its most important provisions was the requirement that all countries – including the UK – report annually on the state of women's rights.

Meanwhile, in 1973, the UK had joined the European Union. Because of some of the defining treaties of the EU, particularly the Treaty of Rome and of Lisbon that constitutionally reference equality between women and men and the need for gender mainstreaming, EU laws have been particularly progressive. The European Parliament's voting system requires a form of PR and therefore the proportion of women MEPs is comparatively high. British women MEPs represented 41 per cent in 2014, higher than most national parliaments, including the UK's.[136]

According to Joanna Maycock, Secretary General of the European Women's Lobby:

The EU has been good for women because of hard campaigning by women's organisations, trade unions, lawyers and allies in governments and parliaments pushing for gender equality. Also, the use of the courts has had an impact. Networking, lobbying, campaigning and exchange of practice across Europe (like the work of the European Women's Lobby) has been vital. The relatively higher number of women in the European Parliament has also contributed to a different balance in committees and in leadership positions such as heads of political groups and in the culture of collaboration and committee work seeking consensus.[137]

Momentously, in 2016 the UK voted to leave the EU. Though education, age and socio-economic position had a bearing on the vote, gender as a single category did not seem to, although a poll just before the vote suggested that women were more likely to vote to remain.[138] Emmeline Pankhurst's name was brought into the referendum by the Leave Campaign. My family refuted the idea that Emmeline would have backed Leave, arguing firstly that we have no idea how Emmeline would have voted, and secondly that if anything, our instinct was that her internationalism, particularly her love of France, would have swayed her the other way.[139]

From 2017 to 2019, the Brexit quagmire continued to take up most of the government and parliament's time and energy. The EU Withdrawal Bill ensured existing EU laws remained in force during the transition process, and up to the expected leave date of March 2019. From within Parliament, the Women and Equalities Committee lobbied for an embedding of gender equality in any changes to legislation.[140]

Activism and Civil Society

A study entitled 'When do governments promote women's rights?' found that across different countries, the biggest single factor in achieving progressive policies is a strong, autonomous women's movement holding government to account. It argued that this had even stronger influence than the proportion of women in Parliament.[141]

Over the last century, the variation in the UK of women's political activism running alongside or challenging formal politics is breath-taking. We could start with those who, a hundred years ago, had soft-power as society hostesses. These 'grandes dames' brought together the great and the good at dinner parties and receptions. They included Lady Edith Londonderry, a suffragette who had set up the Women's Legion; Lady Sibyl Colefax who became a prominent interior decorator; Margaret Greville, a philanthropist who bequeathed her jewels to the Queen Mother and her estate to the National Trust; and Lady Emerald Cunard who was also influential in the arts. Many of these women used their political influence in targeted ways, for example to support pro-appeasement policies in the 1930s, although Mrs Laura Corrigan subsequently became involved in funding the Resistance in France.[142]

Individual reformers also left their mark through work on royal commissions and departmental committees, such as Beatrice Webb on the Poor Law Commission 1905–9, which inspired the formation of the welfare state in the 1940s. Likewise Margery Fry had an enduring influence on, and was the director of, the Howard League for Penal Reform in the 1920s.

Beyond the individuals, innumerable associations and organisations advocated for women's political roles and provided training and support. These include the National Women Citizens Association from 1917 to 1975, Women for Westminster, between 1942 and 1949, and the all-party 300 Group, set up in 1980 by Lesley Abdela. She explained:

> The obstacles to women being elected are partly a consequence of *traditional cultural attitudes* and partly a consequence of *institutional procedures*. I call these challenges 'The 6 Cs': Culture, Cronyism, Candidate selection processes, Cash, Chronic lack of time and Confidence. The 300 Group contributed to changing the attitudes. 300 Group supporters went on to become mayors, local councillors, Members of Parliament, Members of the House of Lords and Government Ministers.[143]

In 2013 the 50:50 Parliament Campaign was initiated by Frances Scott calling for a gender-balanced Parliament. An 'Ask Her to Stand' call and an ambassador programme have followed. As Frances summarised: 'We cannot have men dominating the corridors of power for another century. 50:50 Parliament aims to take action and put pressure on those in authority to do something about this historic and ongoing democratic deficit.'[144]

Women's activism has sometimes been very localised and time-bound, for example rent strikes in the East End of London in 1921 by the suffragette and alderman Minnie Lansbury and Susan Lawrence, then a member of the London County Council. Lawrence was imprisoned in Holloway for refusing to set a rate she felt was unaffordable. She subsequently became an MP. Similarly, the Women of Quinn Square of 1938 won an agreement on the maximum rent, regular repairs and the recognition of a tenants' association. There was also the Bengali Housing Action Group of the 1970s co-founded by Mala Sen, a young Indian activist who was involved in the fight against racism and the demand for safe housing.[145]

In mining communities, women supported their husbands against pit closures, organising food distribution particularly during the 1984–5 strike. Many became radicalised in the process, not just through a class struggle but also through finding female solidarity.

Women have also been involved in international lobbying outside formal channels. For example, Helen Bamber's tireless work for Holocaust survivors, asylum-seekers, and victims of conflict and genocide. Women were also centrally involved in the Anti-Apartheid Movement in South Africa and the Nicaragua Solidarity Campaign. In these examples, the attention was on social and economic justice, not on gender inequality per se.

Most famously and visibly, women undertook direct action on a much larger scale. After the suffrage agitation of the first wave there came the Women's Liberation Movement (WLM) of the second wave, from the end of the Sixties. Its demands were equal pay, equal education and opportunities, twenty-four-hour nurseries and free contraception and abortion on demand.[146] The movement gener-ated political activism but also a profusion of feminist writing, visual and cultural initiatives, social experiments in more egalitarian households and communities, and refuges for mothers and children fleeing domestic violence. It lasted until 1978, then ground to a halt because of internal schisms. Ultimately, the movement raised consciousness and fostered a language that remains current today, for example that sexism and sex-stereotyping needs to be countered and 'the personal is political'. The popular response to the 'women's libber' was that of ridicule.

The interests of women have also been championed by organisations such as the Women's Rights Committee of the National Council for Civil Liberties, subsequently renamed Liberty, which took on some of the first cases following the Equal Pay and Sex Discrimination Acts. The examining of laws and policy from a women's perspective was undertaken by feminist bodies such as the Women's Publicity Planning Association (WPPA), active between 1939 and 1956. Likewise the Women's Budget Group, operating since 1989, provides a scrutiny of the financial implications of policies, including of the UK's budget.

Often, women have come together through formal joint forums to push for change. Examples are the Consultative Committee of Women's Organisations formed by the National Union of Women's Suffrage Societies (NUWSS) in 1916, then taken on by Nancy Astor, initially as its president. It operated between 1921 and 1928 bringing together forty-nine women's associations before disbanding in the 1930s.[147] The government's advisory body Women's National Commission (WNC) operated between 1969 and 2010 to make recommendations to government and link women's groups, until abolished in the 'bonfire of the quangos' when many such bodies were axed. In 2007 Harriet Harman, as Minister for Women and Equalities, consulted the Commission on what they felt she should be doing as minister.[148] One final example is the National Alliance of Women's Organisations (NAWO), founded in 1989 to increase women's skills and engage with policy, including in United Nations negotiations.

There are also innumerable philanthropic or charity organisations in which women have played a central role. These have provided social welfare support but also campaigned for policy change, not only for women and girls, but also for orphans, the urban poor, the elderly, those fighting a particular disease, and so on.

Throughout the period, up and down the land, women have quietly undertaken public roles, usually unpaid, providing the glue that keeps communities together. David Cameron sought to harness this in his 'Big Society' project, and Theresa May with the 'Shared Society'. To pick one more example, in 2016, around four hundred child contact centres provided a safe environment where separated families could meet. These centres were staffed by paid employees and 6,000 volunteers – mostly middle-aged and elderly women.

When we think of politics, all these diverse forms of women's activism are rarely put centre stage – yet, often in invisible ways, they have continuously nourished the democratic sphere. Although women's activism persists, the fear is that the voluntarism on which it depends is under threat, for many reasons including women's increased role in formal politics and in the paid economy, the busy-ness of life and the increased demands and shrinking resources of the voluntary sector. Something is going to have to give, if the contributions of millions of women are going to be part of the ongoing story of social change.

The Media

One last area to look at and which informs the whole political scene is the media. The relationship between citizens and politics is mediated by communication between the two. To a massive extent this has been through the media and particularly through the BBC. What role have they played in the story of women in politics?

One of the five founding governors of the BBC in 1927 was Ethel Snowden, a leading suffrage campaigner. She set the precedent at the BBC of there being one – usually only one – woman governor.[149] Hilda Matheson, as the first Director of Talks, conceptualised *The Week in Parliament*, which became *The Week in Westminster* and continues as an influential radio programme today. It was initially made by women for a female daytime audience, and focused on the new women MPs after the 1928 Equal Franchise Act. Male MPs were included only a few years later. The *Today* programme was also developed by women, Janet Quigley and Isa Benzie, in 1957.

As the BBC became established, women's influence shrank, newsrooms became male-led spaces, with women assisting as secretaries and support staff.[150] Women as newsreaders did not figure much until 1975, when Angela Rippon put her stamp on the role. Even then, in 2011, she was told to make way for younger presenters by the Director General, John Birt, himself exactly the same age as her.[151] Despite often calling out and giving coverage to the fight against gender discrimination, the organisation itself unsurprisingly reflects society as it is and is steeped in its prejudices. The financial lens on this reality was revealed in 2017 when for the first time the BBC published its pay list.

Although the BBC was state-owned, it aimed to be non-party political. By contrast, newspapers have long been dominated by 'press barons', wealthy men close to political elites who could be rewarded for favourable media coverage with a peerage or title. The Canadian-born William Maxwell Aitken, 1st Baron Beaverbrook, was the proprietor of the *Daily Express*, the *Sunday Express* and the *Evening Standard* from 1916 to his death in 1964. Alfred Harmsworth, the owner of the *Daily Mail* and *Daily Mirror*, became 1st Viscount Northcliffe. George Riddell owned a number of newspapers and even donated a summer house to Lloyd George – which the suffragettes firebombed – and was knighted and made a peer. The *Observer* belonged to Waldorf Astor, husband of Nancy Astor. The couple were in the two Houses of Parliament and *The Times* was owned by another branch of their family. The influence of 'press barons' continued with Robert Maxwell (until his death in 1991), Rupert Murdoch and Richard Desmond. None of these barons could by any stretch of the imagination be called feminists.

In the past, since newspapers were not free, the choice of what people read was determined by their income, social standing and political views. That had a cyclical effect in that what you read influenced your views, and possibly your status, and vice versa. By the 1930s almost all households bought a newspaper, at least on Sunday; women were generally not the primary readership. The exception was the *Daily Mail*, which specifically targeted women from its beginning in 1896. By 2016 and even after all the changes, including the development of free and online newspapers, it was still the only newspaper with a majority female readership at 53 per cent.[152] Despite this, even in 2017, only 20 per cent of the *Daily Mail* and General Trust plc board members were women; and the newspaper has always been edited by a man.

Women were first allowed temporarily into the Parliamentary Press Gallery to cover the admission of Nancy Astor in 1919, but not on a permanent basis until the Second World War.[153] Even in 1983 only 5 per cent of lobby journalists were women. In Harriet Harman's words, Parliament was 'a boys' club being reported on by a boys' club'. The boys – MPs and journalists – went on Friday-afternoon golf sessions or played football matches against each other.[154] However the club was slowly being infiltrated. The proportion of women increased to 26 per cent and at last, in 2015, the BBC appointed its first female political editor, Laura Kuenssberg.[155]

In the 1960s, columns specifically targeting women appeared in newspapers. Before long there were whole pages, edited by women. Arguments about whether or not these pages were in fact keeping women's interests to a low-status part of newspapers raged from the beginning. Mary Stott was one of the most influential editors of the women's page in the *Manchester Guardian* from 1957 until 1972. Lena Jeger, a colleague, wrote: 'Mary Stott . . . knew from her own experience the struggle women had in balancing love, family and their professional lives, and she ran her page . . . opening out the possibilities for women, forming supportive networks, creating solidarities. [Her page] operated as a community notice board on a giant scale.'[156]

Many other women journalists have since provided a female perspective on the world. Even so, the mainstream media continues to be reported through a traditional white male gaze which affects the way women are reported on. This includes the focus on their appearance rather than on what they are saying. On budget day in 2016, parts of the media focused on how much of Theresa May's cleavage was showing; and interest on her shoes has spawned #newsnotshoes on Twitter. Her £995 leather trousers were media news; David Cameron's even more expensive Savile Row suits were of no interest.[157] 'Never mind Brexit, who won Legs-it!' was the headline of the *Daily Mail* showing a photo of the meeting between Theresa May and Nicola Sturgeon.

When it involves women, the topic under consideration is trivialised and sexualised. Forty-three main recommendations were made in 'The Good Parliament' report of 2016. The media zoned in on breastfeeding, which had been mentioned as a sub-point to a proposal for a clear policy on maternity, paternity, adoption and care leave. As the Liberal Democrat MP Jo Swinson commented: 'It's the journalistic equivalent of pinging a girl's bra-strap and thinking it's hilarious. "Boobs! They mentioned boobs!" You can almost hear the puerile chuckles in the newsroom.'[158]

Television, radio and newspapers link citizen and state and play a central role in people's lives. For most of the last century, the media would fail a gender-neutral test in terms of who, what and how the news has been reported. Some individuals, institutions and networks such as Women in Journalism have continued the drumbeat for women's rights and the democratisation of society from the gender perspective, yet overall the media presents more as obstacle than solution. How women fare with social media is something that we will turn to in future chapters.

Conclusion

The big change in the political world a hundred years ago was the granting of the right of women to vote and be voted for on the same terms as men. It ushered in the right to take part in all the other parts of the democratic system. Thanks to the determination of pioneers, we have seen not just an acceptance of the legitimacy of women's presence, but also an acknowledgement of their capabilities – within institutions and by society more generally. The more visible and valued parts of the political scene now look and feel very different, but it has been tough and continues to demand dogged determination. In the words of one feminist in the Women's Liberation Movement: 'Women's politics are like an iceberg. Only the tip shows and it never looks like much. But underneath is a vast mass of women, always moving – usually very slowly.'[159]

At Westminster, in the assemblies, local councils, trade unions, the judiciary and the media, barriers to women still remain. This also applies in areas such as the civil service. Susanna, the first British woman ambassador to Ethiopia Djibouti and the African Union, reflected:

> I have often heard men say that they would very much like to have more women in the most senior positions in the Diplomatic Corps, but they regret or fear that there are not yet enough women who are ready [implicitly – for such difficult, important, sensitive and demanding roles]. It's worth pausing to reflect how odd that statement is in twenty-first century Britain and how loudly it chimes with what the suffragettes were told.[160]

Institutionally and socially, and in positions of leadership in particular, women still occupy the margins and their influence remains muted. Even when institutions open up, patriarchal attitudes have continued, with a sense that there is a certain audacity in women inhabiting male spaces. Women are still judged by how they look, what they wear and how they speak. Moreover, the different lens through which we perceive political men and women is normalised in culture and perpetuated as much by women as by men. Meanwhile, women continue to provide a backbone of support with less visible – and for the most part unpaid or underpaid – services that society has always taken for granted.

Overall, looking at the feminist trinity of objectives, real inroads have been achieved on equality of representation. Some progress is also visible regarding policies and practices that address gender difference. There is less evidence of women being able to put a transformational stamp on the whole system of governance, on changing the mould. The state and its institutions are both at the heart of patriarchy but also pivotal in the fight against it. To speed up the rate of change, we cannot wait for the establishment to evolve on its own – it has always been behind the curve.

Politics: how did we do?

If we had to give a single score to progress regarding women in politics, what would that be?

Having weighed up the evidence, I have gone for a 3 out of 5 for progress. What would you say?

2

MONEY

'I am working in what remains a man's world – and this is hard in many ways that continually reinforce each other.' (Elaine Lister, professional working mother)[1]

What has happened during the past hundred years for women in terms of their financial situation and to their access and control over money? The battle for equal pay, job segregation and the relationship between work and home loom large in the story. Questions also need to be asked about wealth, tax, access to finance and how these have changed over the century; we can also look at economic cycles on a more macro level. But we start with immigration and education – critical areas that have changed beyond recognition.

Immigration

Because of the increased diversity of the British population and the history of migration, who we are talking about when looking at the lives of women in Britain has changed over the century. Irish immigration to the UK was always commonplace, with young single women in particular escaping comparative poverty, vulnerability and a restricted life.

A descendant of refugees on both sides of my family, I am one of the estimated 13 per cent of citizens not born in the UK according to 2015 figures.[2] My paternal grandfather was an anarchist who escaped persecution in Italy. As my father explained: 'Your grandfather arrived in London with no funds to speak of but found occupation as a journalist and printer. His very active opposition to fascism, undertaken with your grandmother Sylvia, protected us to some extent from being treated as enemy aliens.'[3] Italian immigration increased after the rise of fascism in the 1920s. Italians, like so many other immigrants, clustered in particular areas; so, for example, in 2012, one-fifth of the population of Bedford was estimated to have Italian roots.[4]

My mother escaped the rise of anti-Semitism in 1937. She explained:

> My father foresaw that Romania would go the way of other countries under German control. As for thousands of others, we came to the UK to escape discrimination by Romanian Nazis, only to face intimidation as enemy aliens. As a young school boarder, I had to report every week at my police station.[5]

Refugee women who entered Britain escaping both world wars found work, particularly as domestic servants, replacing British women who were seeking other forms of employment. In the 1940s, these included women fleeing the Baltic States, called evocatively the Baltic Cygnets, mostly white middle-class women, who were recruited to work as domestic cleaners and mill hands.[6]

Around 300,000 migrants then came – most by invitation – from the Caribbean, to fill the increasing demand for labour. This started with those on the *Empire Windrush* in 1948 and went on until the 1960s.[7] From its early days, the National Health Service relied on cheap female immigrant labour as insufficient nurses were being trained locally. More nurses arrived from the Philippines and Nigeria from around the 1970s, doctors from Europe and India. Around the millennium young single women came from Eastern Europe to work in the service sector in towns and in agriculture. Women made the UK their home having migrated for economic reasons and to join family, as well as fleeing conflicts in Hungary in 1956, Czechoslovakia in 1968, Uganda and other parts of Africa from 1972, and Afghanistan and the Middle East since then.

Experiences of immigrants vary, but in the process of making Britain their home many faced overt discrimination based on faith, colour, accent and the 'otherness' of their customs. Job adverts used to openly exclude certain categories of people. Until the 1970s landlords would perfectly legally put up signs saying 'No Irish, no blacks, no dogs'. Racial harassment took different forms. Christine shared:

> When I was four, in 1963, we moved to a three-bedroom council flat. We experienced a fair amount of racial hatred. One day a group of youths put dog poo through our letter box and my dad snapped, he went outside, caught up with the group and threw one of them against a wall with a warning that if anything like that happened again or if any member of his family was threatened or harmed he would not be held responsible for his actions. Although the verbal abuse continued, there were no more physical incidents.[8]

On the other hand, many personal histories are framed more positively. Cecilia for example shared:

> I am a Kenyan and I am proud of my heritage. I always renew my Kenyan passport, and go back regularly. However, I have long lived here, having married a British man I met in Kenya. My experiences in the UK have been overwhelmingly positive, I have loved the openness of people, made many friends and have rarely experienced any discrimination, and definitely nothing compared to some of the internal conflicts between different ethnic groups in Kenya. Although my roots are different, my family, including my adult children, are British, and this is where I belong.[9]

Likewise Azmara, from Ethiopia and Eritrea, speaking of her experiences as a woman, commented:

> Here there is democracy, you experience equality as a woman and respect. That's not the same back there. I'm not sure, it might

have changed over the years, but I don't think so. Here too there are issues, differences in pay at work for example, but at least it is being looked at, it is being addressed. As a woman, it is not a bad place to call home.[10]

Legislation around immigration has often reflected the male bias of the state. For example, in 1914 the British Nationality and Status of Aliens regulations made the wife of a British subject British, while the wife of an alien became an alien. This law remained in place until 1933.[11] So, my grandmother Sylvia, if she had wanted to marry her Italian partner in the 1920s, would have either been made stateless or been forced to seek Italian nationality and after fighting so hard to win it, would have lost her right to vote in Britain.[12]

In 1962, following the Commonwealth Immigration Act, Commonwealth citizens no longer had the automatic right to come to the UK. They needed an employment voucher from the Ministry of Labour or to be the dependant of someone with a voucher. Men could bring their spouses as dependants but not vice versa.[13]

Sexual discrimination in laws about immigration persisted. The British government lost on a ruling from the European Court for immigration-related sex discrimination in 1985.[14] Indirectly this continues even now, since to qualify for immigration a person has to be earning a minimum amount (£35,000 pa in 2017) to stay in the UK on their own merits. Given the global inequality in earning potential, the financial criterion continues to favour men.[15]

Education

Too much education was, from the Victorian perspective, not to be approved of; it could be dangerous to the girl, making her ill and unsexing her.[16] Moreover, innocence depended on ignorance. Education was seen as wasted on girls and the expectation was that girls should get married and boys have a career. For girls, education provided basic instruction in the 'three Rs' (reading, 'riting and 'rithmetic) and domestic subjects such as sewing, cooking and housekeeping. However, from 1918 onwards a number of education Acts raised the school leaving age from twelve to eighteen and initially primary and then secondary state schooling became free. Nevertheless, the steering of subjects by gender, classroom dynamics, stereotypical materials and literature, the different status of male and female teachers and the whole school environment fuelled gender inequality and overall girls did poorly academically.

Many adult women have memories of school as a place where they experienced gender inequality. Liz and Maxine shared:

> I wasn't allowed to take chemistry O level and was told that I had to do needlework instead. I'm proud of my 'U' (unclassified) gained at the end of the course. In the written paper I was asked: Your husband is going on a business trip, what do you pack for him? My answer: I don't, he does it himself. I wasn't trying to be clever, it just had no connection with my life – my dad was an electrician, when would he ever go on a 'business' trip? I was meant to say that I would pack his socks into his shoes, which would be at the bottom of the suitcase. This was 1981! I am very proud of my younger self.[17]

> The blatant preferential treatment of boys at my secondary school meant the real-life chances for girls were hugely diminished. For example, the school had five old BBC computers. Only the boys were allowed to use them. Girls were completely excluded.[18]

Wider societal transformation and action to address the problem in schools resulted in a complete turnaround. By 1988, girls were performing around 10 per cent better in the top grades in at least five GCSEs, compared with boys.[19] They also increasingly stayed on to do A levels, where the difference in attainment narrowed to only around 1 per cent. In 2017, for the first time in almost twenty years, boys were back at the top.[20]

The story is not a simple one of exclusion followed by outperformance but one that is much more nuanced. Some educational establishments had allowed women to train for a career. Edge Hill College (subsequently University) opened in Liverpool in 1885 as the first non-denominational teacher-training college for women. The university adopted the suffragette colours and retained a sense of pride in their pioneering connection with women's rights. This progressive vision was unusual; the UK's oldest teacher-training college, King Alfred's College, subsequently part of the University of Winchester, had trained teachers since 1840, but it was only in the 1960s that women were admitted.

By 1918 women could take degrees in numerous colleges and universities but often with restrictions. King's College London limited the range of subjects, Cambridge allowed a maximum of only one woman to every six men, and it was not until 1948 that all universities were awarding full degrees to women. And not until the 1980s were women allowed to do engineering degrees.[21] Even in 2016, women represented only 25 per cent of those graduating in a STEM subject – science, technology, engineering, and mathematics – and it remains difficult to dislodge the gender stereotype of those being 'male subjects', while the arts, languages and humanities continue to be seen as 'female subjects'.

The real education revolution has been in the massive uptake of higher education by both women and men. The pace of change is demonstrated by Helena, who commented: 'I was the first person in my family to go to university yet my maternal grandmother was not able even to sign her own name.'[22]

Between 1920 and 2011, the number of students doing first degrees increased from 4,000 in fourteen universities to 350,000 in around a hundred and thirty institutions, including the Open University set up in 1971, targeting adults of any age, not least women with family obligations. Jacqueline recalled:

If I had to choose an image to sum up my experience of the Open University it would be sitting at home on my sofa, nursing a baby in one arm, and writing notes from a text book with the other. I thrived on the distance and the flexibility. The distance fed my independence, was non-threatening to my Asperger's brain, and enabled my total immersion. I knew the dates of all my tutorials, examinations and assignment deadlines a year in advance, so was able to schedule study around work and family commitments. I got financial assistance, which allowed me to continue my studies. The OU helped me to develop knowledge, skills and confidence.[23]

Women were 28 per cent of students in 1920 and 56 per cent by 2011; in higher degrees, the proportion rose from 25 per cent to 50 per cent.[24] In accessing education, women have moved from the fringes into the very centre, thereby transforming their economic opportunities.[25] Until recently this was underpinned by government grants; however, with the increasing cost of higher education we have started to see a retrenchment.

Moreover it would be wrong to present educational establishments as no longer being a location where gender discrimination flourishes. Hierarchical gender socialisation is imprinted onto young people from nursery onwards. As they grow up, it is also where girls face abuse, and is a breeding ground for peer-pressure-related behavioural problems including ones around food and image. Nevertheless, the overall increased access of women and girls to education is a major contributor to the story of the changes in their opportunities and in their working lives.

Work

Prior to the First World War, most women's lives were determined primarily by the status and health of the head of their household. In poorer families, young girls and women became live-in servants or found casual work in domestic service, in agriculture or in the mills. Women in middle-income and richer households were not expected to seek employment outside the home. However, as well as the voluntary and political work mentioned in the previous chapter, middle-class women found jobs teaching, nursing or working in offices and shops.

During the First World War, the number of women counted as being in employment almost doubled from 24 per cent in 1914 to 47 per cent by 1918.[26] Women took over work that men had vacated and entered new jobs created by the war. Among these were the 'canaries', women whose skin turned yellow from handling TNT in munitions factories. Working conditions and pay were often poor, yet still seen as a liberation by those gaining some freedom and new horizons. Additionally, without actually creating a right to work, the 1919 Sex Disqualification (Removal) Act finally allowed women to take up certain civil professions or civic service, such as becoming magistrates, Justices of the Peace, barristers and solicitors.

Then, within one year of the armistice, an estimated 775,000 women left formal employment, either voluntarily or having been dismissed, and half a million women registered as unemployed.[27] The period was one of great male unemployment, so women who wanted to continue working were criticised, and those who refused domestic or laundry work in the hope of something better had their benefits cut by the Employment Exchange. Most gave up their hopes and by the 1930s the number of women registered as unemployed dropped to 29,000[28] and women's unemployment became invisible once again.

With few other options, a third of working women reluctantly returned to domestic service.[29] The textile industry in the North of England and the linen industry in Northern Ireland also continued to employ over 250,000 women.[30] New industries also emerged employing women on assembly lines. The 'white blouse revolution' expanded their opportunities in clerical and retail industries. Nevertheless, by 1931, women's formal employment had dropped to under 8 per cent and only increased gradually thereafter; then, because of the Second World War, all women aged eighteen to sixty became legally required to register for work in industry, civil defence or one of the auxiliary services – unless they had children under fourteen.[31] By 1943, an estimated 7.75 million women, 43 per cent of whom were married, had been conscripted into work.[32] From having been barred and considered unsuitable for and unsuited to work, suddenly everything had changed. In many households, women in essence became single parents juggling work and home. Wealthier women did so without or with less help from the servants they had relied on in the past. The then standard twelve-hour day and fifty-four-hour week became impossible and part-time work became more common.[33]

Yet even in times of war, some traditional gender divisions remained: single women could be assigned work away from home, unless they had a widowed father to look after – but not a widowed mother. Furthermore, although war disrupted assumptions about who could do what, the Restoration of the Pre-War Practices Act 1942 legislated that women's work was 'for the duration only'. The government's obligation to soldiers fighting on the battlefields was greater than to women on the home front.

Demobilisation this time was more gradual and there were some successful attempts to fight women's redundancy. Most importantly, the economy was growing due to infrastructural investment and the growth of the welfare state, so employment opportunities for women remained high.[34] By the late 1940s, there were significant labour short-ages, partly caused by the raising of the school leaving age and the post-war economic boom. Automation was also opening up new job opportunities, although jobs considered appropriate for women remained limited. In the course of the century, the economy moved from one dominated by blue-collar industrial male workers to one of white-collar clerical male workers, with lower-paid female secretarial and clerical employees. By 1951, most young women were working, including 79 per cent of fourteen- to twenty-year-olds.[35]

Most of the new jobs available to women involved leaving home every day. They gained financial autonomy, freedom from the house, and opportunities to meet others. The disadvantages were the juggling of domestic obligations and childcare. The pattern is more complicated when we look at the experiences of married women.

Before the First World War, except in poorer households, a woman was socially expected to stop work when she got married. A marriage bar was in force in companies and parts of the civil service. After the war, this was extended to include teachers, clerks and nurses. Legislation reinforced the view that married women's responsibilities should only be the home and that they were incapable of making their own choices. This position did not go unchallenged. In 1927, a private member's bill tried to remove the marriage bar. Nancy Astor MP pointedly commented: 'When I listen to the opponents of the Bill, I feel that I know women who could have twins every year and still be more efficient than some Members of Parliament.'[36] The bill was nevertheless defeated. Those who chafed at the bar were sometimes accused of taking jobs away from men as well as from younger, unmarried women.

Overall it was estimated that in 1931, only 5 per cent of married women worked in the formal economy, as opposed to 30 per cent of all women.[37] Some tried to sidestep the bar by hiding spouses and even children. Exceptions for the most part were class and poverty related. Cotton-mills had long employed mothers, and women continued to work formally and informally in the service industries in caring and cleaning work. Unusually, the Managing Director of the newly established BBC also declared in 1926 that women should 'be on an equal footing' and some prominent BBC female employees were not just married but also mothers. The policy did not last and a marriage bar was introduced in 1932; however, exceptions that suited the BBC were negotiated through a Marriage Tribunal. In any case, 'lavatory attendants, charladies and wardrobe women' were also exempt.[38]

The 1944 Education Act removed the bar on teaching and because of labour shortages some employers continued employing trusted staff. Like many, Judy Page stopped work at the Post Office and took a 'dowry' – a cash gift from her employer – when she married in 1954. She was told she could have continued working by forfeiting the dowry, and starting again at the bottom of the salary scale, but this did not appeal.[39] Similar dowries existed with other companies, including the civil service and the Church of England, and were taken up by millions of women. They looked well intentioned, but translated into a financial loss to the women, who were signing away their rights to benefits based on insurance contributions.[40]

The cultural expectations that women should give up their jobs on marriage continued in many circles. As Jackie explained:

> In 1975 when working for the civil service I told my manager, a 'spinster' in her 50s, that I was about to marry. She said I would need to write to the Civil Service Commission for *permission* to continue working afterwards. I settled for *informing* them that I would be staying on and this was accepted. My mother in law saw this as progress, as she had been obliged to resign when she married in the 1930s.[41]

So far I have looked at women's employment without touching on the question of attitudes to their value and their pay. The struggle in this area mirrors that for equality in the political world. However, unlike the vote where all it took were two laws in Parliament ('Ha! All it took?!' I hear my ancestors saying), in terms of pay many more laws were needed, closing loopholes as they emerged.

Since government policy and social norms were premised on the assumption that men were the breadwinners for the family, if a woman worked, it was assumed that she had no dependants so she did not need to earn as much. However, in reality many families did not fit the norm, and women wanted both financial autonomy and to be paid equally.

Even before 1918, some women workers, such as welders, were demanding equal wages. Welding was an occupation where men and women did exactly the same work. During the First World War, the Society of Women Welders (in which suffrage activists were involved) successfully campaigned to reduce the wage gap.[42] During the Second World War, many more women took up welding given the increased need. Trade unions supported them in ensuring wages were not cut, fearing that on the men's return, their jobs and wages would be threatened. Wages were maintained and at the end of the war women were simply fired.

Figure 3: 'We Can Do It' poster used by the War Production Co-ordinating Committee and designed by J. Howard Miller, artist employed by Westinghouse

Welding work is an interesting case because of the association with feminism, partly through the 'We Can Do It!' American poster by J. Howard Miller[43] regularly recreated and posed for. The poster was produced in 1943 for the Westinghouse Electric and Manufacturing Company in the United States as part of a series to boost the morale and productivity of the primarily male workforce. Most of the other posters were of men, but Howard Miller decided to paint one of a woman, without realising the symbolic importance it would take on.

The welders were not alone in their battles. In 1918, 27,000 women worked as bus conductors, including over 3,500 at the London General Omnibus Company. Women at the Willesden depot went on strike for a war bonus being paid to the men but not to them. The strikers' demands grew under the slogan 'Same work – Same money'. Within a week 18,000 women conductors had stopped work. The strike was settled a few days later, and the women won the five shillings' war bonus – but not equal pay.[44]

During the Second World War, when the government decided that there was a need to conscript women, activists tried but failed to ensure that women would be guaranteed equal pay under the 1941 National Service (Number Two) Act.[45] There were some successes, however. In 1943, with the support of Pauline Gower, women pilots in the Air Transport Auxiliary took their case to Parliament and won the right to equal rank and pay. The ATA was possibly the first organisation in the UK to have a policy of equal pay and treatment.[46] Likewise, when compensation for work injuries was introduced for men and not women, there was an outcry and a cross-party parliamentary revolt involving nine of the ten women MPs. The result was an amendment to the 1939 Personal Injuries (Emergency Provisions) Act in 1943 in favour of equal compensation.[47]

Campaigns were established to push for economic equality more widely, spurred on by the defeat of an amendment to the 1944 Education Bill proposing equal pay for teachers. This had been quashed by Winston Churchill and a Royal Commission set up to delay legislation.[48] In 1946, the Commission's tame report recommended equal pay – but only for lower grades in teaching, the civil service and government. The three women on the committee published their own minority report but the Labour government rejected even the limited recommendations of the main report, citing the inflationary pressures that equal pay would generate.[49]

From 1951, following the Equal Remuneration Convention, international human rights law and institutions such as the International Labour Organisation also started to encompass the principle of equal pay.[50] Lobbying continued in Britain and in 1952 the London County Council agreed to introduce equal pay for civil servants, local government officers, teachers and nurses. The limited legislation was delayed and only became law in 1963. Then, in 1968, a strike was started by 187 female sewing machinists at the Ford Dagenham plant. Their jobs had been classified as unskilled, despite the fact that they needed to pass a skill test to be employed. They earned less than the men in equivalent work. Although they won some concessions and, momentously, laid the foundations to the 1970 Equal Pay Act, they did not achieve this themselves until after another strike in 1984.

Other factors behind the 1970 Act were the negotiating skills of Barbara Castle, then Secretary of State for Employment and Productivity, the actions of the National Joint Action Committee on Equal Rights and the plans to join the European Union. The 1975 Sex Discrimination Act, championed by Nancy Seear in the House of Lords, was also passed, focusing on ending discrimination in the public sphere, in appointments, promotion, dismissal, training and regarding other benefits.

The Equal Opportunities Commission[51] was established to help enforce gender equality legislation although, in practice, there were very few successful claims. One of these was initiated by Belinda Price, who challenged the maximum age of twenty-five for joining the civil service. This was ruled to discriminate disproportionately against women who took career breaks and had children. The age limit was only abolished in 1978.[52]

Implementation of the Equal Pay Act relied on individuals taking employers to tribunals – at personal cost – and failed to address the systemic gender inequality. The 'genuine' occupational qualifications element could be used as a get-out clause; and it did not cover discrimination regarding social security, tax and pension rights. Furthermore, employers used the period before the implementation of the Act to avoid increasing women's wages by changing job descriptions.[53] Nevertheless, the threat of legislation seems to have been important, in the signals it gave, and the pay gap fell significantly in subsequent years, as can be seen from Figure 4.[54]

GREAT BRITAIN'S GENDER PAY GAP 1970-2008
% difference between Male and Female earnings

Note from 1970-83: Data for men aged 21+, women aged 18+

Figure 4: Gender pay gap 1970–2008 ONS Data. Source: ONS (New Earnings Survey/Annual Survey of Hours and Earnings)

Nevertheless discrimination at work continued and, in 1982, the European Court of Justice ruled that Britain was violating the EEC Equal Pay Directive, so the 1984 Equal Value Amendment to the Equal Pay Act was passed. However, the work most men and women did was different and cross-industry comparisons could not always be made. Furthermore, the regulations allowed unequal pay if it reflected a material factor other than sex. 'Market forces' was one such factor, allowing anything to be justified on this basis.[55]

Similarly, employers could assign work to agencies to make them different from non-agency work.

Taking a case to an employment tribunal was expensive, so the support of a trade union was essential. Immigrant women in particular had a difficult time (and are still less likely to belong to trade unions).[56] In 1976, in the Grunwick film-processing laboratory in London, Jayaben Desai, a small, middle-aged woman, led the 'strikers in saris' on a two-year battle that included a hunger strike. Famously she summed up the workers' determination, saying to her manager: 'What you are running here is not a factory, it is a zoo. In a zoo, there are many types of animals. Some are monkeys who dance on your fingertips, others are lions who can bite your head off. We are those lions, Mr Manager.' She also commented: 'Trade union support is like honey on the elbow – you can smell it, you can feel it, but you cannot taste it.'[57]

In 1988, 1,300 women working for a council serving school meals in Yorkshire were dismissed and then re-employed on lower rates, cutting holiday entitlement and abolishing a sick-pay scheme. This happened despite the council accepting a job evaluation study that had found the women's work to be of equal value to that of road-sweepers, gardeners and refuse collectors, who were mainly men. Only in 1995 did the Law Lords unanimously agree that the council had contravened equal pay legislation. The council had argued that it was trying to reduce costs to keep the service in-house and protect the women's employment. Another test case found that it was unlawful for a private tender to introduce inferior conditions for ex-council employees. The legal decision, gained with the support of the trade union Unison, had repercussions for many thousands of largely low-paid women workers.

The Equality Act of 2010 provided an important additional layer of legislation. It allowed for positive discrimination where two people had equal qualifications and one had a protected characteristic such as race or gender, and required public authorities to eliminate discrimination and promote equality of opportunity.

Differential bonuses, across different working environments, were another element that had to be addressed from the 1970s onwards. For example, 4,000 women workers took Birmingham City Council to an employment tribunal for excluding women such as cleaners from bonuses, which meant that men such as refuse workers could earn four times as much. The women won eventually, in 2011, but only after the council had appealed at every stage. Differential bonuses are found at all economic levels. Louise Barton, for instance, took an investment firm in the City to a tribunal for a lack of transparency in how bonuses were awarded. A subsequent Treasury Select Committee report in 2010 on Sexism in the City ended with the comment: 'Transparency and public scrutiny are important ways to ensure that discrimination does not persist.'[58]

The overall gender pay gap in 2018 was the lowest on record at 17.9 per cent overall and 8.6 per cent for full-time work.[59] The trend is positive but the pace is very, very slow. In ground-breaking legislation, from 2017 companies with more than 250 employees were required to report on their gender pay and bonus gaps. Although a very positive step forward, only a third of the workforce is covered, and many of the factors that create the gap remain in place.[60] It was calculated that by 2025, full gender parity could potentially add £600 billion to Britain's GDP.[61] At the present rate, we will have to wait until 2069, ninety-nine years after the Equal Pay Act, for the gap to disappear.[62]

One critical factor interwoven with that of pay is segmentation of the labour market, with women and men expected to fit particular stereotypes. Sarah, a firefighter, shared:

> I was the first female firefighter for my area in Hampshire. Once, when I was waiting in the fire engine, a man came to the window and said, 'It's not a woman's job love,' and walked off. Later the same man was talking with my colleague and feeling the weight of our large hydraulic cutting tool. The man was struggling to hold it with two hands so my colleague called me over and asked if I could place it back on the fire engine; I picked up the tool with one hand and walked off, quietly making my point.[63]

Dany Cotton became the London Fire Brigade's first woman chief commissioner in 2017. She commented: 'As a woman in the fire service, I sometimes feel that part of my role is about myth-busting.'[64]

Although women's paid work has increased substantially, it continues to be segmented, with women at the bottom of some jobs, clustered in specific low-pay occupations and working more in the lower-paid public sector. For example, at the beginning of the last century, and still to some extent today, women were mostly relegated to service and support roles, monetised versions of their domestic roles. These have been called the five Cs: caring, cashiering, cleaning, catering and clerical. Even in these areas, however, a few men dominate at the very top for example as cooks and hairdressers.

According to a 1980 'Women and Employment Survey', 63 per cent of women were in jobs done only by women; while 80 per cent of men were in jobs exclusive to men.[65] Sometimes what was seen as a male or a female job changed over time; for example in 1911 women represented 18 per cent of the clerks but by 1981 they were 78 per cent as men moved into higher-paying white-collar jobs. This changed again with the replacement of typewriters by computers.

As a further example of the hierarchies, according to data from 2015, although the numbers of men and women entering universities are now on a par, women comprise only 24 per cent of professors and 45 per cent of academic staff but 81 per cent of non-academic, clerical staff.[66]

Women in the Police

The first female police officer, Sofia Stanley, was employed in 1919. Policewomen initially patrolled in pairs, followed by two policemen under orders to keep them in their sights and provide support when needed. Women officers had no power of arrest until 1923 and could not carry handcuffs unless instructed by a senior officer. In 1973, the first Woman Detective Constable (WDC) was appointed, and the different rank structure and

---

separation of tasks and office space was subsequently abolished. Equal pay for police officers began in 1974 and part-time officers started working in 1997.[67] Judith Gillespie, the Deputy Chief Constable of the Police Service of Northern Ireland, commented:

> Given the terrorist threat in Northern Ireland, from the early seventies male officers were issued with both a Personal Protection Firearm and a baton. Female officers were issued with a handbag. Female officers weren't routinely armed until 1994 – ironically the same year as the first IRA ceasefire.[68]

> The first female Assistant Chief Constable, Alison Halford, was appointed in 1983. She developed new standards for abused women and children to be interviewed by women officers. In 1999 women officers started to be called PCs rather than WPCs, a battle still not won in some professions. By 2000 women made up 17 per cent of the police force. Sue Sim rose up the ranks over thirty years and in 2011 became the first woman to lead a Metropolitan Police Force (Northumbria Police). She retired following a Police and Crime Commissioner probe into misconduct, which she put down to her challenging the sexist boys' club within the force.[69] In 2017 Cressida Dick achieved the highest-ranking position as the Metropolitan Commissioner in London.

One of the causes of job segregation has been careers advice that perpetuates gender stereotyping. Baroness Patricia Scotland QC remembers being told she should aim to become a supervisor in Sainsbury's.[70] Similarly Jayne recalled:

[My teacher] said I should look into the law. At 14 we got sent to a careers fair in the town hall. I wanted to know where the table was for the legal profession. The unforgettable response was, 'Why do you want to do law, someone like you will never get anywhere. The hairdressing table is over there.' It is frightening to think how many people have had their career dreams shattered by a 'careers advisor'.[71]

According to the Women's Engineering Society (set up in 1919 and adopting the suffragette colours), in 2015 only 9 per cent of the engineering workforce was female. For Jackie:

> When I graduated in 1967 I was lucky enough to get a job in the applied physics department of an engineering company. I was the only technical woman in my department, the first woman to attend my Trade Union conference and the only woman at the vast majority of meetings I went to.[72]

The segmentation of labour is constantly being 'reinforced and reinvented'.[73] Even today many young men expect longer and better training than their female counterparts.[74] Tradition, culture, schools, the media, women's domestic roles, all play their part.[75] Vicious cycles are created, which now and again are challenged but often also reformulated.

Work segregation not only contributes to pay gaps, it also feeds into sexism and abuse. As Elaine explained: 'I work in construction where women must power dress and/or use their sexuality, work extra hard, have a lot of confidence and tolerate a fair amount of what is called "banter" to be taken seriously.'[76] The sexualisation of certain 'female' jobs has been reinforced by the kinds of uniforms that, for example, waitresses and female cabin crew are required to wear. This is sometimes being challenged, as shown by the successful 2016 legal battle against British Airways by staff who were not allowed to wear trousers. Even so, in many workplaces labour segmentation, pay differences and sexual harassment are often intertwined.[77] Lucy shared:

I commenced training in obstetrics and gynaecology (O&G) in 1989. It was then a male-dominated speciality and I was firmly put in my place. A male consultant told me in 1990: 'My female juniors do not wear trousers', ergo if I wanted to remain I should wear skirts.

My sexuality was entirely closeted at the time. Some senior doctors with suspicions made disparaging comments about why a lesbian could possibly want to practice O&G, forgetting the contradiction of being a heterosexual male practising O&G.

Times really have changed: in 2017 O&G is now dominated by female doctors who make up more than 80 per cent and we have specific policies on lesbian and bisexual health.[78]

In the legal profession, the segregation is such that women tend to work in social welfare and employment law – at the lower end of the pay scale – while men work in corporate law with more status and money. At the Bar, although women comprise only 36 per cent of barristers 61 per cent of them specialise in family law.[79] Among solicitors, as Jayne explained:

Women are put off by the whole 'corporate' environment. Our department is literally 90–95 per cent men. In fairness, it's not intentional. The company is very good about encouraging a work–life balance. But some firms, especially in London, expect availability around the clock. Most have showers but some have beds as well. Even some local firms expect people to be in until 8 p.m. every night. It is virtually impossible to work these kinds of hours and juggle childcare.[80]

Work and Family

The need to balance work and family is often the crux of the matter. For Janet:

How times have changed! In 1984 I was pregnant with my first child and it transpired that I was the first teacher in the 110-year history of the school who wanted to return to school after her child was born. Miss Moon had to get her book of 'rules' to find out what maternity leave I was allowed. Yet the bursar still asked why I was not staying home to look after my baby.[81]

Although the marriage bar had gone by the 1970s, expectations of women changed from being a wife and mother, to a hybrid form accommodating paid employment before marriage, to one in which mothers could move in and out of employment, with the possibility of some support from family members, employers and the state.

Maternal health benefits were first recognised in the 1911 National Insurance Act; then the 1946 National Insurance Act introduced thirteen weeks of paid maternity leave.[82] Nevertheless, many employers including the civil service still forced women to resign or dismissed them when they became pregnant until, in 1975, the Employment Protection Act made this unlawful. Maternity pay was introduced for six weeks at nine-tenths of normal pay for those who had worked in a company for two years or more and mothers could extend their leave to twenty-nine weeks after giving birth. Maternity protection was eroded in the 1980s and extended again in 1993 to comply with an EU directive. Many women still fell through the cracks. In Juliet's case:

In 1994 I was working for a marketing agency. You only had to work for an employer for six months before the birth of your child to get maternity benefits. I had been there four months when I fell pregnant and was made redundant within a week of informing them. Because my partner worked for the same organisation we felt I couldn't take them to the EOC.[83]

The UK policy on statutory paid and unpaid maternity leave has for the most part improved since its introduction in 1975, and statutory paternity leave also started in 2003, including for those adopting and surrogate parents but without any special provision for complications or pre-term babies. Many families, especially the poorest, find it difficult to take the unpaid element at a time of additional financial burdens, and the take-up of unpaid paternity time has been less than 10 per cent.[84] Nevertheless, the number of stay-at-home fathers increased from 111,000 in 1993, when the data was first collected, to 229,000 in 2014, while stay-at-home mothers decreased over the same period from 2.91 to 2.04 million.[85] If the total leave entitlement were divided more equally, as it is in Iceland for example, employers would have one less reason to discriminate against women.[86]

Although at interviews it is now illegal to ask a woman if she is pregnant or planning to be, many employers continue to do so. They would never think of asking a man if he was planning to become a father. In 2015, an estimated 11 per cent of women lost their jobs due to pregnancy discrimination. Of these, 20 per cent experienced harassment or negative comments related to pregnancy from their employer and/or colleagues and 10 per cent of mothers said their employer discouraged them from attending antenatal appointments. Some were demoted or not put forward for promotion during their pregnancy or on their return to work.[87]

Joeli Brearly was sacked by her employer when she was four months pregnant. She hired a solicitor but discovered she was having a high-risk pregnancy and decided to focus on her baby. In 2015, after having her child, Joeli set up the campaign Pregnant Then Screwed, with a website for people to post their experiences anonymously and seek mentoring or free legal advice. When the Equality and Human Rights Commission found that less than 1 per cent of discrimination victims raise a tribunal claim,[88] the campaigners looked into the reasons. They found that, firstly, as with Joeli, the three-month time limit is restrictive when pregnant women are least likely to cope with the stress of litigation. Secondly, many women might not have the information or support to pursue a claim. Joeli reflected:

Discrimination can be overt and ruthless, but often it is slow and insidious. Bullying and harassment is very common as most employers know that sacking someone for pregnancy or maternity leave is illegal so they look for alternative ways to force you out. Women return to find they don't exist on staff diagrams, that their hours have changed to make it impossible to work and access childcare. I heard from one woman who returned to find she didn't have a desk for two months; another was told her post had moved 100 miles away. Her old office was still operating but they decided she needed to be based elsewhere. I have lost count of the number of women who have told me their employer asked them to have an abortion.[89]

At least, in 2017, the upfront fees to take a case to a tribunal introduced in 2013 were ruled to be illegal. However, more needs to be done. This could mean closer oversight by the government, support with returners' programmes, and measures to foster working environments where women have the confidence to speak up.[90] Many solutions have no significant cost implication, such as providing a quiet place where women can express and store breast milk. But some do require a financial investment. As Kate argued: 'small companies can ill afford the extra costs and disruptions incurred when employees become pregnant, even if they are supportive and appreciate the long-term benefits of being good employers. We have experienced this and seen other companies suffer.'[91]

Unless norms change, small businesses in particular are pitted against women. In all this, an attitudinal shift towards joint responsibility for parenting and improved childcare is pivotal. Yet throughout the century, childcare provision has been inadequate, except possibly during the two world wars. There were more than 1,500 government-funded local authority-run nurseries by 1944, which were set up to enable women to work outside the home.[92] When peace came, the nurseries were closed, but not without protest. In Pudsey, Yorkshire, women locked themselves in a nursery over a weekend until police stormed the building. Thirty women also went on strike at the local textile factory, but without success.[93]

Lack of childcare surfaced again during the 1970s. Ruth Lynn Fraenkel, later Baroness Deech, recalled her experiences: 'In the 1980s, I fought a decade-long battle to get more staff nurseries at my university, facing the hostility and fear expressed by working men and "homemakers".'[94] In 2007, the Conservative–Liberal coalition government made a commitment to provide fifteen hours a week free childcare for three- to four-year-olds. The Conservative government increased this to thirty hours a week in 2017. Although a great improvement, support beyond the statutory levels remains patchy and costly and the impact is primarily on mothers. Madeleine, for example, shared: 'My now ex-husband never did a fair share of the childcare. Being a father has had no effect on his work patterns whereas my life as an actress changed completely as I could no longer work in the theatre.'[95] Sheryl Sandberg's summary was that 'the most important career choice you'll make is who you marry'.[96]

While women's opportunities to work and pursue a career are generally better than their grandmothers' and great-grandmothers', those who choose to have a family face a pattern of working full-time before the children arrive and, increasingly, after they have grown up; and in between working part-time or in more flexible ways. The situation results in a motherhood-related pay gap. In 2016, as can be seen from Figure 5, on average before motherhood there was a gap of around 13 per cent between women's and men's pay.[97] This gradually increased until the first child was twelve, when women's hourly wages were around 33 per cent below men's.[98] The differences were found to be cumulative until women are in their fifties.[99]

Differences in pay carry through into differences in pensions. These for women were the highest level to date in 2017, yet they were still estimated to be 27 per cent less than men's. The gender gap hasn't always narrowed; for example, it increased between 2015 and 2017, partly because of changes in state pension requirements and the underpayment of national income contributions.[100] This in turn was the result of the government handling of the equalisation of pension ages demanded by European legislation.[101] The women

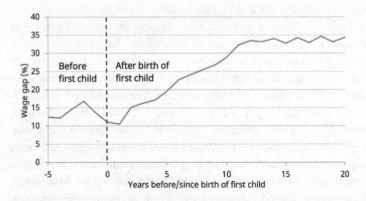

Figure 5: Gender wage gap by time to/since birth of first child. Source: BHPS 1991–2008

caught up in the transition process who had planned to retire at sixty found that they had to keep working and sometimes could no longer do so. They felt that the government failed to deliver a smooth transition and they established the WASPI (Women Against State Pension Inequality) lobbying group.

The need to care for elderly, sick and disabled relatives is another critical demand on many women's time. From the 1950s, carers formed pressure groups and, as a result, in the 1960s and 1970s, limited tax concessions and pension credits were introduced. In 1976, the invalid care allowance excluded married women until, in 1986, Jackie Drake took the government to the European Court for unlawful sexual discrimination, and won. The initial Act acknowledging the work of unpaid carers only became law in 1995. This was followed by a string of Acts, including the one in 2014 that increased local authorities' obligations and put a cap on individuals' liabilities for care costs. The problem was a hot topic during the 2017 election campaign. Yet despite increasing acknowledgement of the social and economic vulnerability of carers, attention and support for something that affects mainly women remains perfunctory.[102]

In the story of the caring economy, women immigrants play a central role as those relieving wealthier women from domestic care.

A study in 2015 found that 20 per cent of the social care workforce in England was born outside the UK, including 150,000 working in private homes and 81,000 in adult domiciliary care.[103]

Another aspect of the care that women provide is that which lies behind the success of many men's careers. Katharine Whitehorn described how her father was a housemaster at Mill Hill School but it was her mother who, among other jobs, prepared the food for around fifty people in his charge. Her role was neither officially acknowledged nor paid. Her father's predecessor had left when his mother, who did all the cooking, had become ill.[104]

Similarly, MPs, diplomats and vicars have relied on their wives to answer the telephone, host parties, receptions and so on. Joint sharing of roles between husband and wife is becoming more common but there are few examples of a man forfeiting a career to help his wife's. Perhaps the most notable exception has been Prince Philip supporting the Queen for almost seventy years.

If we look at the world of farming, men have dominated as the owners of the land and the business. The role of a farmer's wife has always been critical but in a support role, often unacknowledged – and as usual with some exceptions. Very often the farmer's wife's role has expanded to include responsibilities such as managing B&Bs, shops, food processing and community activities.[105] For reasons to do with emotional ties and cultural norms it seems that many farmers' wives reinforce their husbands' position as bread-winners, even when their work is the primary source of income. Researching the issue, Sally Shortall wrote: 'Change has occurred, but women and men do gender identity and work identity in a way that allows the family farm discourse to persist.'[106]

Minimum wages and flexible work

Given that women are over-represented amongst low-income earners, the battle for minimum wages and improved conditions has been particularly relevant to them – a concern even during the suffrage campaign, as depicted by the poster on the following page.

Figure 6: *Waiting for a Living Wage poster designed by Catherine Courtauld and printed by Suffrage Atelier 1913. Source: Museum of London*

During most of the century, home-based piecework provided employment that could be done while rearing children or care-giving, and this was a common source of cheap female labour, until at least the 1980s.[107] More recently it has returned to prominence, particularly linked to high-tech work. From the 1970s, contracting to agencies became another way to reduce obligations to employees, particularly in the low-paid cleaning and catering industries, in which women predominate.

Minimum wage standards were introduced for specific sectors following the Wages Council Act of 1945. Another half a century later these were replaced by the National Minimum Wages Act in 1998. At least 1.5 million workers, disproportionately women and BAME communities, benefited. Thereafter the rates were amended and a National Living Wage was introduced, with phased increases and a review mechanism involving the Low Pay Commission. The rates applied not only to direct employees but also to agency staff and home workers.

Working conditions also improved over the century thanks to a tightening of legislation and, particularly in the second half, through the EU and the concept of a floor of rights. This included the 1998 Working Time Directive setting a maximum forty-eight-hour week.

The main trend in the last half-century has been the expansion of part-time and more flexible female labour. In 1951 there were 20 million employees in Great Britain and women accounted for 12 per cent of the labour force. By 1986, this had increased to 44 per cent. Over the same period, the percentage of women workers in part-time jobs increased from 11 per cent to 44 per cent.[108] The rates then dropped marginally for women and increased for men. By 2015, 41 per cent of women workers and 11 per cent of men were working part-time.[109]

Women have wanted part-time work for many reasons including pregnancy, childbirth and their role as carers. This preference was particularly evident after the Second World War, when more part-time jobs and even some job-shares started to become available. Employers have also benefited from this 'marginal' or 'reserve labour' as it has meant a reduction in the loss of output for meal-breaks, less commitment to training and fewer employee rights. Although there are many exceptions, part-time work is disproportionately available for jobs with the lowest pay and most limited career paths. It also perpetuates labour segmentation.[110]

A survey of 800 female solicitors in 2010 found that half of them felt there was a stigma attached to working part-time; those doing so were viewed as less serious about their careers and therefore less likely to be promoted.[111] Conversely, a woman in full-time work 'leaving' her children with their father or other care-givers, was seen as prioritising herself above the children's needs and having questionable maternal instincts – a judgement that men rarely face. Nevertheless, although many of the problems continue and the pay gap in part-time work remains higher than in full-time work, legislative support has reduced some of the discrimination. Moreover, the full-time/part-time dichotomy is being eroded with the advent of flexible working.

Another pattern, especially since the recession of 2008, concerns those caught in a cycle of repeated short-term contracts. Some employers use this approach to reduce employees' entitlements, including maternity leave and overtime. In 2016 more than 900,000 workers were registered on so-called zero-hour contracts – which have been compared to Victorian sweated labour at minimum rates with no guarantee of work, no security and no protection.[112]

For those with more secure employment contracts, the Employment Rights Act of 2002 gives employees the right to request flexible working if they have a child under seventeen (or eighteen if disabled) or responsibilities as a carer. The benefits became evident and in 2014 the right to request flexible working was increased by the Children and Families Act, so that any employee with twenty-six weeks' continuous service could ask to work flexibly – with a duty on employers to respond in a 'reasonable' manner.

As well as part-time work, women have tended to be attracted to self-employment because of the greater flexibility it provides. Sometimes they have defaulted to being self-employed, as many did after the recession of 2008.[113] By 2013, women represented one-third of the self-employed and accounted for 17 per cent of business owners.

One last point about flexibility is that, culturally, women are still expected to adapt their working lives to the needs of their families. When the family relocates or women lose their jobs it is considered acceptable for women to apply for any other job, even a significant demotion – there is no 'floor' around their expectations. For men, there remain stronger taboos against downward progression. However, even this is beginning to change, with the pattern of full-time guaranteed jobs for life becoming something of the past.

Women Leaders

In the 1950s, female graduates were often recruited as secretaries with the assurance that other jobs would be available to them later. Conscious or unconscious bias was at work and this rarely happened.[114] Many women have tended to get on with their job, and expect to be rewarded for it, lacking a mindset that requests recognition. According to Sheryl Sandberg, the 'tiara syndrome' involves: 'Keeping your head down, delivering excellent work and hoping that the right people will notice – and place a tiara on your head.'[115]

In 2004, women made up only 9 per cent of board members of the FTSE 100 companies. To solve the problem, in 2010 the '30% Club' demanded pledges to get a minimum of 30 per cent of women on boards. Then in 2015, a lower voluntary target of at least 25 per cent female board members was set by the government's Davies Review, with an indication that tougher measures would ensue if things did not change. The modest target has been achieved: as of April 2016, the overall figure had risen to 26 per cent.[116]

Attention has also focused on paid women directors rather than non-executive positions. The FTSE 100 companies had less than 10 per cent female executive directors in 2016. Helena Morrisey, who founded the 30% Club, reflected: 'A lot of progress has been made, but I often still feel very isolated . . . We haven't got true inclusion until women feel they don't have to be honorary men and gays don't feel they have to be honorary straights.'[117]

Vanessa found that her working-class accent was scorned. In her earshot, when she first got a job in a City bank, she heard a female colleague say: 'I don't know why we take these council rejects in the first place.'[118] Her sense of not fitting in continued as she moved up in a career in the City, so she decided to take voice coaching lessons. Even for someone proud of her working-class heritage, the only way up was to sound like those at the top. Vanessa could change her voice but not her gender. She decided to create a platform for women to advance their careers, WeAreTheCity, which in 2016 had 120,000 members and 8 million hits on its website per month.

Support Networks for Women in Business

The Women's Organisation, established in 1996, has provided a vibrant hub for women in Liverpool, helping to develop new business ventures, or strengthen existing ones by providing a range of business services.[119] Other networking and support initiatives include the Forward Ladies Network formed in 1999, the Women in Business Network in 2005, Enterprising Women founded in 2006, the Women's Business Council in 2012 and the Women's Business club in 2013. Groups catering to women of specific backgrounds include Asian Women Mean Business and there are location-specific ones such as City Women's Network.

Terms associated with the barriers to women in their fight to get to and stay at the top in business include the glass ceiling, or, more evocatively, the leadership labyrinth with its invisible barriers and prejudices that women have to navigate alone.[120] Another term is the glass cliff, where women are promoted to difficult jobs, either because the old-boy network do not recommend the job to each other and someone with less social capital is appointed, or because women are actively sought because of the stereotype that women are good at sorting out a mess.[121] An example was the appointment of the CEO at the English National Opera, Cressida Pollock, who turned its fortunes around in 2015.[122]

Overall it feels like we have reached a pivotal moment in understanding the benefits of including women in all aspects of business. The economic argument for diversity was strongly supported by an influential 2015 McKinsey study, which found that in the UK a 10 per cent increase in gender diversity in senior management corresponded with a more than 3 per cent increase in business income.[123] Other studies have also found that the collective intelligence of groups increases where women are included.[124] Ruby McGregor-Smith, a peer in the Lords and a leading figure in the Women's Business Council, reflected:

> I was really surprised in 2007 at the interest in me when I became CEO at Mitie. That was because I was the first Asian female to run a UK listed company. Sponsoring and supporting their people to do well is something all businesses should do. It is amazing what talent you will find that does not tick the conventional boxes. Cultures need to evolve to be inclusive of all talent and respectful of it.[125]

Looking back over the period, Margery Hurst was one of the first business leaders to make it to the top, founding the Brook Street Bureau in 1946, which became the largest secretarial bureau in the world and was the first employment agency listed on the London Stock Exchange.[126] Another success story was that of Dame Stephanie Shirley, an Austrian refugee who arrived on the Kindertransport. In 1962, she started a software business employing women working from their own homes, consciously creating opportunities for women with dependants. She called herself 'Steve' to increase her credibility in the IT business. In an interview with the *Guardian* in 2017 she explained that she was a feminist 'in deed but not in word'.[127]

For the most part women entrepreneurs have become success-ful primarily in very feminised areas of fashion and beauty prod-ucts including Laura Ashley, Vivienne Westwood and Cath Kidston. Jacqueline Gold, in 1987, became the MD of the Ann Summers lingerie and sex-toy business owned by her father. Prior to this, only around 10 per cent of the company's clientele were women; she turned this around and by 2016 women were 80 per cent of customers, the products having become more explicitly geared to women's sexual interests.[128] By 2016 the company boasted over 140 shops across the UK and a turnover of £140 million, and Jacqueline Gold had become one of the richest women in Britain.[129] Also in the lingerie business, founding the Ultimo brand of bras in 1996, was Michelle Mone, ranked one of Britain's most successful businesswomen.[130]

Fewer women have succeeded outside these fields. The sports journalist Karren Brady became the MD of Birmingham City Football Club in 1993 and then vice chair of West Ham United and a TV personality, particularly through *The Apprentice*. She has spoken out about her experiences of sexism and is renowned for encouraging women in business. Similarly, Deborah Meaden's entrepreneurial successes started in 1992 with a family holiday park. She also acquired a textile mill and other investments and is best known for her appearances on the television programme *Dragons' Den*, initially as the only woman investor. Women entre-preneurs who have made their fortune from the internet include Martha Lane Fox, who co-founded Lastminute.com in 1997 and was made a cross-bench peer in 2013; and Denise Coates, who from 2000 made a fortune from the online gambling company bet365, becoming in 2017 the highest-paid woman in corporate history.[131]

Wealth and the Wider Economy

Accumulated wealth and access to capital are more fundamental to one's livelihood than people's employment – and capital has mostly been held and passed on between men. Susan told me that her grandmother did not inherit when her father died:

> My mother left Ireland in 1956 to get away from how unfairly she was treated as a woman. Her five brothers all inherited or were bought farms on marriage. My mother was given nothing and often said she couldn't leave my dad if she wanted as she had nothing in her own name, although she worked her fingers to the bone. The story repeats. My younger brother inherited the farm in Tyrone, Northern Ireland, even though he had lived away for many years. His seven older sisters inherited nothing . . . This was in 2012![132]

Historically, inheritance passed from father to son. Wives and their property belonged to their husbands. Exceptions have always existed such as where women inherited because there were no men, as in aristocratic and entrepreneurial dynasties. Even when laws changed and were not prescriptive, the cultural assumption remained that fathers, brothers, husbands or sons should be making financial decisions and owning assets. In Dinah's case:

> Back in 1969 my husband and I bought our first house. The solicitor drew up all the documents in my husband's name. I objected and insisted the documents were drawn up in joint names. The solicitor was not happy. Fortunately, because we could not proceed without my financial input, I was able to bring pressure on my husband and in turn, the solicitor.[133]

However, the laws of male entitlement and female subjugation were being eroded even before 1918. The first Married Women's Property Act, in 1870, initially drafted by my great-grandfather Richard Pankhurst, ensured that money earned by a wife through her own work would be regarded as her property. The Act was subsequently expanded in 1882 to include all her property. From 1935, married women were allowed to bequeath property through a will on the same terms as single women, and a husband was no longer liable for his wife's debts and vice versa. The revised Married Women's Property Act of 1964 also ensured that, when divorced, women became legally entitled to keep half of what they had saved from housekeeping allowances given to them by their husbands. Nevertheless, it was not until 1996 that the courts decided a fair division of assets was more appropriate than maintenance payments based on needs, which tended to favour men.[134] Many of the legal discriminations have long gone but dig a bit and the cultural mores still remain.

Institutions such as banks were part of the problem. Although a woman could inherit money and therefore have a bank account, until around 1975 it was quite common for banks to require a male guarantor to open the account or sign for any loan, and it was difficult for women to take out a mortgage. Jean and Ann shared:

In 1960, I was working as a legal secretary where I had a good wage. I wished to buy a TV with my money. The shopkeeper wanted my husband's name on the HP contract. I stuck to my guns, said that if I could not buy it in my own name only, I did not want it. He eventually relented but when the date of payment neared, this guy was gleefully on to me expecting I could not pay. But I proved him wrong and moreover I have never forgotten how proud I was at exercising my right to financial independence.[135]

When I started my own business, in 1974, I encountered difficulties when I asked for a loan, the bank manager admitting to my face that if I had been a man he would not have refused me. As soon as I started making good money I moved banks.[136]

With the growth of women's independent income, banks started to cater more for them. The National Commercial Bank of Scotland, which later merged with the Royal Bank of Scotland, opened a 'Ladies Branch' in Edinburgh in 1964, which continued to operate until 1997.[137] The first credit card was introduced by Barclays in 1966, and although it was initially targeted at men, it didn't require a male guarantor and became popular with women. Yet women are sometimes not given a credit card because they don't have a credit rating independent from their husbands. If they divorce or the husband dies, they have to start from scratch to obtain a credit history.[138]

Finance and banking were and to a large extent remain male bastions. For example, women were only allowed to join the London Stock Exchange in 1973. It appointed its first female chief executive, Clara Furse, in 2001. Some of the biggest wage gaps have been in the finance sector, particularly in areas like high-risk hedge funds most associated with risk-taking behaviour. When the 2008 banking crisis ricocheted around the world, governments stepped in with taxpayers' money to protect the banks. Amongst the casualties was the whole banking industry in Iceland, affecting many in the UK who had invested there. The only Icelandic bank that fared well was one run entirely by women.[139] More recently, a study by Yorkshire Building Society in 2015 found that women were not so likely to take risks, were much less confident about financial matters and therefore were wary of share schemes, which are in fact there to help employees save for their future. Some companies have woken up to the differences.[140] As Janet explained about Marks & Spencer:

With over 75 per cent of Marks & Spencer employees being female, the company made conscious efforts to ensure that their share plan engages with women. This has been through listening to its employees and as a result changing the perceived very masculine and corporate styled communications to one in which the language and the presentation was more akin to what women would find attractive and less 'scary'. This led to double-digit increases in participation, with a greater proportion of women now participating in the plan.[141]

Generally, access to capital remains in the hands of men. A study of the top 100 venture firms in the world in 2016 found that only 7 per cent of the partners were women. Widening the net to include both accelerators and corporate venture firms, women held just under 12 per cent of the partner roles.[142]

Taxation

Who and what gets taxed is also far from gender neutral.[143] Married couples were initially taxed as a single person and even when married women were earning, it was the husband who was responsible for taxation matters. Annie shared: 'Mum was sent a tax rebate from her earnings in the 1970s. The cheque was made out to my dad.'[144] The tax system could also cause complex problems for women's lives following relationship breakdown. In the early 1970s, according to Dinah: 'The tax office threatened to take my husband to court as my accounts had not been filed by my errant account-ant. In law, my husband was responsible for any tax due and I was treated as his property with no rights over my own financial affairs.'[145]

Independent taxation finally came into force in 1990, following years of discussion.[146] This resulted in all taxpayers, male or female, married or single, being taxed on their own income or capital gains, and receiving the same personal tax allowance. The introduction of separate taxation suited both the radicals who argued for gender neutrality and the conservatives who were pleased to remove a disincentive for marriage.

In 2015, the transferable personal tax allowance was introduced by the Conservative–Liberal coalition. This, with certain limita-tions, allowed unused tax allowance to be transferred from one spouse to the other.[147] The allowance benefited many families; however, it reduced the incentive of the spouse with the lower income – usually the woman – to enter or remain in paid employ-ment. Eighty-four per cent of beneficiaries were men and it created a difference between married and unmarried couples.[148]

Regarding indirect taxation, in 1940 the government introduced purchase tax to help fund the war effort. This required small-scale producers such as tailors and dressmakers to pass on purchase tax to their customers. The *Northern Daily Mail* from 21 October 1940 reported the positive spin on the new tax made by a clothing sales manager, who commented:

A new hat is regarded by the average woman as one of the best tonics she can buy and all the taxes in the world wouldn't stop her keeping her spirits up in this way. So if long-suffering husbands find that they have to make their socks and shirts last twice as long, they can perhaps comfort themselves with the knowledge that the money thus saved is going to pay the tax on the wife's spring hat, or rather hats.

In advance of budget day in 1950, the *Sunday Post* reported the views of women, most of whom wanted a cut in purchase tax. Mrs G. C. Marshall said:

The housewife has been more hurt than the husband by taxation. The housekeeping allowance doesn't stretch beyond Tuesday for the average housewife. I would advise Sir Stafford to make washing machines, vacuum cleaners, household linen, curtain material and other necessities tax free. Also cosmetics. What husband doesn't want his wife to hide her tired looks after Monday's washing? One-sixth of the husband's income should be tax free so that he can give his wife a sum for her personal use.[149]

Purchase tax was replaced by the introduction of Value Added Tax (VAT), when the UK joined the European Community. The ability of the UK government to set the rates of VAT on various items became subject to EU law. One exception was the so-called tampon tax, of which more in Chapter 6.

Companies have also long marketed and charged the same products such as stationery and toiletries to women and men differently.

Consciousness about sexist surcharges, also called the 'pink tax', has been growing and in 2017, following a campaign on the matter, companies such as Tesco equalised their prices.

The relationship between government and companies in taxation regimes has also been under the spotlight, particularly since the millennium, because of the tax avoidance strategies of giant multinational corporations such as Amazon, Apple, Google and Starbucks. Tax inequalities are a feminist issue for many reasons. When countries don't raise revenues through taxation, a majority of the savings are made by men while the costs are borne predominantly by women, who tend to be more dependent on publicly funded services. This affects women in the UK, but the impact is greater in the global context, where some of the poorest countries are losing more from tax avoidance than they get through aid.[150] As Margaret Casely-Hayford, then chair of ActionAid UK, explained:

> Tax avoidance strategies used by some multinational corporations deprive the world's poorest communities of vital revenues. It compounds underfunding of public services such as health, education and transport, and is holding back women's and girls' chance to thrive. Collectively we need to put the spotlight on this global injustice.[151]

Of the £82 billion in tax increases and cuts in social security spending announced in 2010, it was calculated that women would bear at least 81 per cent of the total burden. By contrast, 85 per cent of the top 1 per cent of earners in the UK were men and since 2010 they have received £3 billion in tax cuts. Also, the reduction in childcare benefit resulted in 24 per cent of mothers giving up work to care for their children.[152] Based on data from 2010 to 2016 and projections to 2020, lone mothers were projected to be the most affected by cuts, followed by lone fathers and single female pensioners. Among lone mothers it was BAME women who lost out the most.[153]

The Economy

Looking at economic crises through a feminist lens highlights first the obvious point that the cause of the problem and its solutions have so far been determined almost exclusively by men. Women Women have been vulnerable to job losses directly because of insecure employment and – in the past – minimal trade union support. They have also been affected by job losses of the men on whom they have been financially dependent. In the 1920s and 1930s many women who lost their jobs joined marches organised by the National Unemployed Workers Movement – yet did so at the back or in separate women's marches as they were not welcomed alongside men. This was no longer the case by the time of the financial crisis in 2008. The subsequent indirect effects are also gendered, as public-sector cuts affect women's employment more than men's. And the effects of austerity cuts tend to impinge on women more, for many interrelated reasons including the fact they tend to be the main users of services.[154]

Income inequality should also be looked at from a feminist perspective for similar reasons. Overall, inequality, which had reduced in mid-century, increased again after the 1980s, and then around the millennium returned to levels not seen since the 1920s. Between 1960 and 2005, income inequality increased by 32 per cent, more than in many other countries including the United States. The top 10 per cent of all UK earners accounted for 35 per cent of GDP in 1938 and this fell to 21 per cent in 1979, before increasing to 30 per cent in 2010.[155] The growth in inequality has been explained in particular by the increase in the incomes of the top 1 per cent.[156] In the last decade inequality seems to have levelled off due to reduced unemployment and the national minimum wage rates at the bottom end coupled with the recession affecting the middle and richest quartiles. At the same time, absolute poverty levels have not fallen, due to cuts in benefits.[157]

In 2015, the ratio of pay of the FTSE 100 CEOs to the average pay of their own employees was 129:1. Most of these same companies were not accredited by the Living Wage Foundation for paying the National Living Wage to all their UK-based staff. Women are over-represented among the poorest and appear least among the richest – with no woman CEO included in the top ten companies.[158] In 1995, 20 per cent of the top 10 per cent of earners were women; by 2013 this had increased to 28 per cent.[159]

Wealth inequality has been even greater than income inequality; in the UK in 2010 the richest 10 per cent owned 45 per cent of the country's wealth.[160] This led to protests and campaigns, including under the slogan 'We are the 99%'. Young women were very involved in these campaigns. However, the message was gender neutral: the fact that women are overly represented in the bottom 1 per cent and under-represented in the top 1 per cent was not central to the protest. Social asymmetry and gender inequality are often not analysed together. The same applies to the concept of the JAMs or the 'just about managing', squeezed in the middle-income house-holds that Theresa May's government pledged to support in 2016. The JAMs are most likely to be female-headed BAME households, but this has not been a central part of the narrative.

According to the Joseph Rowntree Foundation, in 2014–15 there were 13.5 million people living in low-income households (21 per cent of the UK population). At the most extreme, this comes with homelessness which affects men much more than women; in 2016 women represented 26 per cent of the homeless and around 12 per cent of rough sleepers in London.[161] Given women's economic vulnerability up to the point of becoming homeless, it is interesting that there is a point below which fewer women seem to fall. Why is this? Is it because of the greater dangers of being on the street for women and/or the fact that they are more likely to be able to call on someone, even to sell favours for a bed? Those who do end up homeless tend to have compound vulnerabilities including mental health problems, experiences of sexual abuse, drug and alcohol dependency and childhoods spent in care. Both the vulnerability and resilience of women in these circumstances was powerfully portrayed in the 2016 film I, Daniel Blake.

Recently, absolute food poverty, of the kind witnessed earlier on in the twentieth century, has re-emerged and resulted in a huge increase of food provision via breakfast clubs, hostels, community centres and refuges. Whereas once food banks existed primarily for homeless people, now more and more people are dependent on them at times of crisis. Food banks are a non-monetised feminised area of livelihood support. Women do most of the work, both voluntary and paid. It is predominantly women who get the supplies and cook the meals for themselves and their families, and they are the ones who are more likely to turn up with their dependants.

Sarah, a volunteer at the Pankhurst Centre's Emmeline's Pantry food bank explained: 'I think what this food bank offers is brilliant. We can provide some meat, halal products, dairy, baked goods, fresh fruit and veg. Nutrition is important no matter who you are. Also, unusually for food banks, we offer women a choice, so they can come in and select what they need from the shelf or fridge. It gives them a sense of agency and control that they may not have in many other places.'[162]

Conclusion

Over the century there have been massive positive trends regarding women's access to employment of all kinds and at all levels resulting in increased horizons and financial independence. For many the changes have been transformational and there is no looking back.

Yet for those stuck in low-paying jobs in a segmented market, having employment does not feel like liberation but a necessity of life. Not all would see the changes as progress. Furthermore, most women have not yet broken through the barriers of the gender pay gap, the glass ceiling and the greater precariousness of their working lives.

Moreover, women joining the labour market in 2018 expect to be worse off than those retiring at this time. The same applies to men as well, so the whole situation has changed, yet growing inequality and times of economic stress affect women disproportionately.

Women have found that they can often have it all, but not all of the time, and not on the same terms as men.

As with women's political rights, the working environment is still an unequal playing field. There is an increased understanding of the potential value of diversity in transforming the economy, and the increased requirements to address inequality and ensure transparency are yielding results, but traditional patterns are hard to shift.

Money: how did we do?

In the end, I decided on a 3 out of 5.
What would you say?

IDENTITY

'To airbrush age off a woman's face is to erase women's identity, power, and history.' (Naomi Wolf, *The Beauty Myth*)[1]

One of the greatest differences between the lives of women and men is the extent to which women's lives centre on their family, their position within it, and social attitudes to what being a woman means. Annie's words echo through the ages:

> My aim is to raise my children to be happy and healthy. Yes, it's not very equal to be home whilst my husband is working, but it's what I want. Maybe I've been conditioned that way after seeing my mother and grandmother do the same but I have also seen the successes they achieved and their quiet power. They are my heroes, I would like to follow in their footsteps.[2]

Families perpetuate tradition and incubate diversity. They are where class, economic position, colour, ethnicity and religion reproduce and intersect over time. More obviously, gendered experiences begin in the family, where its hierarchy is first felt.

The family is evolving but is as much part of the story in 2018 as it was a hundred years ago, despite the fact that some thought the family would not last. In the 1940s Engels argued that, with the end of capitalism, the state could take over social reproductive tasks, and deal with its citizens directly, doing away with the source of women's oppression.[3] Moral panics about the family's demise have abounded. Increasing divorce rates, the number of children born outside marriage, falling birth rates, delinquency, have all been seen as contributing to the end of family and the breakdown of social order. Yet the family survives and women's identity and their sense of self continues to be moulded by the relationships therein.

Life Expectancy and Women

After the birth of my father in 1927, Sylvia Pankhurst was told by her doctor: 'If you had not come into the home when you did, baby could not have been born.' A few months later in a book called *Save the Mothers*, she wrote: 'The words came to me as a challenge: "Seek to obtain for others the care you had!"'[4]

She found that 4.42 women per 1,000 were dying in childbirth, 40 per 1,000 were stillbirths and 31 per 1,000 infants died within one month of birth. The figures hid massive regional and wealth-related disparities. A medical officer told her that childbirth was the main cause of death in mothers of childbearing age. Yet the view among hospital physicians was that: 'Midwifery is of very little importance and childbirth, being a natural process, can be left to look after itself . . . the obstetric physician has been the butt of his colleagues, on whom they have expended their poor wit, if such it could be called.'[5]

Even into the 1930s, some blamed working-class women for not looking after themselves properly, but organisations such as the Townswomen's Guild and the Co-operative Women's Guild pointed to the vicious cycle of poor housing, poverty, mothers' malnutrition and ill health.[6] The dangers of childbirth remained high until 1935 when a national midwifery service began and better living conditions also reduced infections leading to maternal and infant mortality.

Over the century, women's life expectancy at birth increased dramatically, from fifty in 1918 (forty-five for men) to eighty-three in 2014 (seventy-nine for men).[7] When looking at the differences to women's lives this is no small point.

Another massive change is that the physical drudgery of life, which far too often defined a woman's existence, has lessened. As Susan shared:

> My mother, born in 1927, left her farming home as no one paid her any notice. She had five brothers and their work on the farm was everything. She was awake before them, made bread and breakfast, helped around the farm all day and was the last to go to bed.[8]

In 1918, it was common for large families to live in one or two rented rooms, with shared outdoor lavatories, and no hot water or electricity. For most women, much of the day could be taken up with relentless chores – on laundry, cleaning, buying food, cooking and looking after the family. In the depression of the 1920–1930s, and during the Second World War, women's lives became even harder with the departure of men to war, the destruction of more than a million houses, and the introduction of food rationing. See Figure 7 for an example of government propaganda around making food last.[9]

At the end of the war, 33 per cent of rural households still did not have piped water, 12.5 per cent lacked at least one basic amenity such as a kitchen sink, or indoor toilet.

Conditions started to improve with the building of new housing estates. Further liberating changes came as gas became more common, being used in 80 per cent of households by the 1940s,[10] and electricity in 66 per cent of households in 1938 increasing to 95 per cent by the late 1950s. By 1948, 86 per cent of households had replaced heavy flat irons with electric irons, 40 per cent had vacuum cleaners, 19 per cent cookers and 15 per cent electric water heaters. In 1948, 4 per cent had washing machines and 2 per cent had fridges; by 1965 freezers were in 3 per cent of households. By 1995, 90 per cent or more of households had washing machines, tumble driers, fridges and freezers,[11] dishwashers were owned by 25 per cent and microwave ovens were new on the scene.[12]

Supported by the growth of consumerism, more and more ready-made goods were available in shops and supermarkets, and then more recently also became available online in ways that simplified

BETTER POT-LUCK

with
Churchill
today

THAN HUMBLE PIE

under
Hitler
tomorrow

DON'T WASTE FOOD!

*Figure 7: Government propaganda poster encouraging women to
support the war by making food. Source: Imperial War Museum*

domestic life. For most women, the physical work and time taken on household chores has been massively reduced. It was not just the gadgets at home that made life easier. Mobility also increased dramatically and this brought a reduction in isolation. Ownership of cars helped, although driving was culturally constructed as a male preserve and men sometimes resisted women's desire to drive. Dinah remembered:

> In the sixties, my husband so objected to the fact that I wanted to drive that he wouldn't look after the children to enable me to have lessons. It was only once the youngest started nursery school at aged three that I was able to sneak out and have lessons.[13]

The proportion of women with driving licences reached 50 per cent in the 1990s.[14] To some extent there remains an assumption that women are less keen on, and not as good at, driving, and that the car is predominantly a masculine space.

The Family and Domestic Work

Until 1925 men had sole rights over children. This changed with the Guardianship of Infants Act, which in theory gave fathers and mothers equal rights over their children. As Mari Takayanagi found, it had many limitations:

> The Guardianship of Infants Act 1925 ended up a compromise. One problem was vaccination – a father could exempt a child from vaccination but a mother could not, and the 1925 Act didn't change this. More fundamentally, it only applied in the event of a court order, so women denied access to children had to go to court to get redress – not practical for many mothers. However, working class women could go to a magistrate's court, which was helpful – it was an improvement even if it wasn't ideal. Overall, what was important was the concession of principle in the 1925 Act even if the practice left something to be desired.[15]

The assumption that men were the heads of families, the ones with authority, the breadwinners who 'kept' their wives and family, while women played support roles, was and to some extent remains prevalent. For women, being the homemaker could be fulfilling, but not always. As Ann Feloy put it:

> Somewhere around that time I started to slip into a rather undefined world, where I became less of an individual and more a support to others. I was there for my husband, for my children and for my ageing parents and while this evolving kinder, more caring persona developed, another side of me lost definition and direction.[16]

Women who had tasted a different, more public function, and then had to retreat into exclusively domestic roles for social or economic reasons, found it particularly hard. Clare said:

> My granny lived an expatriate life until the end of WW2, with domestic staff. She was an indomitable character and, for example, was awarded an honour for services in rescuing Allied airmen from the North African Desert. After her return to the UK, in the 1960s, she was unable to afford a cook and parlour maid. Like many of her generation and social class, she had very little idea of how to keep house. Those who were keen relied on *Good Housekeeping* and the newspaper columns that flourished. But in my grandmother's case, she had little interest in a domestic role, and although being extremely able and energetic, her heart wasn't in it.[17]

Most domestic work was self-negating, no sooner done than undone, and with little perceived value. Yet comfort, security and love remain encapsulated in the idealised figure – the primary role of a good wife and mother being to provide the bond that holds families and communities together. Religion and culture are likewise celebrated and enforced through food and dietary laws.

Home-made meals 'feed into' the ideology of the ideal family. Ursula reflected on the difference between image and reality:

> My husband's parting shot when we separated was that I was a bad wife because I couldn't even cook properly. But I didn't want to be domesticated like my mother who was unhappy, asking what do you want for dinner, always stirring the pot, standing there, always in the kitchen, every day. I didn't cook because I wanted to be free – consciously not tied like she was. I still cannot cook the dishes my mother cooked, and I think it's because I associate them with a limited life, with my mother's life.[18]

As a generalisation, although women's financial contribution to the family increased significantly over the century, this has not been paralleled by an increase in men's labour in the home. Jean mused:

> Not many men in the 70s would be seen pushing a pram, even if they were accompanying their wives. There were more engaged fathers, but they would not change a nappy for example. In my case, I think my husband only changed one single nappy, for our third child, in 1985. I once asked him to and he did, but never volunteered again and I did not push him either – it just wasn't expected of men.[19]

Ann, now in her eighties, reminisced: 'I worked, but my husband always said that work was his role in life, mine was the house and children and, therefore, he never helped, no matter how tired I was.'[20] The situation has changed a bit for her daughter, Andrea, in her fifties:

> My friends and I are picking up jobs and careers again after having had children, we are trying to get husbands involved in taking more responsibility in the home, but are meeting a great deal of resistance. I am lucky as my husband will shop and cook, but he is still very *macho* with other chores and likes to think he is the head of the household.[21]

In the UK in 1974, the time working fathers spent with their children each day was recorded as five minutes.[22] Forty years later this had increased to thirty-five minutes. Also in 2014, it was estimated that British women spent 4.3 hours compared with men's 2.3 hours a day on unpaid domestic work.[23]

Women's work within the family is one of the more unshifting aspects of life in the twenty-first century. At one extreme, even where women are the main earners, men sometimes talk about babysitting their own kids.[24] At the other, there is a 'New Man'. Jackie said: 'Our younger son is a staunch feminist – makes me look wishy-washy. For example, at work he ensures that extra meetings are no longer scheduled between 5 pm and 7 pm as he's putting the children to bed then – and he is.'[25] However, men who 'share' rather than 'help' with domestic work, and completely 'symmetrical' families, are still rare.

Turning to look at the children themselves, traditionally and generalising within a wide set of specific experiences, boys were regarded as an investment, a pride – girls a worry and a cost. Daughters were expected to move with their husband on marriage, whereas sons were more likely to stay and take over a father's business for example. Girls were, and to some extent still are, expected to be self-effacing. Ursula mentioned the conflicted attitudes she grew up with:

> My father was open minded, he would say if you read you have knowledge and you can do anything, but at the same time he would give a bit more attention and treats to the boys and it was never equal. His idea of himself was that he was treating us fairly, but the practice was about control and making me something that was a bit less, somehow.[26]

The differential valuation is linked to expectations. There are families that assume their sons will have a career and their daughters a family. A number of girls and women have told me that their parents or grandparents ask if they have boyfriends and why they are not married and having children yet, with no interest in their education or career – in marked contrast to how their male siblings are interrogated. The emotional scars and the impact are not always visible, but they are felt. Anu told me:

> When I was 13 we went to visit my father's family in India. My father's friend commented to my parents: 'She is just like an Indian girl, she is pretty, sits quietly and smiles.' More than thirty years later, I still remember those words and how horrified I was that my parents took this as a compliment.[27]

In families today, boys' higher status and greater privileges are less common, and many youngsters ridicule the idea that girls and boys should not be treated equally. Even so, the differences in treatment and attitude are still there. These surface particularly when girls start their periods. The idea that menstrual blood is shameful is an undercurrent and cuts across many cultures and religions globally. This view can be linked to the fear of women's reproductive power and a need to control it, with mothers and other female relatives perpetuating the negative interpretation of the physical process as polluting. 'The curse' has been a burden women were expected to bear without talking about it.[28]

In the 1920s women in the UK used rags. Disposable, but leaky, pads tied to a reusable sanitary belt were introduced by the innovator Valerie Hunter Gordon. (She also invented part-disposable biodegradable nappies with a waterproof outer element made from old parachutes left over from the war.) Tampons became common in the 1930s and sanitary pads with adhesive strips in the 1970s. Options have massively increased, and attitudes have changed. Lesley reminisced:

> I remember in the 1960s the subject of menstruation was still a taboo subject with my mother hiding her Dr White's sanitary towels in the bottom of her wardrobe. Compare that to today where we see graphic images on our TV screens advertising the properties of the latest slimline protection.[29]

Yet in 2014, Apple's new health-tracking app forgot to mention the menstrual cycle – causing some embarrassment to the company, given that an estimated 53 per cent of iPhone users were women. For most of them, their period was a regular concern and period apps were becoming a popular way of keeping track of cycles for many practical reasons.[30]

According to the NHS in 2016, 90 per cent of menstruating women experience pain because of their periods.[31] More widely, PMT (pre-menstrual tension) is the subject of jokes and put-downs. For the most part, talking about periods is no longer socially muzzled in the UK, options have improved and support has grown, but the undercurrent of shame is still there.

Virginity and Sexuality

The view that women's virginity was something that men had rights to and which should be controlled was a common one in 1918. Women were kept in relative ignorance about biological matters, their vaginas being referred to as their 'private parts' or their 'down below'. This attitude contributed to millions of women finding sex within marriage 'something between a boring duty and a nightmare of pain and revulsion',[32] with mothers advising their daughters on their wedding nights to 'lie back and think of England'. However, in 1918, Marie Stopes's book *Married Love* was published, articulating the importance of women's sexual desires. It had sold 500,000 copies by 1925, and was shared and read by many more.[33]

The flappers of the 1920s also changed things, bringing ideas about sexual freedom and liberation, and an understanding that pleasure was political. By the mid-1930s, sexuality, particularly women's heterosexuality, had become much more evident and open, fanned by the development of mass entertainment in cinemas and dance halls. Even the Church of England, in 1930, recognised the importance of sex as part of the joy of marriage and not just an act of procreation.[34]

During the world wars, because of the spread of venereal diseases associated with prostitution, any woman could be forced to undertake a medical examination on the word of one or two men. Men's role in the spread of infection was totally ignored, and women could not accuse men.[35] Meanwhile, a soldier's needs in wartime were considered understandable, while wives of soldiers abroad were expected to be faithful to man and country. Nevertheless, with around 2 million American soldiers in the UK, relationships were formed and an estimated 70,000 British women became GI brides and left for the United States. A significant number of the American soldiers were black, and their estimated 1,500 babies challenged racial prejudices on both sides of the Atlantic.[36]

From the late 1950s, for more women, sex moved from being a duty and obligation to something that could provide mutual pleasure. But the underlying double standards remained as did the theme that a wife's responsibility was to satisfy the sexual needs of her husband and make herself attractive to him. Heterosexuality was still the default, and men were supposedly more knowledgeable and sexually experienced than women, and were therefore expected to be the drivers of sexual encounters. A study in 1971 found that on marriage only 26 per cent of men were virgins, compared with 63 per cent of women – women's virginity, inexperience and vulnerability were considered appropriate.[37]

There are still today vestiges of the view that young girls' virginity needs safeguarding while young boys can do as they please and 'sow wild oats'. The same behaviour by girls attracts censure, even by her peers. At the same time, sexual identities are ever more important to millennials and post-millennials. They are more sexually aware than previous generations, sometimes presented as hyper-sexualised because of greater pressure to have sex at a younger and younger age. In 'raunch culture' sex not only precedes marriage but also in some cases precedes intimacy, and taboos such as those around female masturbation are being broken. Messages and images linking happiness, wealth, beauty and sexual desirability are ever more pervasive.

Looking at the changes in sex education through the century, from the 1920s, some girls in schools were provided information on hygiene, modesty and sexually transmitted diseases. Formal sex education became more common in the 1950s when biology classes covered the reproductive system not just of plants and animals, but also of humans. By the 1970s, teaching about contraception was also common, the underlying message being that women's role was to help men act responsibly.[38] The contradictions were satirised in the 2004 American film *Mean Girls*, where the coach cautions: 'Don't have sex, because you will get pregnant and die! Don't have sex in the missionary position, don't have sex standing up, just don't do it, OK, promise? OK, now everybody take some rubbers [condoms].'[39]

More recently, in particular through Personal and Social Health Education (PSHE) lessons in years 5 and 6, issues of consent, relationships, bullying, homophobia, pornography, sexual assault and dealing with peer pressure are also addressed. However, in 2015, 40 per cent of schools were judged to have poor sexual education teaching.[40] Laura and Maggie reflected: 'All I remember was a childbirth film and condoms being blown up and thrown around, that's about it really.' And: 'We now have to practise by putting condoms onto bananas.'[41] The content and delivery of sexual education classes varies hugely and is affected by the school's ethos and teachers' beliefs. According to Louisa, a teacher:

The introduction of the HPV (human papilloma virus) vaccine in 2008 was the perfect moment to start talking frankly but the opportunity was missed, and we are still sending the message that girls are responsible since boys aren't yet, to my knowledge, being vaccinated. HPV is discussed in terms of girls' reproductive health in adult life rather than of joint responsibility.[42]

For many years, experts have called for statutory, age-appropriate, non-optional programmes on sexual education in all schools, to give children the language and knowledge to promote sexual health and healthy relationships. In 2017, after years of debate, an all-female cross-party group of MPs won the battle for this to be government policy.[43] By September 2020, a written policy must be in place in all schools.[44]

Sexual and Gender Identities

A hundred years ago, when male homosexuality was a criminal offence, there was a silence about female homosexuality. Some suffragettes were lesbian or bisexual, or just preferred to live with other women. The composer Dame Ethel Smyth had passionate feelings for a number of women, including Emmeline Pankhurst. Suffragettes Eva Gore-Booth and Esther Roper were buried in a single grave in Hampstead.[45]

In the 1920s, with a generation of men lost and a rejection of Edwardian values, an element of the flapper identity provided greater visibility to the lesbian subculture. At the same time, in 1921, there was an attempt to make 'acts of gross indecency' between women illegal. However the House of Lords did not find sufficient grounds for the amendment, arguing that by making it illegal it would help advertise something 'unbalanced', 'neurotic' and 'decadent' to women who would otherwise have 'never thought of it, never dreamed of it'.[46] There were other sanctions, however. In 1928, the novel *The Well of Loneliness* by Radclyffe Hall,[47] about a love affair between two women during the First World War, was banned in the UK.[48] The book continued to be published in the United States, but was only republished in the UK in 1949. From the late 1950s, the Gateway Club in Chelsea among others resulted in a more visible public lesbian presence. This grew and in 1963 also comprised the Minorities Research Group and a lesbian and bisexual publication, *Arena 3*.

For some in the feminist movement in the 1970s, heterosexuality was seen as underpinning patriarchy. Avoiding sexual relationships with men and becoming a lesbian was argued to be what a real feminist should do. This created conflict with those who did not feel that their heterosexuality undermined their feminism.

Pride marches came on the scene in Britain in the 1970s. They started as Gay Pride marches and were renamed 'Lesbian and Gay Pride' in 1983. This saw a large political mobilisation around gay and lesbian identities, but the HIV-Aids pandemic revived prejudice and discrimination. Following awareness-raising campaigns, particularly by Stonewall, the Terrence Higgins Trust and celebrities such as Diana, Princess of Wales, people began to come out in greater numbers and social acceptance returned, though to different degrees in different cultures and locations. The marches became Pride in 2004, then LGBT+ Community Pride in 2012. Initially a few hundred people took part in London. By 2017, which saw a return to the simple title 'Pride', more than one hundred events[49] were celebrated around Britain and over a million people were thought to have attended in London alone.

Nevertheless, away from the pomp and ceremony, the discrimination continued. Sarah commented that in 2013: 'A colleague discovered I was gay and stated he knew people like me and had fixed them before; he wanted to fuck me as he saw me as being unwell.'[50]

Where earlier generations boxed people into male or female, heterosexual or homosexual, or at a push asexual or bisexual, from the 1970s transsexual, transgender and even non-gender identities began to be more openly discussed in the UK. Transgender identity has long been recognised elsewhere, particularly in South Asia.[51] Legal recognition in the UK came with the Gender Recognition Act in 2004 and the Equality Act of 2010.

At a cultural level, 2015 marked the entry into the mainstream of transgender, gender reassignment and the idea of fluid sexual identities following the appearance of Caitlyn Jenner, formerly Bruce Jenner, an American TV personality and Olympic athlete, on the cover of *Vanity Fair*. That same year a survey found that half of eighteen- to twenty-four-year-old British adults defined themselves as 'not totally heterosexual'.[52]

The reasons behind body dysmorphia are complicated; however, people born male have tended to want to transition because of an association with the feminine and a disassociation with traditional masculinity. Young girls' desire for transition has been linked to a dislike of female puberty, with the development of breasts, the start of menstruation, the sexualisation of the female body and the cultural subordination of girls.

The more famous transgender celebrities have tended to be those transitioning to women and the media's obsession is in those perfecting the female look with the commercialised, sexualised world of glamour jumping on the band wagon. However, numerically there have been more females transitioning. The Tavistock Referral Clinic in London, one of fourteen gender identity clinics in the UK, showed an increase in gender identity patients from 97 in 2009–2010 to 1,398 in 2015–2016. Of these, 485 were born male and 913 were born female.[53] By 2016, there were over 15,000 patients, with estimates that around 130,000 people in the UK were likely to have gender incongruence at a level where they would want to seek medical intervention.[54]

For Andrea, it was simple. She explained: 'approaching 50, I had to transition to live the rest of my life as my true self'.[55]

So how did society transform from one in which heterosexuality was the only option to one where at least 1 in every 250 people define themselves as non-binary, and the acronym LGBTTQQIAAP (lesbian, gay, bisexual, transsexual, transgender, queer, questioning intersex, asexual, ally and pansexual) just about covers most options and yet where Facebook has increased the number of gender options to seventy-one?[56] Whatever the individual stories, a significant number of people have found the courage to reject social straitjackets and challenge heteronormativity. Their journeys can be transformative for all.

Some feminists – including famously Germaine Greer, one of the feminist gurus of the 1970s – have argued against the inclusion of trans women in women-only events, arguing that it devalues the female experience. There is in addition a warning that the changes will skew data and is dangerous – citing examples such as the transgender inmate who in 2017 sexually assaulted prisoners after transferring to a women's prison. However, there is an increasing appreciation of the difficulties that transgender people face in trying to work out where they fit and a growing acceptance of people in the gender that they self-identify in.

In 2018, we are entering a time of shifting sands regarding perspectives on gender, biology and sexuality. What we know is that sexuality includes socially constructed elements. For most of the century these gave pre-eminence to heterosexuality and constructed gender differences in ways that involved men's domination over women. It is increasingly clear that there are other ways of being.

Marriage and Divorce

In 1918, the idealised marriage was based on a courtship, women's virginity and chastity – symbolised by the white wedding. Because of unplanned pregnancies, 'shotgun marriages' were also common. So were arranged marriages in both rich and poor families. Susan, for example, explained: 'My grandmother used to tell the story of being "sold" off in the 1920s to her husband. Granny's family had borrowed money and couldn't repay the debt, so she was sold to pay back the loan.'[57]

Once married, women were expected to serve their husbands. In 1923, the headmistress of Manchester High School for Girls, despite having been a suffragette, held the view that:

To be sure [educated girls] should marry. It is the nicest thing for them to do – to marry well and happily. They give to their husbands the benefit of their cleverness and academic training which should help the men in their careers and rebound to the credit of man and wife together.[58]

By the 1950s the courtship process had become less ritualised and 40 per cent of first sexual encounters were prior to or outside marriage.[59] The trend continued and different forms of dating evolved. By 2013 it was estimated that, in the UK, 20 per cent of relationships started online and almost half of single people had searched for a partner online.[60] Marriage also moved from being the expectation of young women, to a choice, with options about who, when and how to wed. Rates of cohabitation prior to marriage started to be common from the 1970s, and by the 1990s 70 per cent of women who married for the first time had cohabited prior to marriage, compared with less than 10 per cent in the 1960s.[61]

Figure 8: Total Marriages in '000. Source: Office of National Statistics 1918–2014

Overall marriage numbers in England and Wales since 1918 show spikes and troughs linked to the world wars, and slight increases over the first half of the period, followed by more reductions up to 2009. Ironically, there were increases during the 'swinging' Sixties through to 1972. In the more recent past, when marriage became available for gay couples it created a minor surge in the marriage statistics.[62]

In the UK the legal minimum age of marriage was twelve for girls until 1929 when it was raised to sixteen. The mean age difference between husband and wife has varied within a narrow band, with the wife on average between two and four years younger.[63]

Not surprisingly, since it has been conceived of as the union between a man and a woman, almost all aspects of marriage have gendered elements reinforcing the idea of male agency and authority. For example, traditionally the man asks the woman's father for permission before he asks her directly, a practice that has for the most part disappeared. The practice of a father giving away the bride at the ceremony remains current. The groom is hardly ever accompanied by a parent and is not 'given away'. The marriage supplicant bends down on one knee in subjugation to the woman he wants to marry. The only other time in our culture we expect this symbolism is in church, when knighted, or in the past when begging forgiveness. The giving of the ring by the man to his intended and the choice about whether or not to accept him, the prerogative of women, is all sometimes played out in public. The exception is the tradition that women can propose on 29 February in a leap year.

A hundred years ago, when female industrial workers left to get married, some general ribaldry would take place in the workplace and among friends and family. 'Hen parties', as a more formalised event, became part of popular culture from the 1960s onwards. Stag nights were culturally more important, seen to be the 'last night of freedom'. Even the terminology is telling: a wild stag and a domestic hen.

Until 2018 marriage certificates in England and Wales included the names of the fathers of the bride and groom but not the mothers'. This inequality has not existed in Scotland since 1855. It is particularly galling when a mother has brought up the bride or groom on her own. In some cases, mothers have ignored the wording, as with Sylvia putting her name on my parent's marriage certificate, adding '(Mother)' for good measure.

Another example of asymmetry is the concept of a 'maiden' name. Most women who got married in 1918 or before took their husband's name. However, some challenged the tradition and added their surname as a middle name or double-barrelled the name, including many suffragettes such as the Pethick-Lawrences in 1901. In 1994 an estimated 6 per cent of women kept their names; in 2013, the figure was still only 25 per cent.[64] The Olympic gold medallist hockey player Kate Richardson-Walsh explained:

> Helen and I had our Civil Partnership ceremony in 2013, surrounded by friends and family . . . We are more than a little perplexed when people ask us whether we double barrelled our surnames to make a statement about our relationship. We can't say for sure, but we'd like to bet nobody asked Jess Ennis-Hill the

same question. We, like we imagine most people who choose to double barrel their surnames, did so because neither of us wanted to give up our family name and history. We could have stayed with our own maiden names but if we decided at any point to grow our family we would want the children to share both parents' names. And the order of our surnames wasn't the result of a power struggle or long debate! We chose Richardson-Walsh quite simply because it sounds better to us than Walsh-Richardson.[65]

I kept my surname as has my daughter Laura, with her father's surname as her middle name, and vice versa for my son. This was our attempt to honour and take forward both surnames. Laura did some family tracing and wrote a blog commenting on how even in our own family, tracing women back over time is more difficult because they change their names and they are therefore more likely to become invisible.[66]

In March 2017, I met another Pankhurst, Caroline. She explained the story behind her name as follows:

After I divorced my husband, I decided I didn't want his name, but then I didn't want my father's name either. Why should the default be a patriarchal name? I wanted my own name. I then started to think. Why not choose my own surname? If so, whose name stands for things I believe in and has values that align to my beliefs? Emmeline sprung to mind almost immediately, and the Manchester connection instantly made it feel right. So, I changed my surname to one I could be proud of! I love the conversations it springs with people: 'Are you . . .?' 'No, but I chose it because of what she stands for . . .' 'Yes, amazing.'[67]

Many strong feminist women still continue to take their husband's surname and pass it on to their offspring for a number of reasons: as a sign of love and commitment, wanting the social approval, so as not to make a fuss, and sometimes because they don't like their own name. Some professional women also use both names to separate their personal and professional identities.

Another of the gendered traditions concerns titles. A century ago girls and unmarried women – whatever their age – came to be called 'Miss'; when they married they became 'Mrs'. Divorced women were supposed to return to the 'Miss' appellation – a social downgrading in status. Also, wives were traditionally addressed by their husband's first name – to make the stamp of ownership clear. Jill reflected:

> My granny used to always refer to herself as Mrs R. E. Humphries – which was her husband's (my grandad's) initials. She also used to address post to my mum, using my dad's initials on the envelope. I remember thinking that if I ever got married, I'd never use my husband's initials. Interestingly, I did get married but I did not need to make the point as we have the same initial![68]

The neutral 'Ms' is a term revived by feminists in the 1970s and used by many so as not to disclose whether or not they are married. Yet Vivienne commented: 'Just last year I gave my name using Ms and the young man behind the counter said: "Is that Miss or Mrs?" I really thought the UK had moved on . . .'[69]

Recently 'Mx' has also started to be used, primarily by those who identify as non-binary. Overall there is some social confusion around titles, with women finding different solutions; some are 'Miss' irrespective of marital status, in schools for example. In my case I have long used my 'Dr' title to avoid the problem but thankfully the direction of travel is to do without titles altogether.

Some marriage contexts are more unequal than others. For instance, older men buying younger brides through mail order, a process facilitated by the internet. The women come primarily from Eastern Europe and Asian countries, where women have fewer prospects. Although there are successful stories, the transactions can create an isolated and vulnerable category of women. The pattern of older men looking for younger wives shows up in different forms. Take the seventy-year-old aristocrat Sir Benjamin Slade advertising, in 2017, for a wife to help look after him and his estate, making it clear that anybody past their reproductive age, termed their 'sell-by date', should not apply.[70]

Another example of enforced dependency concerns the wives of servicemen, as reflected in Samantha's story:

> I was married at 21 in 1988, on arrival in Germany. I had a steep learning curve. Officers' wives were discouraged from working and jobs were difficult to find. It was explained to me by the Battery Commander's wife that my role was to attend weekly flower-arranging classes and to take part in and host coffee mornings with officers' wives and separately soldiers' wives. I wasn't ideal officer wife material – I went to a comprehensive school, my father was a miner and my mother a receptionist/barmaid and I have a northern accent. I felt more at home with the soldiers' wives.
>
> The army medical facility wasn't great as there was only one male doctor who we also socialised with. For example, my smear test result came back for the attention of 'Wife Of' and my husband's army number, my name nowhere to be seen.
>
> Women were not allowed to approach the bar and in the sergeants' mess there was a strip on the floor to denote where we must not pass. Only men could order drinks and they had mess chits with which to pay.
>
> I shared these stories with my daughter who is 15. She was appalled that I had accepted the situation, I had merely been amused by such archaic military rules.[71]

Over time the pattern is one of more and more variations, with women showing greater agency rather than adhering to a scripted narrative. As Coral, Jo and Anna show:

> My feelings about marriage have all been smooched because we got married and it was for keeps but that's not happened with our

four children. The oldest, they lived together before they eventually got married. Our second daughter married, she lived with him before, but now that marriage is no longer. Our next one didn't ever marry and they are still together. Our youngest married late and that's another story.[72]

When I married my long-term partner in 1978, my manager rang me to congratulate me on now being 'respectable' . . . I got my own back by telling him I hadn't changed my surname.[73]

Some people seem to feel that we are somehow cheating, or that we are eroding the institution of marriage, because we are married but don't live together. We didn't do this as any kind of rebellious statement (we're both too old for that) but simply because it worked for us. After many years 'together' we decided to get married and we were both caught unawares by how much the act of getting married deepened our relationship – it became the start of a whole new chapter in our lives. Now, after seven years of marriage, we've bought a house which we will live in together. It seems we just did things in a different order . . .[74]

Feminists have the option of rejecting the institution and all its accoutrements outright, or they can accept it and be strategic about the subsequent choices, in ways that resist the unequal social norms it comes with. No easy task. Today few women would see marriage as an end goal, or the function of a girl's education to enable her to support their husband's career in the way that the headmistress of Manchester High School for Girls did in 1923. A survey at the school carried out in 1974 found that 93 per cent of the girls expected to continue their career if they married. The figure went up to 95 per cent in 2017. To the additional question of whether they would expect to continue their career if they had children, 92 per cent said they would.[75]

Turning to patterns in divorce over the century, in 1918, according to national statistics in England and Wales, 1,111 couples divorced, 66 per cent petitioned by husbands. Adultery was sufficient grounds for a man to divorce his wife. A wife had to prove her husband had committed incest or subjected her to an unacceptable level of cruelty. The few women who did manage to secure a divorce had the full agreement of the husband or were wealthy and protected by supportive families.

Until the Second World War, it was mainly men who initiated divorce, thereafter it has been the other way round. In 2013, in a complete reversal from the starting point, 65 per cent were petitioned by the wife. The two largest spikes were in the mid-1940s because of the war and following the Divorce Reform Act in 1971. Since 1993, the general trend has been a decrease in divorce numbers.[76]

Figure 9: Total number of divorces. Source: Office of National Statistics 1918–2014

Changes in divorce laws over the last hundred years illustrate how Parliament began to reduce institutionalised inequality but also the perpetuations of some of the inequalities in practice. From 1949 onwards the provision of legal aid made it feasible for poorer women to seek a divorce. Divorce also continued to be simplified, so that, following the 1969 Divorce Reform Act, it became enough that a marriage had irretrievably broken down, and cases could be heard in county courts rather than the high court in London. The Child Support Act 1991 introduced the Child Support Agency so that the absent parent – usually the father – could be forced to pay maintenance for the upkeep of the children and in certain circumstances for the ex-partner. This was replaced in 2016 by the Child Maintenance Service, with weaker powers. During the transition, there was more than £4 billion of arrears, mainly owed by fathers. They were not asked to pay up; the mothers were advised to write off the debt.[77]

The 2014 Children and Families Act is gender neutral and there is no longer a presumption that the prime carer is the mother, after the first few breastfeeding months. It encourages both parents to be involved, evidence of how much society has changed, particularly in regard to the best interests of children. But discussions during and after the drafting of the bill highlighted the dangers that could arise if equal parenting was presumed where parents lived far apart or in cases of domestic violence.[78]

Similarities in women's experiences of separation and divorce and sometimes remarriage echo through the ages and across generations. Denise shared:

In 2017, I published *Suddenly Single* about women suddenly finding themselves separated or divorced, based on my own experience and those of women I had met through my work as an executive coach. No matter what the circumstances, the pain of lost relationships, wider fractures within families and the lost ideal often resulted in long-term emotional scarring. Yet, it also provided an opportunity for reflection and re-discovery.[79]

Divorce is a stamp of marriage failure and is almost always surrounded by hard times for all those involved. The changes in the law have reduced the stigma, acknowledged realities and allowed remarriage. The fact that divorce happens in all corners and at all levels of society has also contributed to its normalisation.

Sexual and Reproductive Rights

Abortions were dangerous and illegal in 1918: the 1861 Offences Against the Person Act stipulated life in prison both for the mother and for any person helping her with the abortion process. In 1929, the Infant Life (Preservation) Act created a specific crime if the foetus was over twenty-eight weeks, unless the woman's life was at risk. Between 1923 and 1933 an estimated 15 per cent of maternal deaths were due to illegal abortions.[80] The Conference of Co-operative Women in 1934 called for abortion to be legalised and in 1936 the Abortion Law Reform Association was established. In 1938, a case-law precedent was set when a doctor was acquitted after having performed an abortion on a fourteen-year-old who was suicidal after a gang-rape. However, allowing abortion in certain circumstances failed to be ratified because of the start of the Second World War. Women, particularly poorer women, continued to resort to illegal abortions. In the early 1960s it was estimated that 100,000 abortions were still being carried out annually, dispropor-tionately among the poor.[81]

Campaigns to legalise abortion culminated in the 1967 Abortion Act, which the MP David Steel introduced as a private member's bill. The Act allowed women to seek termination of a foetus of up to twenty-eight weeks with the sanction of two doctors for social as well as medical reasons.

The movement for de-legislation has come from the left, while conservative and religious groups have often taken an anti-abor-tion position. A reversal of the law has been attempted a number of times. In particular, a private member's bill to repeal the Act was heading for a parliamentary majority in 1975, when a National Abortion Campaign was founded to protect and reinforce it. Among other activities, they organised marches, with support from the TUC and the British Medical Association, such as the one in 1978 attended by more than 100,000 people, labelled the largest women's rights demonstration since those of the suffragettes.[82] Abortion rights remained as they were, until 1990 and the Human Fertilisation and Embryology Act, when the time limit was reduced from twenty-eight to twenty-four weeks – a change supported by the then prime minister, Margaret Thatcher.

The 1967 Abortion Act applies in all parts of the UK except

Northern Ireland. In Ireland, following the successful 'Yes' campaign, from the 1st of January 2019, abortion has become permitted during the first twelve weeks of pregnancy, and later in cases where the pregnant woman's life or health is at risk, or in the cases of a fatal foetal abnormality. The same rules apply in the Channel Islands. In the Isle of Man it is only allowed in the case of rape or mental health concerns, though decriminalisation is on the cards for 2019, and in Scotland women are now allowed to take abortion pills at home. As part of the bargaining between the Conservatives and the DUP following the 2017 general election a bill to allow women in Northern Ireland to access NHS abortion clinics for free in England was passed. It was estimated that around a thousand women were making the journey, although since the age of the internet women were also accessing online services such as those provided by Women on Web. Those taking this route risk medical complications and/or prosecution.

As well as campaigning for abortion rights in all parts of the UK and beyond, feminist organisations like We Trust Women, set up by the British Pregnancy Advisory Service, have been lobbying to get rid of the twenty-four-week cut-off and to de-medicalise the process. They point out that in Scotland, where there was no term limit until 1990, late abortions were not more common, and that in Canada, where all abortion has been decriminalised, the number of late abortions is comparatively small and rates of abortion actually fell.

Abortion remains common. In 2015 it was estimated that one in three women had had an abortion by the age of forty-five.[83] The difference from the beginning of the century is that abortion is now likely to be carried out earlier and in safer conditions. Legislation in 2018 brought England into line with Scotland and Wales in allowing the second pill in an early abortions to be taken at home, avoiding the risk of miscarriage on the way home.

On a par with women's political emancipation and economic autonomy through work has been the journey for women over the century towards greater control over their fertility. This has meant no longer being at the mercy of repeated pregnancies throughout their reproductive lives or having to resort to back-street abortions, not once but many times in their lives.

Marie Stopes published her second book *Wise Parenthood: A Book for Married People* in 1918. It advocated the use of birth control in marriage and challenged the association between immorality, prostitution and the use of contraceptives. Traditional birth control methods included withdrawal, sex in the safest period of a woman's cycle and abstinence. The use of condoms was boosted by the development of latex in the 1920s and their mass production in the 1930s.

In 1921 Stopes opened the first birth control clinic in Holloway in North London with support from a number of prominent suffragettes. Consultations were free for the poorest women because of the direct link between a family's size and poverty.

By the 1930s welfare centres and then government clinics started giving birth control advice to married women (and those pretending to be married using borrowed rings or curtain rings). In 1939 Family Planning Associations were formed, again with little or no government backing, and the numbers accessing the services increased throughout the century. The Church of England also stopped condemning the use of contraception in 1958.

A transformational moment was the introduction of the pill in 1961, simplifying family planning, giving women control – but also shifting the responsibility onto them. In 1964 Helen Brook founded the Brook Clinic, one of a number of independent clinics open to unmarried women.[84] By 1966 the pill became available to unmarried women at family health clinics and by 1974 these were mostly free on the NHS. In 1984, the morning after pill also became available on the NHS. With cultural changes also came challenges testing the appropriate boundaries of women's autonomy. For example, in 1985 the courts ruled in the Gillick case that girls under sixteen, if they had the understanding, could be prescribed the pill without a parent's knowledge.

Over the last century, contraception options have increased dramatically: pill, patch, cup, condom, coil, IUD implant, vaginal ring, injection and a contraceptive injection for men. Questions have also been raised about the possible side effects of some forms of contraception, particularly whether the pill may increase and/or decrease the risk of cancer or contribute to mental health problems.[85] Although not foolproof, contraception has allowed women to have lives not defined by their biology. Access to it has not necessarily changed the power dynamics or the responsibility for the most part laid on women to not get pregnant, but it has given them greater control over their reproduction and made it easier, with ripple effects impacting on all aspects of their lives.

Motherhood

In 1918, embarrassment and shame was attached to feminine health matters, particularly gynaecological ones, and many women and girls had very little knowledge about their own bodies. Married women would often conceal their pregnancy because of the general taboo and fear for the health of the mother and baby – a global pattern.[86] Visibly pregnant women could be confined, for their own health and that of the baby, and literally kept out of view. Now, although too simplistic a contrast, the opposite is often the case; there is a public ownership of pregnancy, with people feeling they have the licence to touch the stomach of a pregnant woman and ask personal questions.

Around the millennium, Britain had some of the highest teenage pregnancy rates in Europe. Because of the link to poverty, reduced opportunities and dependency on the state, the government initiated a strategy to tackle the problem. By 2016, teenage pregnancies in England and Wales fell to their lowest since 1946: 20 live births per 1,000 between the ages of fifteen to nineteen. Although the moral panic has abated, the figures remain among the highest in Europe.[87]

At the same time, the average age of mothers has been increasing from less than twenty-seven prior to 1966[88] to thirty in 2014.[89] The other moral panic is therefore a fear that women are leaving it too late to have babies, compromising their chances of pregnancy and endangering the health of the foetus. To the pattern of older fathers, considered acceptable in British culture, the older mother is being introduced, though with much higher levels of public disapproval.

Where and how children are born has also changed. In 1918, almost all childbirth took place in the home; by the 1950s about two-thirds of babies were born in hospital, and by 1990 around 99 per cent.[90] This has resulted in much better support and outcomes. The growth in medicalisation, and in particular the increase in caesareans from around 10 per cent thirty years ago to 25 per cent in 2015, has undoubtedly saved lives but also raised concerns about whose interests were driving the trends. However, as Lucy, a consultant obstetrician, explained, the pattern is above all one of a mother's greater choice: 'Compared to a few decades ago, a woman's voice is now heard loud and clear embracing the whole spectrum of those who want an elective Caesarean section, "nothing is passing through my pelvic floor", to those who want to breathe through the "waves", and have a home birth.'[91] Fathers are also more likely to be present at the time of delivery and both parents have started to be centrally involved when a baby is in intensive care.

Fashions around how to be a good mother have come and gone, pushing women to conform to the latest theories. These included, after the introduction of formula milk in the 1940s, whether or not to breastfeed, feeding on demand or by the clock, whether to cuddle infants or let them cry, whether to use pacifiers and when to introduce solid food. As new mothers have become more visible and less housebound, some of these ideas have been played out in public.[92]

One of the big differences over time has been the level of support available. The National Childbirth Trust (NCT) was set up in 1956 to support parents through pregnancy and childbirth. Many young parents also draw great support from online networks and information sources.

In addition to adoption and fostering, one option for those unable to have children and which represents a fundamental change in women's lives over the last century is in vitro fertilisation (IVF). Since the inception of IVF, and the birth of Louise Brown in 1978, more than 250,000 children have been born through this method in the UK.[93] In 2016 2 per cent of babies in the UK were born through IVF.[94] Baroness Deech shared:

> I was of the generation that was overjoyed – liberated – to have the benefit of contraception, so that we could plan children and careers with greater ease. What escaped me, until I was appointed chair of the Human Fertilisation and Embryology Authority, was the great misery of women who could not have babies. It was a wonderful experience to be part of helping infertile couples, although I was always careful to emphasise that every woman is a worthwhile person in her own right, whether a mother or not.[95]

Artificial fertilisation raises hope for families but also concerns about social, ethical and legal implications of the technology. The cost of IVF was and remains a major constraint for couples, despite some limited NHS-funded support. By the late 1990s an international 'reproductive' or 'fertility' tourism had emerged due to shortages in sperm or eggs, for those wanting sex selection, those with specific medical conditions and for gay couples.

What IVF offers is the possibility of motherhood for more women and in different contexts, across ages and family compositions. Sometimes this has happened with disturbing elements around the international commodification of women's bodies.

The Invisible Women

The traditional clear blue water between the life of men and women is blurred by women who do not marry and/or do not have children. Following the deaths of millions of men during both world wars, there were spikes of so-called 'surplus' unmarried women. For example, in the 1931 census, there were over 1.5 million women over the age of thirty-five who were unmarried. There are many other reasons why women have stayed single over the period: if they were not heterosexual; because of not finding or losing a partner; having to look after elderly relatives; not having had time due to career or religious commitments, and sometimes as a deliberate choice. Whatever the reason, although still looked at askance, living alone has been on the increase: going from 12 per cent of all households in 1961 to nearly 34 per cent in 2012, the highest figures being among the forty-five to sixty-four age group.[96]

Childless women are another growing social anomaly – portrayed traditionally as 'barren', unnatural and even as evil. And yet it was estimated that in 1938 11 per cent of women were childless, 20 per cent in 1965 and by 2018 it is projected that 25 per cent of forty-five-year-old women will be childless.

If you had children but outside marriage this also would not do. In Clare's case: 'My family disowned me, they were strong Catholics and didn't believe in sex before marriage so I had no family, no backup, nothing. It was: "You made your bed and you lie in it." '[97] Even my great-grandmother Emmeline – not exactly the bastion of traditionalism – was distraught that Sylvia had my father 'out of wedlock' and she refused to see her daughter or grandson, despite the fact that Sylvia was making a feminist point about gender relations in the home.

By 1945, the birth rate for unmarried women had doubled from the pre-war figure to 9 per cent. And gradually, as with other trends, the stigma is subsiding.[98] Ann and Nikki shared:

I had my baby before I got married, that was very hard in the 1960s, now it's not thought about. I didn't get sent away, but they, mum and dad, did try and stop me. But then they relented and I lived with them before I married my baby's father and we could afford our own place. My parents did help during those early years.[99]

I had a child out of wedlock, a mixed-race baby. Frowned upon, I raised my son alone. I worked, I went to college and then university. I graduated and now work with young single mothers raising their aspirations.[100]

Unlike two-parent families, perceived as the backbone of a civilised society, lone mothers – but not lone fathers – have been regarded with suspicion and their families as a burden for the state, the women seen as likely to neglect their children and prey on married men. Yet, Ursula shared her – very different – preoccupations:

After I had my daughter I decided to work locally and not pursue a better job in London. I didn't want to be at the station at 6 a.m. and only back at 7 or 8 p.m. to make a career for myself, that would mean not having any time with her. My daughter doesn't have another parent so that would mean a stranger would be the main influence in her life. As a single mother, it was important to me that I brought her up with my values, with respect, and encouraging her to aspire to everything she could achieve.[101]

And being treated as an independent adult could be difficult. Margaret remembers:

When I was about 12 my mother and father split up. She was a working woman, had an income and could afford to buy her own property for us to live in. The house needed some refurbishment so she agreed with a builder the scope and specification of the work. When she was ready to sign the paperwork, he insisted that he wanted my father's signature on the paperwork. My mother asked why, and was told 'because he is the man'. The builder would not accept the signature of a mere woman, on her own. We eventually used another builder. That was in the early 1970s.[102]

Widows form another category of women who have often been stigmatised and ostracised but with more complicated social associations attached to them. In some traditions, as well as wearing mourning clothes and not wearing jewellery, widows were supposed to retreat and not be seen in public places. They were likely to be vulnerable if they had depended on their husband. On the other hand, they could become powerful women if they inherited from their husbands and become honorary men as well as 'merry widows' released from their roles as wives.

It has been estimated that by 2020, 50 per cent of the UK population will be aged fifty or above.[103] Many older and very old women feel lonely and invisible. For those who have family nearby, one long established role for older people – women in particular – is providing childcare support for their grandchildren. According to a poll published by Grandparents Plus, in 2017, one in four mothers would give up work if it were not for the help of grandparents and only an estimated 7 per cent did not receive any help from them.[104] At the same time older people also continue to be the backbone of care in their communities, as discussed in Chapter 1. In some senses, the work keeps them young and reduces isolation. Nan explained:

> To people who might say 'you're 86, you should be at home with people visiting *you*' I say it's not something you can put into an age category. If you're able to do it, you go on doing it. Also, once you develop a relationship with someone you don't just abandon them.[105]

Some, like Gill, do eventually say that's enough:

> After retirement, I worked as a steward at a festival for a number of years, and have been involved in voluntary work on various committees including driving local residents to hospital appointments for a charity. I have now blessedly retired from absolutely everything and am thoroughly enjoying just pleasing myself![106]

The Female Image

Throughout the twentieth century women have had a complicated relationship with their own image and that of the male gaze, with innumerable companies working to feed idealised images, and centuries of cultural obsessions with what women look like rather than who they are and what they think and do. This relationship has carried over to how they present themselves, such as their posture, attitudes and even the way they speak being part of the constructed image. With different degrees of agency, as customs and fashions have come and gone, women have operated within these wider parameters to navigate their own images.

Make-up

Make-up in 1918 remained risqué because of the connection with prostitution and the theatre. Bright-red lipstick was also used by some suffragettes as a symbol of defiance, and in the 1920s and 1930s its use increased. This was boosted by the manufacture of new products and the use of colour photography in advertisements and the cinema.

During the Second World War women were encouraged to use make-up to keep up morale; it was considered a necessity, with a high value on the black market.[107] After the war, cosmetics remained an important commodity, especially given the continued rationing of clothes. Then, in the 1960s, use of make-up increased. Joan told me:

> My mother always put lipstick on before our dad came home for dinner. One day, in the late 1960s, I asked her why she put this on every day, even when she was cross with him; her reply was, 'That's what you do when your husband is due home.' She did this right up until she died.[108]

From the 1980s onwards the beauty industry seemed to target a wider age range of women and from the 2010s even very young girls were enticed in increasing numbers through tutorials by vloggers on YouTube. Overall, the trend seems to be one of greater use of cosmetics by more women of all ages – though the beauty business is also increasingly targeting boys and men. There are numerous very tangible dangers, including black women using whitening creams, and white women tanning themselves, both of which can be carcinogenic. Skin can react to all the products it is exposed to, eyes can be damaged during the process of shaping and colouring, pain is endured when eyebrows are plucked and there is the potentially bottomless financial pit of buying into the cosmetic world.

Many feminists, including Naomi Wolf, in her ever more relevant book *The Beauty Myth*, eschew the idea that women need to be made up, as though the way they are naturally is not good enough. She argues that the whole focus – in fact obsession – with women's body image by society, the media and big business feeds into women's subordinate position – becoming a 'political sedative'.[109] Many forms of cosmetic surgery, including facelifts and Botox, require keeping up and 'perfecting' further in an attempt to stop the clock. As Wolf put it:

> Airbrushing age off women's faces has the same political echo that would resound if all positive images of blacks were routinely lightened. That would be making the same value judgment about blackness that this tampering makes about the value of the female life: that less is more. To airbrush age off a woman's face is to erase women's identity, power, and history.[110]

Although the social pressures on young girls and women are immense, and in the social media image age ever more so, it need not be this way. For some, make-up has nothing to do with presenting a sexualised image or appealing to anybody else, or even to beauty norms. It is – literally – about adding colour to life, and having some fun.[111] In Maggie's case:

> When I was 12 all my friends wore make-up so I did too. Caking on foundation gave me spots, which I then tried to cover up with more make-up, and it was a horrible cycle. Now I'm 16 and more comfortable with myself, so I save the make-up for special

occasions – it's now an artistic expression – I enjoy trying out different looks for different occasions – putting it on every day would be so boring![112]

Hair

What we do with hair is also an identity marker and reflects historical and cultural factors as well as personal choice. Historically women tended to keep their hair long, and when married, tied up. In public, hair was often partly covered. Short hair from the 1920s and afterwards was an expression of independence of spirit – more recently, a shaved head even more so. The colour of women's hair has connotations and carries stereotypes; for example, fiery redheads and dumb blondes, and the expectation that women should dye their greying hair. For Madeleine:

I remember buying Toyah Wilcox's record 'Brave New World' in 1982. I was immensely impressed with her hair, bright pink and blue, and so I started experimenting with dyeing my hair pink and purple. I then started shaving my hair at the sides. I felt a liberation about experimenting with my appearance. I got teased at school of course but I didn't care, I was just enjoying being different. Now that my daughter is an adolescent she is also experimenting with her hair but it's more groomed curls and high ponytails![113]

For black and minority ethnic women Eurocentric standards of beauty have been at work with straight and wavy hair being valued. Even when the hair is worn short and un-straightened, women tend to compensate with a feminine marker by wearing a hair clip, putting on make-up or earrings. Although in many cultures long hair continues to be considered feminine, body hair everywhere else is considered masculine. And with facial hair there is the 'bearded lady' stereotype of something unnatural. The advent of more revealing clothes probably contributed to the pressure to shave armpits and legs and the mocking of those who didn't. However, some women again resisted by dyeing their armpits different colours in protest (see #dyedpits).

Social expectations of how women should look extends to their pubic hair. It is increasingly expected that young sexually active women remove much or even all of it. There is the extreme 'Brazilian', or the marginally less 'landing strip'. Pressures to conform to this include the influence of hairless genitalia in pornography, and the desirability of pubescent girls as well as sexual preparedness and cleanliness. Not all women comply. Lynn wrote:

> I'm now 45. All my boyfriends have asked me to remove my pubic hair – which shows the entitlement men feel they have with regard to the female body. The only difference is that men over the last five to ten years have asked much sooner than they used to, which I think ties in with their increased exposure to online porn as opposed to the mags of before. I've always said no categorically without hesitation. It's my body not theirs.[114]

Clothes

Gendered differences in clothing start with infant clothing. From around the 1940s the 'pinkification' and other forms of gendering of clothing for babies and young girls increased, with a new boost in the 1970s. In previous centuries infants wore dresses and tended to be clothed in white; earlier in history blue was more associated with women and pink with boys.[115] Girls' clothes became about looking 'pretty' and even at very young ages looking sexual. Claire explained a particular incident:

> My daughter is now 13 and too big for so-called children's clothes, but adult clothes don't quite fit the body of a young girl. Recently she tried on an adult dress and sobbed, 'Mum I just want to wear children's clothes.' Soon after, she wanted a tankini like her friends. But they had padded bras. She has only just started

developing and did not feel comfortable with making her bust look bigger. I don't think I faced the same pressure when I was young. The industry is denying adolescent girls the opportunity to grow into their bodies at their own pace, and I'm horrified at the sexualisation involved. It's affecting the whole peer group and parents go along with it.[116]

Turning to women's clothes, we have to start with the corset. They are the epitome of the idea that women's bodies should be artificially shaped and controlled to suit an image of womanhood, constraining women and making breathing and moving difficult – and they could cause internal damage. They were one of the first mass-produced garments for women.

The elasticated girdle evolved directly from the corset and was made possible by the development of new materials such as Lycra. They were worn from around 1920 to the late 1960s. The emphasis shifted from moulding the body to supporting it. Female underwear went through various transformations, generally using less material, with greater practicality. There was also, particularly from the 1980s, an increase in colour, fabric and design choices. Since then we have moved on . . . or have we? Coming full circle, back to the pre-1918 era, so-called 'shape wear' or 'foundation garments' such as 'waist trainers' or 'waist cinchers' emerged as a new fashion item around 2015. We are told by one UK manufacturer: 'By safely compressing your stomach, waist trainers can effectively curb appetites as the body adjusts to eating smaller portions during meals.'[117]

As for outer garments, the Rational Dress Society, formed in 1881, promoted dresses that liberated women. These gave way in the 1920s to rebellious shift dresses with little shape for everyday wear and evening cocktail dresses. The colour black also entered the repertoire as a fashion option in the late 1920s, as did white shirts. In the 1930s curves were back, with the influence of Hollywood glamour, and a reaction to the economic depression. As the hemline moved up, pantyhose, stockings and tights came into play. More functional clothing characterised the war years, and then in the late

1940s and 1950s the trend was for bright colours, an even more accentuated waist, and wide calf-to-waist skirts. Christian Dior's 'New Look' of 1947 was influential and a direct reaction to the austerity of the war years. The 'feminine' look was back.

One development in 1946 was the invention of the bikini in the United States, popularised in Britain soon after, and initially creating much consternation. More recently, popularity of the bikini has declined, some brands doing away with it altogether. A mixture of reasons has been offered: increased concern about skin cancer, the all-pervasiveness of nudity making it less alluring, more women being overweight and wanting to hide their bulges, women making their own feminist statement, and the rise of fundamentalist views about the display of women's bodies.

Returning to the chronology of outer garments, the late 1950s and 1960s saw more off-the-peg clothes, rather than individually made garments. Before this, girls tended to dress as their mothers did. Then in the 1960s came designers such as Mary Quant who were responsible for the youth revolution. Tights replaced stockings, which enabled the miniskirt to grow shorter and shorter, along with innovations such as hot pants and PVC raincoats in novel colour combinations and patterns. The model Lesley Hornby, 'Twiggy', epitomised the look. She was petite, weighing around 8 stone, 50 kilograms, at the time, prefacing the future focus on zero-size models. Jeans also came in as casual wear from the late 1950s. The late 1960s and 1970s saw the emergence of two looks: the feminine 'ethnic' long flowing dress in Laura Ashley patterns, and dungarees, jeans, shirts and boots. Lesley Covington shared:

> During the 60s, my sister and I represented both ends of the spectrum. I was wafting about in long flowing dresses that I bought from Kensington Market or Laura Ashley, my hair down to my waist and beads around my neck, whereas my sister preferred tailored suits and shirts, short hair and the ubiquitous Doc Martens. We lived under the same roof in – mostly – perfect harmony.[118]

Teenagers and young adults throughout the period drove fashion changes, to some extent overlapping with political and social positions such as the 1920s flappers' post-war escapism. Rebellion then took the form of Teddy Boys in the 1950s; the mods, rockers, hippies and Beatles' fans in the 1960s; in the 1970s the feminist 'libber', campaigners for nuclear disarmament, skinheads, glam rockers, punks and goths – most with variations on a defiant look.

Overall, since the 1970s, mainstream women's clothing has increased in informality and in practicality, as forms of fabric have expanded, and the growth in cheap mass-produced clothes has led to extensive wardrobes. On the margins is an interest in ethical sourcing and the environmental footprint of clothes.

Many anti-suffragette posters had women in trousers and men in dresses showing how ludicrous it would be to give women the vote. The expression 'who is wearing the trousers' still links trousers with power. The practice of women wearing trousers gained ground during the First and Second World Wars. But the notion that it is not proper for women to wear trousers continued.

The same applies for girls and school uniforms. In exasperation Elaine exclaimed to me: 'Why is it that in almost every school it hasn't changed? Even now that the school uniform is skirts for girls and trousers for boys, when look at us adults, here we are all in trousers. That bedazzles me.'[119] Nicola, who has campaigned on the subject, wrote:

> I believe that making girls wear skirts at school against their will is one of the first steps towards teaching them to be ashamed of their bodies. This leads to them inevitably being punished for having skirts too long or too short, and it was certainly the first time that I became self-conscious about keeping myself 'covered' so as not to 'distract' boys or to 'look respectable'. Whenever I get asked why this is so important to me, I always say . . . 'So that girls can do cartwheels, isn't that reason enough?'[120]

On the other hand, there are also many girls hiking their skirts up as high as possible, often against school rules, wanting to display their emerging sexuality, while others keep their school jumpers on and overheat because they feel self-conscious about see-through school blouses.

Over the last twenty years, more schools have included trousers as an option for girls. In 2016, gender-neutral school uniforms were introduced in eighty state schools, allowing girls to wear trousers and, even more progressively, boys to wear skirts. In 2017 John Lewis also became the first major retailer to get rid of boys' and girls' sections of the store and from the labels on its clothes and launch a unisex gender-neutral clothing line.

A particularly contentious area of women's clothing in the recent past has been the use of the veil. At the start of the twentieth century British women wore headscarves as an informal alternative to a hat, without which they would have felt improperly dressed. Sometimes they used a net veil, especially when in mourning. Women of different faiths still cover up to different degrees. Traditionally Hindu women did so after marriage, particularly in front of men from the husband's family. These mores have largely been discarded among Hindu women in the UK. Many Muslim women still use a scarf and/or veil to make a statement to their own community about keeping the faith. A global rise in more traditional Islamic views has also led to more veiling, including with the burka fully covering the face.

Although the topic of Muslim women covering up had been simmering for a while, in the summer of 2016 it flared up, initially in France. This followed a confrontation on a beach in Cannes where armed police forced a woman to take off her burkini – a full-body swimsuit invented by the Lebanese-born Australian Aheda Zanetti to allow her girls to swim without the constraint of a veil. Cannes had been the location of a terrorist attack a few weeks earlier. Photos of the confrontation were widely circulated.

This incident underscores the relationship between women, families, social norms and the state. France is secular, and the burkini was seen to be politicising the beach and alienating non-Muslims. The official view was that a ban would protect the public and counter the control that Islamic clerics were exerting over women. The opposing view was that forcing a woman to remove her clothes in public was an unacceptable humiliation; it was misogynistic, violated human rights, and reeked of cultural hegemony and islamophobia. Why would a nun's habit or a wetsuit be allowed but not a burkini? What is clear is that conflicting attitudes to the veil are a symptom not a cause of the problem, with women having some agency, but also their bodies being the pawns in a battlefield directed by men.

Advertisements

The battle is also fuelled by money. Mass-market advertising started to see women as consumers from the 1920s because of their growing power over household spending. And after the 1950s the influence of advertisements grew substantially. A male-dominated industry, it largely reinforced stereotypes using women's sex appeal to sell products. Fairy Liquid TV advertisements from the 1960s to the 1990s had a mother and daughter talking by the sink and the jingle 'Hands that do dishes can feel soft as your face' with the tune imprinted on many of us. In 2017, the advert changed to show a father and son wanting to use the bottle as a spaceship, but Mum – now faceless in the background – is still washing up.[121]

The alternative to the mother figure is the sexualised image. A 2015 Protein World poster sold its dieting products with a very thin model and the words 'ARE YOU BEACH BODY READY?' In response, a petition on Change.org was signed by more than 70,000 people objecting to the implications. A Twitter hashtag #everybodysready went viral, many an advert was defaced and the watchdog ruled that the advert could not run again. Meanwhile the advert had done its job with the outrage increasing the company's visibility.

By contrast, some advertisements have been at the vanguard of social change, as epitomised by the #Femertising concept and annual awards. Cindy Gallop, founder of the creative agency Bartle Bogle Hegarty, argued: 'One of the quickest ways to make people think differently about something is to change the visuals around it.' Campaigns such as the 2014 #LikeAGirl by Always, 2015 Sport England's 'This Girl Can' and the 2016 New Boyfriend Maltesers advert have set a tone depicting active women from a diversity of backgrounds just being themselves.[122] From 2018, the Advertising Standards Authority has given warning that new rules will be drawn up to ban adverts reinforcing stereotypical gender views. The chief executive, Guy Parker, explained: 'tougher advertising standards can play an important role in tackling inequalities and improving outcomes for individuals, the economy and society as a whole'.[123]

'Female' Illnesses

One final area to look at in the context of women's identity is their health and attitudes to female illnesses. A hundred years ago and more, female hysteria (the word from the Greek, meaning 'of the womb') was sometimes seen as self-inflicted, 'morbid introspection' and 'motiveless malingering'.[124] People diagnosed with mental illnesses, especially women, were segregated and often incarcerated in asylums; they faced the danger of sterilisation and all sorts of experimental treatments including electric shock treatment. Penni shared:

Both of my grandmothers were committed to mental institutions. One died there in the late 1930s (St George's in Morpeth). She had been incarcerated because of depression caused it was said, by my grandfather's philandering. Some thought she'd died of cancer, though that was often used as 'cover for suicide'.

In my early twenties, I discovered my other grandmother had been in St Nicholas's Asylum in Newcastle but was told she was dead. It transpired she lived on until the mid-1990s, when she was moved into a local nursing home. In 1998 when I was forty-eight I discovered through a chance comment that she had died that year! My dad had never visited, he blamed her for 'leaving him'. It seems most likely she suffered post-natal depression and was sectioned because of that.[125]

A number of mental health illnesses have affected women during the century in ways that are poorly understood. Dr Kate Middleton puts many of the gains of women in perspective, reflecting:

In the UK and other so-called developed and progressive countries, there has been a steady rise in emotional and mental ill health – particularly in women, who are three times as likely to report anxiety and depression as men, and nearly twice as likely to report severe symptoms of emotional illness. Young women in particular are at the highest risk of emotional illness, including eating disorders, self-harm, anxiety and depression. This is not to negate the benefits to women over the century, but to point up some of the more negative realities.[126]

Many mental health problems circle back to ideas about what women should look like. However hard women work to fit the image demanded of them, the beauty industry has been using excessively thin and young models and airbrushing photos to present an exacting ideal. In 2007, the British Fashion Council, led by Baroness Kingsmill, undertook a health inquiry into the matter, which developed protective guidelines. Meanwhile countries such as France, Italy and Spain took stronger action and passed laws to penalise companies that encourage excessive thinness.[127]

The beauty industry continues to be exploitative, with particular fads moving from the catwalk to the streets, as in the case of the 'thigh gap' around 2012. Amy, a model working around the same time, says:

I worked as a model from the age of sixteen up until I was twenty-one. During this time, I experienced the destructive demand the fashion industry places on models' bodies. I lived with girls who tried to keep to the industry standard by navigating each month with a conveyor belt of diets; low-carb diets, coffee-and-cigarette diets, vegan diets and one-cookie-a-day diets. Keeping models 'in-shape' was a lucrative system not only for agencies, but personal trainers who appeared like vultures hovering around the agency doors. These were girls whose bodies had 'transgressed' the boundaries of the industry's desired measurements. I myself got caught in the industry's snare when a week before one London Fashion Week my booker told me I needed to lose two inches off my hips. This moment set me on a precarious slope where a 34-inch hip would follow me around like a spectre, dictating to me what was beautiful.[128]

Individual models and actors such as Kate Winslet have spoken out against the 'anorexic is beautiful' culture and in her contract with a cosmetic sponsor demanded a clause to ensure her photos were never photoshopped.[129] Likewise in 2017 beauty contestant Zoiey Smale, who had been crowned Miss United Kingdom and was a size 10, handed back her crown after being told to lose weight if she wanted to compete for the Miss United Continents pageant.

One of the main food- and image-related problems is anorexia nervosa, the eating abstinence disorder with a genetic component and a cultural one that tends to afflict adolescent girls in particular, but not exclusively, with boys and older women also susceptible. Although documented since the 1870s, public awareness of the condition was limited until the mid-1960s when the obsession with body image intensified. The illness can be exacerbated by social media and celebrity culture, and affects middle-class and highly educated girls disproportionally. Seventeen-year-old Izzy shared:

I come from a happy, supportive and stable middle class background, and yet I have struggled to be happy. It's because the illness is an indiscriminate, irrational beast. It makes victims of the rich and the poor, the old and the young. It blinds us to the blessings in our lives and robs us of our self-esteem. Anorexia is mercilessly controlling. It caused me to lose my hair, weaken my bones, miss my periods, withdraw from my friends, constantly feel tired and for what? Another inch off my already emaciated waist. It's perplexing that it seemed worth all of the consequences.[130]

Beat, the eating disorder charity, found that from 2008 to 2014, the waiting times for outpatient appointments in some parts of England had increased by more than 120 per cent, with some patients waiting over a year, putting lives at risk.[131] The illness has the highest death rate for any psychiatric disease.[132] The fasting that defines anorexia can sometimes be seen as a conscious or subconscious attempt to delay menstruation and postpone sexual development – all this when puberty is happening earlier and earlier. Izzy explained:

> I distinctly remember the harrowing feeling that came each month with the acknowledgement that my period had started. In my sickened mind, this was a signal that I had to restrict what I ate even more. The ultimate goal was to stop having my periods entirely. I was determined to reach this as a way of escaping the need to grow up and face independence, uncertainty and my sexuality – all three of which I found deeply confusing and anxiety provoking.[133]

The gender element of the disease is often not addressed. Yet, as Isabelle makes clear, anorexia is often the result of girls, even as young as eight, wanting a sense of control over their bodies when they are losing their androgynous look and becoming more feminine. A feminist analysis challenging cultural norms around body image is therefore important in the treatment of eating disorders.[134]

Bulimia, another eating disorder with the compulsion to overeat and then vomit, emerged as a problem from the 1970s. As with anorexia it is often associated with outwardly successful people, a hidden fear of becoming fat, allied to self-disgust and self-punishment. Some celebrities have owned up to the illness, most famously Diana Princess of Wales, who explained the illness's grip in her biography. Diabetes has been linked to eating disorders and women in particular have been diagnosed with diabulimia. In 2016, it was estimated that 40 per cent of diabetic women between the ages of fifteen to thirty were suffering from the disorder.[135]

In 1996, orthorexia nervosa, which involves compulsive narrow 'healthy', 'clean' eating habits, fasts and excessive exercise, was added to the family of eating disorders. In this condition, not only is there the usual theme of women trying to fit idealised images, but in addition there is a focus on the purity of the food, using a language that draws uncomfortable parallels with women being valued for their innocence and chastity.

A different but connected mental health problem is that of self-harm. In 2016, the NSPCC reported that the rates for self-harm in young women had tripled between 2007 and 2014.[136] A study by the Children's Society found that nearly a quarter of girls aged 14 (22%) said they had self-harmed in just a year. The figure for boys was less 9%.[137] Self-poisoning with alcohol, painkillers and antidepressants is reported especially among poor teenage and young girls,[138] with LGBTQIA young people also disproportionately represented.[139] Growing problems of obesity also have gender dimensions but less clear-cut ones, with a study in 2015 finding 10 per cent more men being obese compared to women overall, though not in Scotland or Wales, and overall 1 per cent more women being morbidly obese than men.[140]

If we compare the lives of adolescent girls over the last hundred years, there is no doubt that young women have more opportunities to shine than ever before. In contrast to their mothers, grandmothers and great-grandmothers, they are now told that they can do anything they set their minds to. However, there has been an inflation of expectations in what counts as success. At the same time, cultural norms focusing on being attractive and desirable are emphasised. The pressure is on to be perfect, to excel in all areas; as one friend put it, to be 'skinny, smart and hot'. Self-harm can be a response to worries around image and exams, with busier more complex families, the internet and a celebrity culture being contributing factors.

During the 1930s a female mental illness was given the name 'suburban neurosis'. It was a term given to young housewives who felt lonely, trapped and unfulfilled. Apart from depression, it was associated with alcohol and substance abuse. This extreme loneliness was felt particularly by housewives in the new high-rise towers of the 1960s and by immigrant women, isolated by language and culture. With more women in paid employment and having other social links, the growth of the internet and increased multiculturalism, this 'neurosis', or at least the scale of it, seems to have decreased.

A more constant mental illness is severe perinatal anxiety and depression including, at its most extreme, postpartum psychosis. In 2014, it was estimated that one in ten women[141] had some degree of depression and for some this was life-threatening. Those who also suffer miscarriages or are in abusive relationships and/or have financial concerns are at particular risk.

The so-called 'sandwich generation' of women, who care for young and old at the same time, also face particular worries linked to juggling obligations at home and work. A woman's time belongs to others, to a husband, parents, children, employer, colleagues and friends, the house. For many, especially when an additional factor such as an illness comes into play, there can be a feeling of guilt that no one is getting enough of her time. This emerged particularly during the wars when soldiers' wives worked long hours and shouldered all the family obligations, with few mod cons, and had reduced disposable income. Over time, the pattern of delayed childbirth, greater proportions of women at work and longevity of life has increased the likelihood of women being in the sandwich. The internet has both helped and hindered. As Juliet Webster researching this area explained:

> The conventional boundaries between work and home, and production and consumption are shifting and/or being eroded: activities such as making travel arrangements or banking, are now self-service; paid work is increasingly done in the home at sporadic times, so the home is an even more contested space than before, especially for women. Women also have a disproportionate tendency to take responsibility for problems that are actually structural rather than individual in nature.[142]

Another point at which many women suffer anxiety and depression is when children grow up and leave, which can be especially hard for women who have been dedicated to the care of their children without much of an external focus. The response from society, and even the children themselves, couched in humour, can be pain-fully dismissive. This empty nest syndrome can also hit fathers, and grandparents also talk of the pain when they end up parting from grandchildren they had helped care for.

In many of these stories, differences in class, education, women's age and family life cycle and their ethnicity have an impact on the problems manifested and the likelihood of seeking and getting support. For example, a 2006 study of South Asian women showed that between the ages of sixteen and twenty-four they are signifi-cantly more likely to self-harm than white women. Furthermore, they report mental health problems more frequently than men, and tend to feel that mainstream services do not cater to them.[143]

Other Illnesses

In Britain, HIV has a male face; statistically, in 2015 for example, three-quarters of the 107,800 people living with HIV were men. However, a quarter were women and of these 17,200 were Black African women.[144] The reason for their specific vulnerability is a combination of factors: many of the women are migrants from East and Southern Africa where HIV is prevalent, violence against women and girls is high, and sexual health provision low. Poverty, exclusion, lack of awareness and a lack of specific services all play a role. HIV is often transmitted through sexual violence, having multiple partners or transactional sex, forced sex, sexual abuse during childhood and through inability to demand condom use.[145]

A number of women's support services focus specifically on HIV, including cliniQ (run by and for transgender people), Between the Sheets (Sahir House, Liverpool), Salamander Trust's 4M Peer Mentoring Project (run by and for women living with HIV to support women on their pregnancy journey), Project 100 (Positively UK) and Sophia Forum. As Alice Welbourn explained:

Positively UK started as Positively Women, in the late 1980s. In 1992, Positively Women housed the newly formed International

Community of Women living with HIV. We have come a huge long way. Yet despite the huge advances in HIV treatment, which have given us the potential to live fully productive and vibrant lives – even with no travel health insurance excess payments (and to have HIV-free babies through normal vaginal delivery) – the psycho-social dimensions to HIV still overshadow our lives.[146]

Funding shortages threaten the possibility of continued support and many women living with HIV are isolated, terrified of telling even their grown-up children, for fear they will be rejected, or barred from cuddling their grandchildren.

A very different illness, this time one primarily associated with women and where again social attitudes have compounded the effects of the disease, is that of ME or chronic fatigue syndrome. In spite of the evidence for a medical cause since the 1950s, it is often dismissed as 'not a real illness'.[147] A similar pattern appears in the treatment of chronic urinary tract infections where patients are told that their symptoms have a psychological cause.[148] These infections have received minimal research, in spite of evidence of a possible bacterial cause, and the fact that the current urine test misses most cases of the illness.[149] There are also illnesses such as migraines, which can affect people of all ages but are strongly associated with women.[150]

Particularly positive over time has been the pattern of people surviving longer after heart attacks and strokes, having joints and limbs repaired, and managing osteoporosis for many years, with medical breakthroughs improving the quality of life. But this also means that there are more people living for longer with dementia, Parkinson's and other illnesses. In 2015 there were 850,000 people living with dementia, of whom two-thirds were women.[151]

One last disease to mention is cancer, a word so loaded with fear that it was often not made explicit, but referred to in hushed tones as 'the big C'. The fear added to the danger, with the disease often being discovered too late. In my family's case my mother thinks her mother died of cancer:

I was aware that there was a great taboo about what was wrong about my mother, great secrecy. Sometimes in the morning we were conscious that she had been bleeding in the night and there was some cleaning going on in her room, but all this was hush hush and you did not talk about it.[152]

Fortunately, growing understanding and effective treatment have challenged the traditional embarrassment and hopeless silence. When I was diagnosed with the same illness, although the diagnosis was still late, the taboo had lessened. As Elizabeth reflected, with the management of cancer and women's identity there is something else going on:

Before I started chemotherapy, I was sent off to choose a wig. I surprised myself by choosing a long, luscious, brunette wig – nothing like my scruffy, short, undyed grey hair. A little later, I joined a make-up tutorial in a cancer group meeting set up to feel like a pamper party, and came away with a bag full of free lipstick, eye shadow, foundation and blusher. Of course, I didn't have to do these things, but they seemed to be the norm, and somehow I felt that doing them made me more acceptable – a 'good' breast cancer patient.[153]

After mastectomy, women with breast cancer are offered breast reconstruction. This can involve a process over several months using expanders under the skin to create space for an implant, or surgery to take tissue from the stomach, back, thighs or elsewhere to reconstruct a breast shape, with up to seven days in hospital.[154] Most people then need further operations to improve the appearance of the new breast and, finally, further work to create a new nipple. Yet it seems that reconstructive surgery – a long process – is accepted as 'normal'. As Elizabeth put it:

I absolutely respect the fact that reconstruction is important for many women . . . But I knew straight away that I did not want reconstructive surgery – and I feel I have had to explain myself and defend that decision ever since. My decisions to have a second risk-reducing mastectomy and not to reconstruct were somehow on the freakish outer limits of acceptability. Nearly three years on from diagnosis, I'm still being asked about reconstruction in my check-up appointments, the implication being that I should consider it, or that I'll come to my senses at some point.[155]

Culturally, it seems, we still have to play the part and look like 'proper' women.

Conclusion

The last hundred years has brought increased longevity to women's lives through reduction in infant and maternal mortality, fewer deaths from disease, better health services and awareness, improved standards of living and nutrition, fewer pregnancies, and interlinked with all of these, greater control over reproductive rights and sexuality. These factors alone have been massively transformative.

At home, the servicing of others continues to dominate and give meaning to women's lives but also to subordinate them, both symbolically and practically. However, the expectation for the first half of the last century was that women would be married before they had sex, children were conceived and born within marriage, and people stayed married to the same person. Families remain important in women's lives but what families look like has become more and more complex and includes reconstituted families, single-parent households and same-sex couples.

Towards the end of the century, the challenge to binary identities placed sexuality and gender under the spotlight as never before and although this is still on the fringes of mainstream society, there is a kernel of change, with the potential to create a revolution in ascribed and prescribed identities.

Women's body image, their clothes, hair and make-up, are still central to women's identities and lives. Women navigate with their own preferences and face specific health concerns that have often been poorly understood and subject to social taboos which increase the risks. Women's lives operate within what are sometimes dangerous cultural and social expectations linked to a sexualised culture, which feeds into the subject of the next chapter, that of violence and conflict. However, overall, women's individual identities have increasingly been allowed to flourish.

Identity: how did we do?

In the hardback version of this book I gave this chapter a 4 out of 5. However, talking to thousands of people up and down the country during 2018, I felt my initial score didn't chime with the reflections of others. I have therefore now reduced the score right down to 2.5 out of 5. This is for two key reasons. First, the focus on what men say and do, but on what women and girls look like. Women are often amongst the worst at perpetuating the problem, though it is fed by commercial interests in the beauty and advertising industries and magnified by social media. Many anecdotes were shared, of very young girls caught up with perfecting narrow ideals of beauty. A Year 12 teacher mentioned a questionnaire she had developed to look at reducing student stress. Not one boy ticked the option of detox from social media; 80% of the girls did. Secondly, because of the very slow progress in joint parenting and caring. Men are still seen as autonomous, women in relation to their families. This point was summarised to me by an elderly couple who told me they didn't have children; the woman was always asked why, the man never questioned. Overall, we have achieved greater equality in politics and at work than we have in the domestic sphere.
What would your score be?

4

VIOLENCE

'Who knew you could travel so far to stay still?' (Mitch Egan CB, feminist campaigner, ex-prison governor)[1]

Globally in 2013 it was estimated that one in three women had experienced physical or sexual violence in their lifetime.[2] The exploitation of women through the use of force and the threat of violence, particularly the threat of sexual violence, has always existed and underpins patriarchy.[3] Obviously a large number of men are not abusive and not all women molested, but there is a dominant pattern where – to different degrees – many men are abusive of women, and it is their rights and power as men that allow them to do so. Even in its most extreme form, violence is often not about seeking personal pleasure or gratification, but about the assertion of power as an expression of entitlement. Meanwhile the fear of violence defines and conditions women. Some forms are universal, others culturally specific, and women who are seen to be different or are particularly vulnerable for other reasons experience additional forms of abuse, denigration and cruelty. Violence and the fear of violence affect women's engagement in politics, in education, in paid employment, in families and in the wider society.

In 1918, there were fewer than 2,000 sexual offences recorded; most violence towards women was not reported let alone prosecuted.[4] This has changed dramatically. In 2017–18, the number of domestic abuse, rape and sexual offence cases referred to the Crown Prosecution Services was 116,574 and 80,387 defendants were charged (a conviction rate of 76 per cent). Men were 93 per cent of those prosecuted, where the gender of the person was recorded.[5] The massive increases can be interpreted as due to a combination of factors: increased naming of violence as a crime, increased reporting and increased crime, including abuse in new forms, e.g. perpetrated through social media.

Domestic Violence and Abuse

A hundred years ago there was greater cultural acceptance of violence by husbands against wives. It was considered normal for a man to lash out, justified in particular if he had been drinking, or was hot-tempered – a man's right, but only up to a point. First-wave feminists campaigned for the right of women to escape violent husbands, divorce them and acquire the right to keep their children. Angela and Penni shared:

> I grew up in a household where my father ruled with an iron fist; my mum was so scared to make a noise, even whispering sent shivers down our spine in case he heard us, and from watching this as a child I swore I would not allow myself to live this way; I swore no man would beat me down.[6]

> I left home at 18 due to the intolerable situation within my family, including attempted abuse by my dad, being disbelieved by my mother.[7]

Domestic abuse still accounts for most of the statistics on violence against women. In 2017–18, 110,562 cases of domestic abuse[8] were referred to the police of which 70 per cent were prosecuted. Where gender was recorded, 92 per cent of defendants were men and 84 per cent of victims were women. The conviction rate was 75 per cent.[9] Agencies in the UK report that on average two women a week are killed by a partner or ex-partner.[10] In 2015–16, 49 per cent of victims aged sixteen or above were women killed by partners or ex-partners, compared with 6 per cent of men. Domestic abuse has been described as a form of everyday terrorism that operates on the individual in the home – and yet cumulatively it affects the whole of society. It is often also cyclical, perpetrated by those who have witnessed or suffered abuse, particularly in childhood.

In general, legislation to tackle domestic violence has been very slow in coming. It only started with the Domestic Violence and Matrimonial Proceedings Act in 1976. This gave victims the right to obtain an injunction against partners who had been abusive, and gave the police the power to arrest them if the injunction was breached. Although marital rape was explicitly prohibited by law in many countries, it was not criminalised in Scotland until 1989 and in England and Wales in 1991.

Yet consent within domestic settings remains a difficult line to draw. As Lynn in 2017 shared: 'I know a man, a husband and father in his late 40s, who is of the opinion that it is his wife's duty to "spread her legs" – his words – that she has no right to "refuse sex".'[11] Despite the laws against domestic abuse and marital rape, victims often do not come forward; enforcement has been difficult and conviction rates very low.

The lower age limit for domestic violence was reduced in 2013 to include young people aged sixteen and seventeen, following a study that showed the younger age group was particularly likely to suffer abuse.[12] Following successful piloting in 2014, Domestic Violence Protection Orders (DVPOs) started to be issued, which meant a perpetrator could be prohibited from returning to a residence and from having contact for up to twenty-eight days. This was an important change as previously the victim and children had to leave the home. From 2014 'Clare's Law', named after Clare Wood who was murdered by her ex-partner in 2009, enabled anybody with concerns about a partner's past to ask the police if there was a record of abusive offences. In 2017, after much lobbying, improved guidance was provided to judges around the presumption of parental contact where there has been Domestic abuse, to increase the protection of women and children.[13] A Domestic Violence Bill due in 2017 was repeatedly delayed to 2019. It promises to be a landmark transformation of the way domestic violence is tackled.

Domestic violence has increasingly been understood to be about control. It is a crime against a human right: the right to liberty and security.[14] See Figure 10 on the links between violence and different systems of control.[15] In recognition of these more complex forms of domestic violence, the offence of coercive and controlling behaviour in an intimate relationship came into force in 2015.[16]

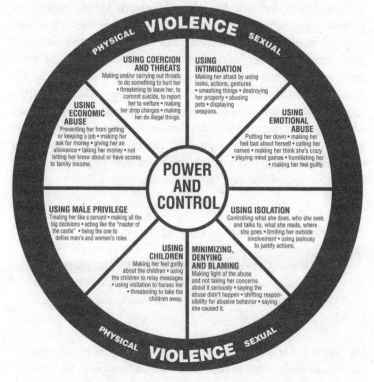

Figure 10: *Violence as Power and Control, Domestic Abuse Intervention Project, Duluth model*

After the 1970s, the help provided to those fleeing violence also improved, with support from the voluntary sector increasingly by government – until around 2010 when, due to austerity measures, funding started to be cut, an estimated 16 per cent of shelters, for example, closing between 2010 and 2014.[17] Legal aid reductions also followed. Even a doctor's letter as evidence of abuse needed to take the legal process forward could cost more than a week's unemployment benefit.[18] Staff in statutory agencies sometimes required women to make statements to the police and provide their own evidence before they could be rehoused or moved to places of safety. Increased shortage of social housing compounded these problems.

Some categories of women are at greater risk: women in rural areas, pregnant, older or disabled, immigrants, particularly those not legally resident in Britain. Some might not speak the language well, or face the threat of their children being taken away from them and deportation. Women's refuges are under extreme strain and they might not take in such women owing to a lack of funding for such cases. There is a growing recognition that because of discrimination LGBTQIA people are vulnerable to sexual violence and abuse, yet are less likely to seek support.[19]

Refuge set up the world's first refuge for women in Chiswick, West London, in 1971. It changed its name from Chiswick Family Rescue in 1993 and is now the country's largest provider of specialist services for women and children escaping domestic violence. In 2018 it supported more than 6,000 women and children on any given day.[20]

Women's Aid, previously the National Women's Aid Federation, was set up in 1975, to provide services and campaign for better support, bringing together around forty independent refuge services for women and children, with Scottish Women's Aid operating independently. In 1987 Women's Aid launched the first domestic violence helpline for abused women and children, which became free in 2003, run in partnership with Refuge. Women's Aid pushed for the establishment of inter-agency support from the 1990s, and supported the first UK-wide public directory of refuges and helplines. Online support has become increasingly pivotal.

SafeLives emerged in 2005 to spread multi-agency work nationwide. They pioneered the DASH risk checklist (Domestic abuse, stalking and honour-based violence), subsequently used by most police forces in the UK. SafeLives also trains independent domestic violence advisors (IDVA in England and Wales, or IDAA in Scotland) working in charities, local councils and hospitals. They run MARACS (multi-agency risk assessment conferences) throughout the country.

The name **Sisters Uncut** references both the suffering of women and the effects of austerity measures. The organisation, which emerged in 2014, encourages women to set up autonomous collectives open to all who identify as women. Men are asked not to attend meetings and protests, but to support in other ways. Sisters Uncut uses non-violent direct action and suffragette imagery. For example, on 7 October 2015, they stormed the premiere of the film *Suffragette*, breaking through the official cordon, lying down on the red carpet, explaining: 'The suffragettes took direct action because they couldn't wait any longer for the right to vote. We are taking direct action because we can't wait any longer for women's safety: our sisters are dying.'[21]

Protests included dyeing the Trafalgar Square fountains red, occupying empty council flats, blocking bridges, and in 2017 occupying the closed Holloway Prison to demand better domestic violence services from the government.

Other forms of violence that have happened within families have included female infanticide – rare in the UK but not unheard of. A category on the rise, by contrast, is that committed primarily by teenage boys, on parents, mainly on mothers, sometimes fuelled by drug dependency and the need for money.[22] One estimate in 2016 was that 3 per cent of families with teenagers experienced severe abuse.[23] According to Karen Bailey: 'Mothers feel additional shame and guilt because they blame themselves for bringing up a child who acts in this way ... and for mothers there is the additional burden of not being able to walk away from their own child.'[24]

Forced Marriage and So-called 'Honour'-Based Violence

In 1918 forced marriage was a reality for some women and girls, including at the highest and lowest echelons of society. The practice is now associated with communities from Asia and the Middle East. In 2007 following the Forced Marriage (Civil Protection) Act, the Forced Marriage Unit was set up. The following year, UK resident and trainee doctor Humayra Abedin was able to return to the UK from Bangladesh after having been imprisoned, drugged and forced to marry a man chosen by her parents. Supported by lawyers in Bangladesh, the British Act protected her, even though she was a foreign national and the abduction and marriage took place in Bangladesh.

In 2014 the law was strengthened, and forced marriage made a criminal offence. The Forced Marriage Unit in 2015 supported 1,220 victims, 80 per cent of them female, most in the eighteen to twenty-five age range.[25] There were 14 per cent of cases with no overseas element. Referrals to the police of forced marriage have been few and far between, for example, 71 in 2017–18 with a 74 per cent conviction rate. Of the defendants, 12 per cent were women, mostly mothers and other relatives.[26]

Another more extreme form of domestic violence is so-called 'honour' killing, something that we now associate with Asian communities, although it is more universal. As with forced marriage, political correctness has contributed to hiding the problem. Usually the crime is perpetrated against women whose relationship or lifestyle choices differ from those planned by the family and are seen to threaten their honour. The women are regarded as the property of the family and community. Much more common than killing is control using bullying, threats and even imprisonment for women who do not conform.

Statistics in this area are poor as there is a great reluctance to testify. In 2015–16 in the UK 216 cases were referred to the police, of which most were prosecuted; half resulted in convictions. Where gender was recorded, 86 per cent of defendants were male and 76 per cent of victims female.[2]

Karma Nirvana was founded by Jasvinder Sanghera, a survivor of a forced marriage and so-called honour-based abuse in 1993. The charity is based in Leeds and supports female and male victims across the UK with the aim of increasing the reporting of cases, reducing isolation and saving lives. It also provides guidance to police, health-care and social-work professionals and awareness-raising events including annual roadshows.

Muslim Women's Network UK is the only national Muslim women's charity with a membership of over eight hundred working within a framework of human rights and Islamic feminism. The charity focuses on Muslim women and girls in the UK, with research and a helpline for forced marriage, domestic abuse and mental health. Key to its success is a broad knowledge base and delivery of a culturally sensitive service. MWNUK also identifies policy gaps and uses this information to inform decision-makers in government and other public bodies.

FGM and Body Surgery

Female genital mutilation (FGM), or female circumcision, affects women and girls in all continents.[28] The prevalence is highest in Somalia, Guinea, Egypt, Mali, Sudan and Ethiopia. It is done to infants, girls and adult women taking different forms depending on specific traditions, and includes clitoridectomy, involving the partial or total removal of the clitoris, infibulation, cutting the clitoris and labia, and sometimes narrowing the vagina with stitching.

Traditionally, older women 'cutters' perform the circumcision on infants or young girls to control female sexuality and to prevent premarital sex, dishonour and difficulties in the marriage. The justification given is that uncut women are thought to be more sexually driven and demanding and may also be considered unclean, immodest and polluting.

As early as the 1920s, the MPs Eleanor Rathbone and the Duchess of Atholl campaigned against female circumcision, but it received little attention because of sensitivities about cultural imperialism. As the practice took place within families it was not seen in the broader context of violence. Others took up the baton in the 1980s, in particular the Ghanaian-British women's rights activist Efua Dorkenoo. The late crime writer Ruth Rendell also protested about the practice. It became a criminal offence in the UK in 1985, and was followed by legislation in 2003 to prevent UK nationals or UK residents taking a child abroad for the operation. Globally there has been increasing awareness of the psychological and physical impact on survivors. The World Health Organisation condemned it in 2010 and in 2012 a resolution was passed by the UN General Assembly aiming to eliminate it.

A 2013 documentary by Leyla Hussein, *The Cruel Cut*, and a petition to eliminate FGM in the UK gained over 100,000 signatures and led to a debate in Parliament. Working with Integrate UK, Fahma Mohamed, a fourteen-year-old girl, launched a successful petition to get the Education Secretary to write a letter about the risks of FGM to all British schools. From 2015, health and social-work professionals and teachers became legally required under the Serious Crime Act of 2015 to report known cases in under-eighteen-year-olds. It was estimated then that over 137,000 women and girls in the UK had been cut.[29]

It is very difficult for girls to report FGM against their own parents. As of the end of 2018 no one had been convicted under FGM legislation. Even so, where there has been concern, prevention orders have been issued and passports taken away to stop girls being taken abroad during the summer holidays in what has become known as the 'cutting season'.

Daughters of Eve was set up in 2010 by Leyla Hussein, Nimko Ali and Sainab Abdi, as a support and advocacy organisation for girls and women at risk from FGM. As well as raising awareness, they work to protect the rights of young people and promote their physical, mental and sexual health. Their holistic approach focuses on girls' and women's needs and not on the gender-based violence itself.

FGM is still sometimes considered as culturally 'other',[30] yet operations to reduce women's sexuality have long been undertaken within Western cultural norms. Clitorectomy was the preferred way to address the illness that was defined as women's 'hysteria'.[31] Then, from the 1980s onwards, as well as a few operations for medical reasons, women have increasingly undertaken female cosmetic surgery on their vaginas, vulvo-plasty to 'correct' their labia minora when it is larger than their labia majora, or labiaplasty – the cutting and altering of the labia minora or majora. In 2010 there were more than two thousand such procedures on the NHS. Girls as young as nine have been asking for an operation.[32]

Casual Sexism to Rape

Outside the domestic setting, women and girls' experiences of harassment is part of an overall culture that presumes male authority and privilege. What Catherine Mayer calls 'the constant tinnitus hum'[33] that women have lived with includes sexual innuendo, wolf whistles, provocative staring, unwanted touching – the list goes on and on. According to a 2016 poll, 70 per cent of women had been harassed in public.[34] Women and girls have the choice of ignoring it, responding humorously, or getting angry. Most choose to brush it off and get on with their lives, accepting that casual sexism is normal and their energies are better directed elsewhere. Many women also don't respond to little innuendos or jokes in poor taste because they feel the focus should be reserved for more extreme harassment.

However, as Laura Bates has made clear through her Everyday

Sexism Project, casual sexism and the fundamental inequality that women experience are connected. There is no line to be drawn between 'banter' and 'serious sexism', or even between words and deeds; they are intertwined. Laura started the online project in 2012. By 2017 it was active in more than twenty-five countries, generating hundreds of thousands of testimonies.[35] After being assaulted, women who speak up are often called 'silly', they are 'making a big thing out of nothing', 'it was mutual', 'I was a bit drunk' or 'she was a bit drunk', 'she is a liar'. The context is one in which, in 1975, the Law Lords could rule that a man was not guilty of rape if *he* believed there had been consent. The woman's voice was unheard.[36]

The Scottish Court, ruling in 1986, first addressed sexual harassment as a form of sex discrimination and therefore made it illegal under the Sex Discrimination Act.[37] The Protection from Harassment Act 1997 then introduced in the UK two criminal offences: a course of conduct amounting to harassment, and putting a person in fear of violence. In addition, stalking was made a specific offence in 2012.[38] By 2017–18, the figure for prosecutions of harassment and stalking offences during the year was 11,922.[39] Research on 350 cases between 2012 and 2014 also found that stalking behaviours existed in 94 per cent of homicide cases.[40] New civil protection stalking orders were announced in 2016, to protect people from harassment by strangers, acquaintances, colleagues and clients.

Nevertheless, the attitude that sexual assault is not a real crime remains embedded in society and even within the Police and Crown Prosecution Service, with the result that reporting and prosecution rates remain very low. To improve understanding of consent and the law, in 2016 Alison Saunders, the Director of Public Prosecutions, spearheaded a social media campaign with the National Union of Students called #consent. They used the cup of tea analogy developed by social blogger Emmeline May, who explained that sometimes you want a cup of tea, and sometimes you don't. Nobody would force you to have a cup of tea if you don't want one. The same should go for sex. The explanation has been further developed in a video[41] used by the Crown Prosecution Service and Thames Valley Police amongst others.[42]

When it comes to rape itself, going back in time, in 1919 in England

and Wales there were 121 reported cases of rape and 1,061 of indecent assault on women. Despite expectations that the return of First
World War soldiers would result in greater violence from men brutal-
ised by their experience, the statistics do not show this.[43] Since that
time, though, the figures for rape and sexual assault have increased
substantially. In 2015–16 they were the highest ever recorded with
6,855 rape referrals, still a tiny minority of the estimated number of
incidents – and only 57 per cent were charged. By 2017–18 the figures
had dropped to 6,012 rape referrals with 47 per cent charged showing
that change is not always unidirectional. Sexual assault prosecution
increased from 1,960 in 1930 to their highest level yet at 12,005 in
2017–18. Conviction rates were 78 to 80 per cent.[44] Where gender was
recorded, 97 per cent of those convicted were men.[45]

Since the 1980s, the treatment of rape victims by the criminal
justice system has improved, with revised sentencing guidelines, the
removal of the right of an alleged perpetrator to question the victim
in court, the right of victims to appeal lenient sentences, and greater
awareness of secondary victimisation in the case of badly handled
procedures. However, policy change cannot always be assumed to
be supportive of women. In 2010 the Liberal Democrats in the
coalition government attempted to introduce anonymity for those
accused of rape. This would have been the only crime where the
alleged perpetrator could be anonymous and would have stopped
linked cases being put together. The attempt failed to become law.

In the past the sexual history of the alleged victim used to be
revealed in rape prosecutions as a way of shifting attention away
from the alleged perpetrator. This was supposed to have stopped
after legislation in 1999, but one clause[46] has continued to allow
cross-examination on the victim's sexual history, as in the retrial and
acquittal of footballer Ched Evans. The case will tend to make
victims reluctant to come forward.

The absurdity of the focus on women taking precautions rather
than men being violent is underlined in the American comedian
Sarah Silverman's Ten Rape Prevention Tips, which went viral in
2016; see Figure 11.[47]

Ten Rape Prevention Tips

1. Don't put drugs in women's drinks.
2. When you see a woman walking by herself, leave her alone.
3. If you pull over to help a woman whose car has broken down, remember not to rape her.
4. If you are in an elevator and a woman gets in, don't rape her.
5. When you encounter a woman who is asleep, the safest course of action is to not rape her.
6. Never creep into a woman's home through an unlocked door or window, or spring out at her from between parked cars, or rape her.
7. Remember, people go to the laundry room to do their laundry. Do not attempt to molest someone who is alone in a laundry room.
8. Use the Buddy System! If it is inconvenient for you to stop yourself from raping women, ask a trusted friend to accompany you at all times.
9. Carry a rape whistle. If you find that you are about to rape someone, blow the whistle until someone comes to stop you.
10. Don't forget: Honesty is the best policy. When asking a woman out on a date, don't pretend that you are interested in her as a person; tell her straight up that you expect to be raping her later. If you don't communicate your intentions, the woman may take it as a sign that you do not plan to rape her.

Figure 11: Ten Rape Prevention Tips, Sarah Silverman.

In 2017, retiring Lindsey Kushner QC spoke about the dangers that women face, especially out at night and drunk. She advised:

A woman can do with her body what she wants and a man will have to adjust his behaviour accordingly. But, I don't think it's wrong for a judge to beg women to take actions to protect themselves. Burglars are out there and nobody says burglars are OK but we do say: 'Please don't leave your back door open at night, take steps to protect yourself.'[48]

Although her comment was a pragmatic one, she was criticised for the focus, once again, on women's behaviour, without commentary on what society should be saying to the abuser.

An important development in this regard was the approach introduced by Nottinghamshire Police to treat sexual harassment as a hate crime, similar to the way racism, Islamophobia and anti-Semitism are addressed. This resulted in it being regarded as a public order offence by the police, logged, analysed and followed up. It also provided women with the language to report the crime in a way that was more likely to be taken seriously. The approach has generated interest among other police forces.[49]

The first **Rape Crisis** started in 1976 to provide specialist, independent, women-led, confidential services for women and girls who had experienced sexual violence. It has provided support, offering counselling and information, and raising awareness of sexual violence. Some also offer services for male sexual violence survivors and men who are supporting a survivor.[50]

Reclaim the Night was born out of an international conference in Brussels on crimes against women around International Women's Day in 1976 at the end of which the candidates held a candlelit procession in the town. Night-time marches followed in many countries, including the UK, in 1977. Leeds was at the forefront, where the so-called 'Yorkshire Ripper', Peter Sutcliffe, had been killing women.[51] Controversies linked to the Reclaim the Night campaigns have included whether or not to include men or trans people, and how to deal with the link between prostitution and violence sensitively. There has been some accusation of a lack of sensitivity to diversity.

Slut-walks started in Toronto in Canada in 2011 after a police talk to law students advising them to avoid being raped by not dressing like 'sluts'. Two residents decided to reclaim the word and to march in anything they wanted to, highlighting the

---

problem of victim-blaming. The walks became a global phenomenon, being held in 200 cities in 40 countries that same year including in the UK. Arguments have raged over whether, with all the male voyeurs that they attract, these walks reinforce sexual stereotypes.

The White Ribbon Campaign started in 1991 in Canada and is now part of a global movement of men pledging to never stand by and ignore gender-based violence. I was involved in the launching of the first White Ribbon Campaign in the UK in 1998. The initiative was part of the sixteen days of activism against gender-based violence observed by most feminist organisations.

At Work and Institutions

Sexual harassment at work used to be normalised, something that just happened and was not talked about. Only more recently have statistics and the #MeToo movement shone a powerful light on the problem. According to a 2016 study of women trade union members, more than half had experienced some form of sexual harassment, 32 per cent had been subject to unwelcome sexual jokes, nearly 25 per cent had experienced unwanted touching and 20 per cent unwanted sexual advances. The perpetrator was usually a male colleague, and in 20 per cent of cases someone with direct authority over the victim. Eighty per cent did not report the sexual harassment to their employer.[52] Christine told me:

During the 1980s when I was in my early twenties I was on a work trip in Germany with my line manager. After visiting the client my boss took me out for a meal, all very professional, but then on the journey home he made a pass at me. I slapped him and explained that was not part of my job specification, accepted his apology and agreed to say no more about it. When we got back to London he started to undermine me in front of clients and colleagues. I had to threaten to report him to senior management to ensure he stopped his campaign to discredit me.[53]

Unwanted sexual behaviour in situations different from the daily environment was also mentioned by Joanne:

> When I started work there was a lot of flirting and innuendo. At Christmas, the parties started in late November at work, and . . . blokes would expect you to kiss them at the end of a party 'cause the alcohol was flowing. People still went to the pub at lunchtime and got a bit drunk and I dreaded Christmas Eve because one of the directors would come down, dressed as Father Christmas and all the women had to queue up, sit on his knee, get a kiss and a present. It's unbelievable now.[54]

Some situations have been so unequal in terms of the voice of those involved and lack of accountability that abuse has been systemic and hidden. In Ireland young single mothers considered to have transgressed by having children 'out of wedlock' were taken, often by their own families, to the Magdalene Laundries and their child removed from them. Magdalene Sisters were more or less incarcerated, exploited in laundry workhouses, and abused within a brutal regime.

Another damning example of the pervasiveness and yet the invisibility of sexual violence was the systemic abuse perpetrated by Jimmy Savile, a BBC personality, beloved figure and English institution, who hosted top-billing radio and TV programmes for many years, including *Jim'll Fix It*, which had him fulfilling the wishes of predominantly young and often disadvantaged children. He also raised significant funds for health- and disability-related charities and was knighted in 1990.

After his death in 2011, it became clear that multiple allegations of sexual misconduct had been ignored. He had been a serial predator of young girls and boys, including disabled institutionalised young people. Four hundred and fifty people made complaints against him for acts committed between 1955 and 2009. The BBC admitted failing in its duty of care and that a 'hierarchical, deferential and macho culture'[55] had allowed Savile to operate unchecked. Other institutions were also investigated, including the National Health Service, the Crown Prosecution Service and Broadmoor psychiatric hospital. The next year Operation Yewtree was set up and other male celebrities were convicted of indecent assault, though a number were released without charge. The integrity of the police forces was undermined by some of its tactics.

Parliament was no exception as an institution where sexual abuse, including of young girls and boys, was allowed to occur. For example, the MP Clement Freud was accused of sex offences in 2013, when a number of women alleged that he had assaulted and raped them, at least two of them when they were children.[56]

In nursing and residential homes, older women, and those with conditions such as cognitive impairment, are particularly vulnerable and invisible because of the assumption that sexual violence relates to the young. One study found that between 2013 and 2015, 2,000 sex offences were reported in these homes, including 1,700 more serious cases such as rape.[57]

There is also a long history of sexual abuse between students and between students and teachers in schools, particularly in boarding schools where children are particularly vulnerable. In the past, incidents usually went unrecorded. A BBC *Five Live* investigation found that between 2011 and 2014, 5,500 sexual offences were recorded in all kinds of schools. Of these, 4,000 were alleged sexual assaults and more than 600 rapes were reported to the police. A Girlguiding study in 2016 found that 59 per cent of girls aged thirteen to twenty-one had experienced some kind of sexual harassment in school or college – not in their lifetime, but in that single year.

An inquiry into the scale of sexual harassment and sexual violence in schools was held by Parliament's Women and Equalities Committee in 2016. Sophie Bennett, co-director of UK Feminista, reported:

> We've heard from girls who tell us you don't leave school as a girl without being called a slut . . . there is that sense of a normalised culture of sexual harassment in schools where girls don't feel able to report it and instead change their own behaviour such as wearing shorts under their skirts.[58]

According to Marai Larai, chief executive of Imkaan, black and minority ethnic girls were abused racially and sexually in schools with terms such as 'black bitch', and girls feared reporting the abuse because of possible reprisals.[59]

At university casual sexism and abuse are also a constant theme. In the past, universities did not collect data about incidents of sexual violence, nor did they have clear policies. A study in 2010 by the National Union of Students found that 14 per cent of students were victims of serious sexual assault or physical violence. In 2016 there was an acknowledgement that universities carried some responsibility and procedures were put in place. Even so, the long tradition of sexual favours as gateways to better grades or promotion[60] has still not been given much attention, despite its prevalence.[61]

In 2017 and 2018, in the wake of the Weinstein Hollywood scandal, the #MeToo movement and the Time's Up campaign, histories of abuse by powerful men in all types of employment hit the headlines. These affected the world of media, politics, business, the arts, education, religion and even charity and international development. This collective voicing of women's common experience seems to have resulted in systemic structural changes within companies with whole sectors improving their human resources systems, their safeguarding policies and codes of conduct. To what extent this is a sea change and how much the attitudes and behaviours of the perpetrators of violence and abuse has really shifted still remains to be seen.

Grooming and Organised Child Sexual Abuse

Data on child sexual exploitation shows an increase of allegations being reported over time, reaching 55,507 children in 2016 – a sexual offence on a child being recorded every ten minutes.[62] In Rotherham, South Yorkshire, a gang of British-Pakistani men were found to have organised the abuse of an estimated 1,400 victims, primarily girls, sometimes as young as ten, between 1997 and 2013. A catalogue of institutional failures – crimes partly ignored through fear of appearing racist – came to light. Other cases emerged in Oxford,

Rochdale and Newcastle hidden in plain view sometimes for more than a decade. Children were being picked, and then offered alcohol and drugs before being abused. When they spoke up, they were disbelieved. Sarah and Jane shared:

> I was only thirteen and he treated me like a queen. He told me he loved me, he made me depend on him. He made me believe he would keep me safe, that he could turn the sky black, [make] the sun shine or make it rain, that he could and would do anything for me and he made me believe that. I made a mistake by telling him that I had been abused, you know, and things were bad at home and stuff. He reached into that and pulled it out of me like I was a puppet on a string. I didn't know he worked for a gang, I ended up having sex with men and he got paid. I thought he was my boyfriend.[63]

> I was being pimped by a gang, I was 14 . . . my Mum kept going to the Police, they didn't listen cause I was known as a runaway before and didn't go to school much, they made me out to be a criminal and I was just a kid, doing something I didn't even want to do, why didn't they help me?[64]

The cases have shown up many failings in organisations meant to safeguard the young and vulnerable. The most glaring of which is the pattern that the victims were disbelieved because of their background, people who did not have any political, economic or social capital, people who so to say 'didn't matter', particularly young people in care who were seen to be 'asking for it'.

Media-based Violence

From the early 1990s, so-called 'trolls' began to make use of the latest platform for cruelty, sending abusive messages, particularly tweets, to those that become visible. The pattern echoes the insults hurled at suffragettes, the voice of the vocal minority now amplified by the internet. In 2016, the *Guardian* commissioned research into the 70 million comments left on its site over ten years.[65] Of the ten most abused writers, eight were women (four white, four BAME). The two men were black, and one of them also gay. Gender, faith, colour, sexuality – the peg on which people hang their hate. Shaista commented: 'Social media has opened the floodgates to verbal abuse and threats when women stand up for their rights. As a Muslim feminist, not only is your personal and moral character attacked but you also get sexual slurs attacking your "Muslimness".'[66]

Another study found that women were twenty-seven times more likely than men to be targeted online and analysis of Twitter over six months in 2017 found 25,000 abusive texts, half of these sent to Diane Abbott MP.[67] Women politicians, journalists and activists have suffered some of the most vicious trolling, including death and rape threats. In the case of Caroline Criado-Perez, who spearheaded a successful campaign to have women on British banknotes, at least one woman was also charged, a reminder that misogyny can be socially internalised and practised by women as well as men. Partly as a consequence of Caroline's experiences, Twitter introduced a mechanism to report abusive tweets.

Some women, such as J. K. Rowling, have become expert at retaliating to online misogyny with wit and dexterity: 'The Internet doesn't just offer opportunities for misogynistic abuse, you know. Penis enlargers can also be bought discreetly.'[68] In a grand fourteen-instalment takedown she thundered:

> . . . I'm sick of 'liberal' men whose mask slips every time a woman displeases them, who reach immediately for crude and humiliating words associated with femaleness, act like old-school misogynists and then preen themselves as though they've been brave. When you do this, Mr Liberal Cool Guy, you ally yourself, wittingly or not, with the men who send women violent pornographic images and rape threats . . . Every woman I know who has dared express an opinion publicly has endured this kind of abuse at least once rooted in an apparent determination to humiliate or intimidate her on the basis that she is female . . . If your immediate response

to a woman who displeases you is to call her a synonym for her vulva, or compare her to a prostitute, then drop the pretence and own it: you're not a liberal. You're a few short steps away from some guy hiding behind a cartoon frog.[69]

Reclaim the Internet, or Recl@im the Internet, was set up in 2016 by a cross-party group of women MPs and also involving 'media platforms, tech companies, campaign groups, think tanks, employers, trade unions, the police, teachers, students, journalists, public figures, youth organisations and young people'.[70] It built on the 'reclaim the night' idea, to make a stand against online 'misogyny, sexism, racism, homophobia, transphobia, intimidation or abuse' and to crowd-source new policies.

There can be and must be better moderation of online abuse or shaming it until things change. Platform providers carry a responsibility for revising algorithms that amplify hate speech and need to take responsibility for the forums they provide. However, the root cause of the problem is underlying misogyny, not the internet.

Activism on Violence Against Women

End Violence Against Women was set up in 2005 and is a leading coalition of specialist women's support services, researchers, activists, survivors and NGOs working to end violence against women in all its forms and challenge the wider cultural attitudes that tolerate and condone violence against women.

A Billion Women Rising started on Valentine's Day in 2012, based on the statistic that 1 in 3 women globally will be beaten or raped during their lifetime. The aim is to break the silence,

> through songs, marches and dances, personal stories, identifying places where violence has occurred, speaking of collective outrage, and demanding an end to violence against women. By 2017, events were taking place in over two hundred countries, involving millions of activists.

To counter violence against women legislative changes have been enacted, such as the ones mentioned earlier, and following the growth of the welfare state, the government has funded services. However, the core of the attention has come from the voluntary sector and from the feminist movement through direct services, testing out new models of support, awareness-raising and advocacy. A number of these organisations are mentioned in the different boxes in this chapter. As Elaine from Manchester Women's Aid commented:

The ship of state is an ocean liner which travels slowly; to change course, it has a massive turning circle. Smaller specialist organisations are quick, we can dart about in the water, and we see what happens sooner, like the rise of people with complex needs around drugs, alcohol and mental health, that is evident to the state much further on down the line; it's us who flag up these things.[71]

In 2012 Parliament finally signed the Council of Europe's Istanbul Convention on preventing violence against women in general, and domestic violence in particular. It is known as the 'gold standard' because it obliges governments to fund services such as rape crisis centres, shelters and sex education in schools, and requires provisions to grapple with the additional discriminations faced by migrant and other vulnerable women. The convention was only ratified by the UK in 2017 following a private member's bill by the SNP's Eilidh Whiteford – despite some filibustering (Philip Davies notably giving a ninety-one-minute obstructing speech) and fifty wrecking amendments by backbenchers.[72]

The Sex Trade

Some women are undoubtedly uncomfortable when it comes to sex and the erotic, even though sexual liberation was supposed to bring empowerment and emancipation in the bedroom – so-called 'sex-positive' feminism. What we are looking at next is the commercialised transactions – what happens when sexuality is taken into the sex trade from the small scale to the global, through pornography, stripping, lap dancing, prostitution and escort services. All these are interlinked and based on a transaction providing income for the woman in exchange for male gratification and what they sometimes see as an enhancement of their masculinity. The problem is not sex but sexism, sexual abuse and the objectification of women's bodies.

Pornography

Erotica has a long history and in 1918 visual pornographic materials were available and accessed by a few. Then came *Playboy* magazine in 1953, the liberalism of the 1960s and the growth and normalisation of the sex industry from around 1990. From 2000, soft porn in particular expanded, with magazines[73] and music videos. Pornography materials have become ever cheaper and easier to access, including on the encrypted dark web. The constant exposure or 'colonisation' of pornography within popular culture has created a society which has been termed 'porn ready'.[74]

Pornography includes child porn. In 2015–16 there were 22,545 prosecutions for child abuse image offences, including prosecutions for 16,672 offences of sexual exploitation of children through photographs.[75]

In general the pornography industry objectifies and commodifies women, reflecting male power and control. Women in the industry are often groomed into it and they earn comparatively little. There are no royalty payments for the number of times that images are viewed. There is some portrayal of mutual enjoyment but little if any representation of discussions around consent or sexual health matters. Women are pressured to take part in acts that they are uncomfortable doing, as part of a need to keep inno-vating and pushing the boundaries. According to one study, about 90 per cent of mainstream pornography scenes contain physical aggression and 50 per cent contain verbal.[76] Most of this is directed at women; it involves 'slapping, hair pulling, choking and gagging'.[77] Anal sex is common as are particularly degrading acts where the message toys with images of aggression as pleasure.

Although there are some female producers of porn who advertise as being different, even this 'feminist pornography' is not sex-positive. Studies have shown these are equally violent, with more aggression between women and more female-to-female sex acts.[78] Changing the director does not address the wider context. As Cindy Gallop explained in her 2009 TED talk 'Make Love Not Porn', most porn is: 'driven by men, funded by men, managed by men, targeted to men, porn presents one world view and it is increasingly important for people to be shown the difference between love and porn'.[79]

In the last decade, internet porn has become a major source of sexual information for children. A survey in 2016 found that 53 per cent of under-sixteen-year-olds had seen explicit material online and 59 per cent of boys viewed pornography by choice, compared with 25 per cent of girls. Forty-two per cent of the twelve- to sixteen-year-olds, more so boys than girls, reported wanting to try what they had seen. However, most thought that pornography was a poor influence and wanted better sex education.[80]

Also linked to young people, consensual or non-consensual 'sexting' – sending sexually explicit images via text – became a grow-ing pattern from around 2005. This starts off innocently enough, but can turn nasty. Similarly, revenge porn is the sharing of private sexual photos or videos without consent and for the purpose of harassment and causing distress. Perpetrators could be taken to court through the Malicious Communications Act 1988, but it needed stronger legislation and became a criminal offence, with the first conviction in 2015. The next year, 1,160 cases of revenge porn (mainly via Facebook) were reported, and over 200 people were prosecuted. All revenge cases referred to the Crown Prosecution Service were by males targeting females.[81] Thirty per cent involved people under nineteen, sometimes as young as eleven.[82]

Adult Entertainment and Prostitution

'Adult entertainment' has evolved over the century – from topless cabarets well before 1918 to the first lap-dancing club in 1995.[83] Such venues multiplied from 2003, following changes in the Licensing Act. There was some restriction applied in 2010 in response to public concern and lobbying, including by UK Feminista, Object and the Fawcett Society.[84] However, 'gentlemen's clubs' combining drinking with stripping, lap and pole dancing still thrive up and down the country. There is even an area of central Edinburgh which is now nicknamed the 'Pubic Triangle'.

The dictionary definition of a prostitute is: 'A person, typically a woman, who engages in sexual activity for payment.'[85] The derogatory term applies to only one part of a transaction that involves two people 'who engage in sexual activity for payment'. Instead, those buying the sex are usually called clients or Johns, another neutral term, or punters – a word also used for a gambler – or sugar daddy. A hundred years ago, one term for the more visible form of sex worker was 'common' prostitute to highlight the working-class nature of the work, in comparison to the wealthier forms less likely to attract the attention of the police. I use the term 'sex worker' because for the most part that is the term the women involved in prostitution want us to use.[86]

The opportunity to treat sex workers differently came with the Wolfenden Inquiry, which in its report recommended decriminalisation of homosexuality. But on prostitution, the report was regressive and led to the 1959 Street Offences Act, which allowed the conviction of women on the testimony of a single policeman. The Act still applies in most parts of the UK today, and makes it illegal for a sex worker to solicit in streets and public places.

In 1975, the English Collective of Prostitutes was founded as a self-help group and to campaign for more safety. Sex workers are often poor and young – according to one source in 2004, 50 per cent of women are drawn into the trade before the age of eighteen.[87] Estimates in 2016 were that there were 72,800 sex workers, 44 per cent in London. Eighty-eight per cent were women, 6 per cent men and 4 per cent transgender.[88] The dominant pattern is that sex workers come from abusive backgrounds. Clare told me of one young girl: 'She said she did it because her dad abused her so she thought she might as well get paid for it.'[89]

Women become trapped for many reasons, including economic vulnerability. Those working in brothels have to pay for the room they use and have no employment rights. Generally, pimps lure in women. A Home Office study in 2004 estimated that up to 95 per cent of street sex workers were drug users.[90] In Sarah's case:

> I was 19 when I met him and he was telling me to start with the drugs, the heroin, have a little bit, then I got a habit and he said you have to make the money so he put me on the beat, every day earning money for his crack and heroin and my heroin. That's how it started and then he got violent.[91]

The sex trade is dangerous and results in a wide range of physical and mental health problems and sexual trauma. Sex workers also experience barriers to accessing statutory support services, which often stigmatise them. Yet women over eighteen who are exploited by pimps, drug dealers and gangs are not seen as vulnerable and their situation is often described as a life choice by statutory services. Dealers and pimps do not want those they control to leave; and the often chaotic lifestyles of sex workers, with limited opportunities to make their own choices, makes leaving extremely difficult.

Fifty per cent of sex workers have been raped and/or sexually assaulted by clients.[92] Getting rape prosecutions is difficult at the best of times; it is much worse if you are involved in prostitution. In addition, in the age of the internet, some clients rate the sexual experience. They give a 'good' score to someone who does what they want, and shows interest, and a bad score to, for instance, someone who refuses to take part in degrading or violent sexual acts. Saying 'no' to a client can mean a poor score, and lead to clients becoming abusive and even losing your job.[93]

Peter Sutcliffe, the Yorkshire Ripper, targeted sex workers between 1975 and 1980, murdering thirteen and attempting to murder nine others. The case drew attention to their vulnerability. Another serial rapist, Steve Wright, nicknamed the Suffolk Strangler, was also caught (in 2006) having killed five young sex workers in Ipswich.

These killers and the fear they generated was one thing, but who are the men who pay sex workers in the normal course of events? According to the National Survey of Sexual Attitudes and Lifestyles conducted between 2010 and 2012, 11 per cent of British men had paid for sex, compared with around 1 in a 1,000 women. Single men aged twenty-five to thirty-four, in managerial or professional occupations, and those with numerous sexual partners, were the most likely to do so. There is a link with heavy drinking and drug-taking and with greater sexually transmitted disease (STD) infections. Among men who had paid for sex, 63 per cent had done so outside the UK at least once – paying for sex seems more permissible away from home.

Male responsibility was first addressed in 1985 through the Sexual Offences Act, which criminalised kerb crawling, and it became an indictable offence under the Criminal Justice and Police Act of 2001 – if it was persistent and caused a disturbance in the neighbourhood. Pimping became illegal under the Criminal Justice Act of 2003 but women have been consistently prosecuted for soliciting much more than men for kerb crawling or pimping.[94]

There are those who argue that prostitution is not a problem, it is a livelihood, that women involved in the trade are making a choice to do so.[95] Brooke Magnanti, also known as Belle de Jour, famously financed her PhD through prostitution. She subsequently wrote about her experiences in a blog in 2003, and then published a number of very successful books, keeping her identity secret for many years. However, for the vast majority of women, it is the lack of choice

that drags them into this most vulnerable and exploited of occupations. Most want out, but as with those facing domestic violence it
is easier said than done.[96]

Kat Banyard highlights the exploitation and abuse that sex workers are exposed to:

> Trades weave themselves into the fabric of society. We know
> this. We place all kinds of restrictions and prohibitions on
> markets precisely because of this. Because the risks, particularly
> to the most vulnerable and marginalised in society, are just too
> high. Sales of human organs, voting rights, bonded labour
> contracts, commercial exchanges that people may agree to
> participate in without a gun being held to their head are
> nonetheless deemed legally off-limits. It's the line in the sand
> societies draw to say that the harm to those directly involved, to
> third parties, or to the bedrock principles necessary for equal
> citizenship, is simply too great. Some trades are too toxic to
> tolerate.[97]

What the appropriate state approach should be to prostitution
remains controversial. Some countries such as New Zealand,
Germany and the Netherlands, and Nevada in the United States,
have legalised prostitution. By contrast, the Nordic model – which
has also been adopted in Northern Ireland – criminalises the buying
and decriminalises the selling of sex, provides social service funds to
help those involved to get out of the industry, and funds education
for the public, police and prosecutors.[98] Critically, sex work is seen as
a form of violence against women. Feminist organisations such as
Object and Eaves and campaigns such as End Demand would like to
see the Nordic model becoming the approach in the UK because it
is seen as addressing the underlying causes. However, so far there is
no standard approach. Zero tolerance to kerb crawling and divert-
ing women away from prostitution and providing support to them
to access services was independently evaluated as being both
successful and cost effective.[99] Managed zones were tried in Leeds,

Birmingham and Tower Hamlets. In some cases, media coverage of these areas made the women more vulnerable and the projects were deemed too expensive to run. After years of deliberation, in 2014 a cross-party group of MPs, peers and civil society organisations published their findings called 'Shifting the Burden',[100] which found that:

> In practice, those who sell sexual services carry the burden of criminality despite being those who are most vulnerable to coercion and violence. This serves to normalise the purchaser and stigmatise the sale of sexual services – and undermines efforts to minimise entry into and promote exit from prostitution. Moreover, legislation does not adequately address the gendered imbalance of harm within prostitution, and as such is detrimental to wider strategies which pursue gender equality.

Prostitution and trafficking are intimately connected and have a long history, with the so-called 'white slavery' fears a hundred years ago and now with women trafficked into the UK from countries as different as Albania, Vietnam and Nigeria. They are recruited with false promises and once in the UK, illegally and without support networks, they are particularly vulnerable. Amid growing concern, the UK enacted the EU directive combating trafficking in human beings in 2011.[101] In 2017–18, 355 cases were referred to the police,[102] though it is assumed that the actual cases are much higher, the UK Modern Slavery Helpline indicating there were around 1,600 women victims, 99 per cent of them in the commercial sex industry.[103] The Modern Slavery Act was enacted by the government in 2015 to strengthen legislation on the matter.

Until a landmark ruling in 2018, those convicted of prostitution would have a criminal record, limiting their education and job opportunities since they were treated as sex offenders and their offences would come up on Disclosure and Barring Service (DBS) checks.

However, government support to address prostitution has been gradually eroded due to welfare cuts, with voluntary organisations trying to fill the gap. Front-line initiatives include Street Talk, which provides counselling and therapy. Pippa Hockton explained:

The women Street Talk works with have been abused and neglected in childhood and live with trauma. In their teenage years, they learn to self-medicate for that trauma with whatever is available to them, usually crack, heroin and alcohol. When they are high or drunk they get a break from tormenting memories and the deep-rooted shame and self-disgust which the victims of abuse feel all the time. They inevitably become addicted and prostitution and theft are ways of supporting their addiction. Most of them know nothing but abuse. They are so used to abuse that they cannot even identify it. I am currently working with a lovely woman of eighteen who has a punter who pays her three pounds a time to defecate into her mouth. She does not see that as abuse. She sees it as one of the few small positives in her life, a regular little earner, safer than the things other punters want to do. The mission statement of Street Talk is to enable women to live in safety and with dignity. The first step is to enable women to recognise abuse and to believe that they deserve better.[104]

That quote is the most disturbing of those I collected during the course of writing this book. The fact that the young girl chooses this abuse as a safer option than others is particularly harrowing. And the stakes are high. As Riannah put it: 'Being involved in prostitution has affected my life, it's psychologically and physically scarred me, but you have to put that behind you and make the best of what you have. Sometimes I am strong and sometimes I am not, but I am alive.'[105]

Society's failure to focus on the demand side of the transaction means that the root cause of the problem is not talked about and criminalisation and blame constantly defaults back to the vulnerable party in the transaction.

Women Criminals

Moving on, what is the story regarding women causing violence, in particular behind women as criminals?

In 1918, there were around 7,600 male and 1,600 female prisoners. By 2016, the numbers, and gender gap, had increased to 87,000 males and around 3,800 females.[106] Both male and female prisoners tend to come from poorer, single-parent and troubled families. According to data from 2014, 46 per cent of women in prison had suffered domestic violence, 53 per cent had experienced emotional, physical or sexual abuse during childhood and 31 per cent had spent time in local authority care as a child.[107] The earlier children become known to social services, the more likely they are to develop a criminal career. Forty-six per cent of women prisoners had attempted suicide at some point in their lives as compared to 7 per cent of the general population.[108] A study in 2012 found that two-thirds of women prisoners had children under the age of eighteen and many were also carers of elderly relatives.[109] Another in 2015 found that most children stayed in their home if their father was incarcerated, compared with only 5 per cent of children with a mother in prison.[110]

In the first half of the century women were criminalised as prostitutes, for having illegal abortions or for carrying them out.[111] Other common reasons were and remain theft, particularly shoplifting, minor fraud and common assault, possession of drugs, and, most recently, radicalisation. Black, Asian and minority ethnic women are also increasingly used as foreign drug mules. Women imprisoned for violent crimes have always been statistically very unusual. The last woman to face capital punishment in Britain was Ruth Ellis, hanged in 1955. She had been in an abusive relationship and had shot her abuser. Other infamous criminals include the child killers Myra Hindley and Mary Bell in the 1960s and Rosemary West from the 1960s to 1980s.

In 2014 women accounted for 9 per cent of prisoners.[112] Because they tend to be imprisoned for lesser offences and serve shorter sentences they tend to have reduced access to rehabilitation. Women's prisons have been less well resourced, more scattered; local support services more difficult to access, and located further away from families. Another problem for women prisoners is the reduced likelihood of getting a job after prison. According to a study in 2013, after release only 8 per cent of women found secure employment compared with 26 per cent of men.[113] The prospect of release from prison can engender fears about where to sleep, personal safety and lack of money. Although prison is said to be a criminogenic factor, for some women it is a relatively safe place to be, with the result that many women are in and out of prison – the revolving-door syndrome.

A number of suffragettes, my grandmother included, were involved in campaigns for prison reform because of what they saw first-hand. Prison reform is particularly associated with Margery Fry who, in 1918, became the secretary of the Penal Reform League, now the Howard League for Penal Reform. Some organisations also provide support and advocacy for women prisoners, for example the charity Women in Prison set up in 1983 by Chris Tchaikovsky and Pat Carlen. In 2006, following the death of six women in Styal prison, Baroness Jean Corston conducted a review and made many recommendations on how to avoid prisons being the 'social dustbins for vulnerable women'.[114]

Community rehabilitation, support to offenders and a 'whole system approach' was piloted in Greater Manchester and North Wales, and found not only to be cheaper, but also to lead to less reoffending and better integration. Support includes detox programmes, parenting help, addressing mental health problems, managing debt and financial literacy. Although there are successes to celebrate, Mitch Egan CB previously a prison governor reflected:

Over the 30 plus years I worked in women's prisons, I saw many brilliant changes. On sober reflection, I think these equate to tidier deck chairs on the *Titanic*. They're all to be applauded and welcomed, but there are still way too many women in prison, and too many children taken away from the family home because of it. I guess the buildings are better. But radical change requires radical measures. Determination (like that displayed by the Finnish administration) can also help keep prison numbers down. If I had to sum up the last 40 years of women in prison, I would have to say – who knew you could travel so far to stay still?[115]

There is a growing consensus that most women criminals are more 'troubled' than 'troubling' and what is needed are small units to enable mostly poor and abused women to find a way out. The decision not to build a prison in the West of Scotland in 2015, the closure of Holloway in 2016 and the government plan in 2017 for a strategy on women in prison might be heralding a change. Nevertheless, there is still the rhetoric about being tough on crime. Furthermore, unless there is housing and social services available when women are released, the likelihood of reoffending remains. Funding cuts, the privatisation of services, and the failure to implement many of the Corston recommendations – particularly the need for greater visible leadership – point to a worsening future for women prisoners.

Women in War and Peace

There is an obvious fault line between those who have experienced conflict and those who have not, and to understand the relationship between women and violence the context of war needs to be added to the tapestry.

During both world wars, the ideology of women's femininity and the need to protect women clashed with the reality. As war encouraged men towards even more masculine roles, women were expected to move along the spectrum, thereby as we saw in Chapter 2 changing perceptions about what they could and could not do. Then, after the wars, at least to some extent, attitudes in society shifted back to allocate men and women their traditional roles.

But focusing on the wars themselves, how much influence did women have on the policies promoted? When the First World War broke out there were no women in either house of Parliament. The war in fact diffused and split the feminist struggle. By the Second World War there were women MPs. A cross-party group of them travelled to Spain in 1937 and drew attention to the rise of fascism, including in Nazi Germany, briefing Churchill at a time when there was limited information about the nature of Hitler's thinking. Meanwhile Nancy Astor was prominently associated with the prime minister's appeasement policy. Following a failed demand for a greater role for female MPs in 1940, she set up the Women Power Committee and all fourteen women MPs met together across party lines throughout the war.[116] Yet, as the MP Edith Summerskill put it: 'the war is being prosecuted by both sexes but directed only by one'.[117] Of the fourteen MPs, only two, with very different political views, were in Churchill's coalition government: Labour's Ellen Wilkinson and the Unionist and Conservative Florence Horsbrugh.[118]

Beyond Westminster, women were involved in lobbying in many different ways. From 1924 onwards my grandmother Sylvia Pankhurst and others such as Cicely Hamilton warned about the dangers of Italian Fascism. Sylvia received threatening letters, one saying the Gestapo would be sympathetic to her if she stopped her editing work, another – see Figure 12 – a threat from Italian fascists in London.

During the wars women were supposed to maintain the social fabric, literally protecting 'the home front', extending the notion of women as carers beyond the family to society. They took part in auxiliary uniformed units, in voluntary and paid capacities, their activities often transformational – both for society in general, but also for those directly involved.[119] In addition, some women took up arms and worked in counter-espionage. Flora Sandes from Suffolk went to Serbia as a nurse in 1914, but instead became a soldier and was the first woman to be commissioned in the Serbian Army. In 1919, her bravery was recognised through a special Serbian Act of Parliament.[120] Other exceptions include Dorothy Lawrence, who disguised herself as a male soldier, obtained a forged ID, and fought on the Somme before being interrogated as a spy and then held in France.[121]

Madame Pankhurst
3 charteris Road
WOODFORD
Essex

Madame Pankhurst

The invasion of England will take place

in a few days. We shall punish you by order of our Leader as you well deserve for the article in your filthy paper against the italian Fascists.

Your house in Woodford will bombed and burned to the ground. Hitler knows your address..

You will pay with your life if you publi sh any name in your paper.

Do not dare to go out in the dark or you will murdered.

Heil Hitler
Viva Mussolini   Italian
London
Fascists.

As requested herewith we reproduce above a facsimile of the envelope and letter sent to the Editor of " New Times and Ethiopia News " by Italian Fascists. The letter from the Nazis has not been returned from Scotland Yard.

Figure 12: Letter printed in New Times and Ethiopia News, *No. 227, 7 September 1940*

In 1936, the first British casualty of the Spanish Civil War was artist Felicia Browne. Many more armed women died during the Second World War, particularly those involved in intelligence and home defence training. Cecile Pearl Witherington Cornioley, a British woman raised in France, worked in the Resistance, leading a unit of 3,500 men. She was recommended for the Military Cross but awarded a civilian medal instead. She returned it with a note explaining that there was nothing civil about what she had done.[122] The French-born Violette Szabo, a mother with a young child, became a member of the Special Operations Executive – this at a time of the marriage bar – but she was useful to the government so the rules were set aside. Her group was betrayed and she was shot in 1945. She was posthumously awarded the George Cross for bravery under torture – again a civilian honour. A Victoria Cross would have been more appropriate, something the French government recognised in their honour of her.

Other women also stood out. Nancy Wake, nicknamed 'The White Mouse', was in the SOE and had a bounty of 5 million francs put on her head by the Gestapo. She ended up as the Allies' most decorated servicewoman, with medals from her native New Zealand, Australia, America, France and the Commonwealth. She was also awarded the George Medal and the military War Medal. These few examples show how some women succeeded in military intelligence and were even sometimes acknowledged for their services. Along the way, however, was an incredible amount of dismissal of their contributions. However, as an indicator of change and the fact that women could make it to the very top, in 1992, Stella Rimington became the first female head of MI5.

In the Second World War more than 7 million women[123] took paid war work and many more joined voluntary organisations, as well as other women's organisations supporting the war effort such as the Guides, the Women's Institute and the Townswomen's Guilds. Their work often cut across class, age and household position. It expanded horizons and gave them a confidence they took into later life. My mother, for example, reminisced: 'I was a child during the war but later I was aware that the women who had been involved were surer of themselves than those who had not taken part. They were more confident and capable. We admired and looked up to them.'[124]

In 1982, the Falklands War erupted with Margaret Thatcher providing the first example of a woman prime minister taking the country to war. Since then an increasing number of women have entered the military, with some involved as combatants in the 1992 Gulf War. At the end of 2018 all combat roles became open to women, including infantry and special forces units.[125] Meanwhile, Stonewall campaigned against the ban on lesbian, gay and transgender people serving in the army and in 1999 Caroline Paige became the first British officer to transition.[126] In 2016, Chloe Allen, who had joined the Scots Guards as a man, became the first transgender soldier and the first woman in the front line.

For Patricia:

The best aspect of service life was the teamwork and camaraderie. I found that women were treated as equals in my unit. It was only when we had contact with male soldiers from outside the unit that occasionally there was some sexism. Ultimately, the authority of the rank would override a soldier's personal feelings about whoever was in charge. That's perhaps the big difference with civilian life. I never came across any incidents of sexual assault or bullying during my time in the services (Navy 1980–9 and Army 1989–99); nor did I ever feel seriously undermined. Occasionally, particularly socially, I felt a bit patronised. But I never found it more than mildly irritating.[127]

The experiences of many other women in military institutions have been less positive, with scandals around sexism and abuse regularly hitting the headlines.[128]

Peace Activism and the Environment

If women for the most part played supporting roles in war, this has not been the case with peace activism. During the First World War the Women's Peace Crusade had 123 branches across the UK and linked feminism and anti-militarism and demanded an end to the war. Many of those who opposed the war were ostracised and vilified. Nevertheless, a prominent supporter was the suffragette Charlotte Despard, none other than the sister of General John French, Chief of Staff of the British Army. She wrote a pamphlet entitled 'An Appeal to Women' against the war, which sold 100,000 copies.[129]

Sylvia Pankhurst edited what became the *Workers' Dreadnought*. As the historian Mary Davis explains:

> With a circulation of around 10,000, the *Workers' Dreadnought* was one of the most important anti-war, non-sectarian socialist papers in Britain, achieving an influential position by opening its columns to all shades of opinion on the left. Its role has been underestimated by labour movement historians, but clearly it was recognised at the time which may account for the fact that Siegfried Sassoon (later an anti-war poet and author) used it for his now famous statement 'Finished with the War: A Soldier's Declaration'.[130]

Many suffrage organisations, including the National Union of Women's Suffrage Societies, were split about attitudes to the war but the Co-operative Women's Guild was against it. Women from different countries came together to work for peace, demilitarisation and global justice through the Women's International League for Peace and Freedom, formed in 1915 and continuing to this day. In 1926 it organised a peace pilgrimage, bringing together twenty-eight different women's and peace organisations under the banner 'Law not War'. A thousand meetings were held in Britain over six months, ending with a pageant with twenty-two platforms in Hyde Park.[131]

Another astonishing feat was the Peace Ballot, in 1934-5, to seek the views of the population regarding militarism. Half a million volunteers – mostly women – went door to door with the questionnaire. Around 11 million people, 38 per cent of the population, voted, more than for local elections. There was almost universal (97 per cent) support for remaining in the League of Nations, and 93 per cent supported the prohibition of the manufacture and sale of armaments for private profit by international agreement.[132]

The International Fellowship of Reconciliation formed in 1914 championed the cause of peace, weaving in women's voices and gender justice. Its ambassador Muriel Lester was imprisoned in Holloway during the Second World War. She was nominated twice for the Nobel Peace Prize.

Among many other initiatives was the foundation by Eglantyne Jebb of Save the Children in 1919, to provide relief for starving children in Austria, Germany and Russia, in sharp contrast to UK foreign policy at the time. The organisation's remit then widened in 1921 to include work on vulnerability in Britain, bringing visibility to a problem that the government was neglecting. Jebb was also the main influence behind the Declaration of the Rights of the Child.[133]

The link between women and anti-war activism continued. The World Committee Against War and Fascism had, in the 1930s, women's branches that attracted many, including Dora Russell who organised a peace caravan that travelled through Western and Eastern Europe. Then, in 1957, as part of the anti-nuclear protests, 2,000 women[134] marched through London with the National Assembly of Women and the National Council for the Abolition of Nuclear Weapons Tests. The Campaign for Nuclear Disarmament was formed as a consequence of that event. It had a women's committee, and strong backing by women celebrities such as Vivienne Westwood.

In 1976, the Northern Ireland peace movement, subsequently called the Peace People, was started by Mairead Corrigan and Betty Williams, involving thousands of Catholic and Protestant women coming together to demand peace and an end to sectarian violence. They received many accolades for this work, including the Nobel Peace Prize, and continued advocating for peace globally.

In 1981 women campaigning against nuclear missiles at the US base of Greenham Common got together. As with the suffragettes, some parts of the press labelled them dangerous lesbians and referred to them in other derogatory terms. It started with around forty women, some of their children, and four men, marching 120 miles from Cardiff to Greenham Common. The group walked with the slogan 'Women for life on earth' to protest against ninety-six Cruise missiles with nuclear warheads at the base. They chained themselves to the gates and lived in a women-only camp outside the base. At times they cut through the fence, danced on the missiles and painted slogans on the planes. An estimated 50,000[135] people came to support them, bringing peace symbols. Again with echoes of the past, a number of court cases followed; the women refused to pay fines and went to Holloway prison. Madeleine and Cathy shared:

My sisters and friends were arrested at Greenham Common, they gave their names as famous women such as Beatrice Webb, Virginia Woolf etc. and when it came to the court hearing, Beatrice Webb, Virginia Woolf, Mary Wollstonecraft, etc. didn't turn up.[136]

I went to Greenham several times for short visits in the 1980s. Once I invited my mother to come. It made a strong impression on her. Although the media tended to portray the protestors as 'woolly minds in woolly hats' she found them seriously commit-ted and well organised. I myself was in awe of the women living there full-time, and all they were sacrificing. I still recall the feel-ing of community, warmth and immense personal security. One weekend, my friend and I invited our husbands to come. They were very supportive of the cause, but it was interesting to see their reaction to being a handful of men among so many women.

In spite of the peacefulness of the camp, they clearly felt intimidated, even vulnerable, a useful experience for them as men to undergo.[137]

The Cruise missiles were removed in 1991 and the camp fully disbanded in 2000 after the protestors won the right for a memorial to the campaign. The Greenham Common camp goes down in history as one of the largest women's peace camps in the world.

More recently, the global Women in Black movement has campaigned for justice and against war, and both women and men were involved in anti-Polaris and Trident campaigns in the 1980s. In 2004, at least a million women and men rallied in Hyde Park to protest over the impending war against Iraq, possibly the largest ever demonstration in London.

Activism has taken many different forms, with marches the usual method to express opposition to war. Women remain a very visible force behind these initiatives for peace. They are also behind schemes such as Mothers Against Violence, the organisation set up in Manchester in 1999 by mothers after their sons were killed in gang wars.

Women are also associated with environmental activism. In 1999 the Soil Association had a 'Women say no to GMO' initiative. Climate Rush, inspired by the suffragettes, campaigned against Heathrow's third terminal and investment in coal energy.

In 2013, six Greenpeace women climbed the Shard as a publicity stunt, with one aim being to counter the masculine image of ecological activism based on what one of the campaigners, Victoria Henry, called the 'beardy boys in boats'.[138] In 2014, with a very different image, the 'anti-fracking nanas' of Lancashire, also known as #OMG – 'Operation Mothers and Grandmas' – fought against fracking plans – ultimately with little success.

Why women have a stronger connection to peace and the environment causes heated debate within society generally and within feminist circles specifically, with many refusing an essentialist position that sees women as inevitably – biologically – more peaceful.[139]

For the most part, the idea that women should campaign separately on peace and the environment, which was common early in the century, seems to have gone out of fashion. What has remained is the argument that their voices and their perspectives need to be heard. In different ways women have carved out a space to link pacifism and environmentalism with feminism – all seen as a resistance to the dominant model of how the world operates. However, with some notable successes, the agenda has often floundered – the world continues to operate in an unsustainable way within a system predominantly constructed by men.

Conclusion

There is a connection between gender inequality and violence at a personal and global level linked to militarism and masculinity. This is not to say only men perpetuate the violence and only women are on the receiving end, but there is an inescapable dominant pattern at work. Casual sexism and physical violence are interconnected in the home, in institutions and socially. There is also a local and global effect through 'honour'-based violence, FGM and the international sex trade.

All waves of feminism, the second wave in particular, have addressed violence against women. Initiatives led and staffed primarily by women have generated debate, provided direct services, pushed for legal changes. Tolerance of blatant sexism and the right to abuse women is now not quite so normalised. More women speak up, laws have improved, and there are more services available.

However, discrimination and violence against women continue to be inflamed by the massive growth in pornography, by prostitution and trafficking, as well as by national and international conflict. Despite the scale and increasing complexity of the violence, there is a paucity of resources to address it, and despite many legislative changes, implementation is patchy and the state and mainstream society continue to be astoundingly careless about the sexual harassment and violence that blights millions of women's lives

– including the few who end up as criminals. Women have been brought into the armed forces but we are failing to conceptualise alternatives to war and the unsustainable plundering of the environment. Violence is reducing the gains made in other areas, muting women's transforming potential.

Violence: how did we do?

Assigning an appropriate score is difficult because policies have improved but the reality remains appalling. Violence against women is still a clear and present danger. It is given impetus in times of conflict, and blocks alternatives to how we could live. On reflection I feel that a score of only 1 out of 5 is appropriate. What would you say?

5

CULTURE

'Like the best mushrooms in the margins we are now showing our heads!' (Frances Morris, Director, Tate Modern)[1]

The right to a voice is political. We have seen how women politicians are less likely to be heard, how girls and women are expected to be quieter, how expressing an opinion has brought forth misogyny on Twitter. However, this reality is no longer so invisible. For example, there are apps that log how much men and women speak in a meeting and/or 'manterrupt'.[2] The American writer Rebecca Solnit, who is attributed with coining the term 'mansplaining' – meaning situations where men condescendingly explain things to women – wrote:

> Most women fight wars on two fronts, one for whatever the putative topic is and one simply for the right to speak, to have ideas, to be acknowledged to be in possession of facts and truths, to have value, to be a human being. Things have gotten better, but this war won't end in my lifetime. I'm still fighting it, for myself certainly, but also for all those younger women who have something to say, in the hope that they will get to say it.[3]

In 2014 some men began a boycott of taking part in manpanels 'manels' – the term coined for men-only panels – and the BBC ruled there had to be at least one woman on its comedy panel shows. Inevitably, this resulted in a backlash by some arguing against positive discrimination.[4]

Written and verbal communications give form and further accentuate gendered social norms. Patriarchal ideas are integrated within the language used to prop it up, something the second wave of feminism drew attention to; the book *Man Made Language* by Dale Spender was particularly influential in this regard. Since then we have become more aware of the conditioning. Writers now often avoid the omnipresent use of 'he', meaning both 'he' and 'she', using the plural 'they', the rather ugly 's/he', 'he and she', or just 'she'. Some sayings have dropped out of favour, such as 'the world and his wife' or 'the man on the street'. Many titles are changing: so 'chair' rather than 'chairman', yet resistance – and accusations of political correctness – continues.

When we look at culture in the widest sense of the term – how we play and socialise, what we read, watch and listen to, our experience of the Arts, of sport and of religion – how has the social conditioning changed? Will women fare any better here than they did in terms of work, conflict or money?

Space – from Playgrounds to Pubs

The occupation of space is gendered and ever changing. In the past, children played outside. For many girls in particular this freedom is now constrained for fear of sexual harm. Louisa shared:

> As a child growing up in the 70s/80s, I was encouraged to go out on my bike and play all day but be back in time for tea. I had complete freedom to explore the physical outdoor space and my inner world and came to no harm until I was a teenager when I was attacked by three boys, in broad daylight, in a residential area, metres from home. That didn't curtail my freedom. What did was a much more violent knife attack in my early 30s, in broad daylight, which has deeply scarred my sense of security. I envy my brother who has no sense of fear walking through a park at night.[5]

The view – real or perceived – of the external world as more predatory for women and girls has become more common. Women manage risks – they don't go out alone at night in certain places, resulting in segregation by time and place; they are blamed if they are attacked for having broken the social curfews.

Male ownership of space applies in other contexts. For example, in mixed schools, the playgrounds tend to be dominated by boys, who in studies seem to occupy as much as ten times the space of girls, who are excluded from their games.[6] On planes, according to an American study in 2012, women tend to 'shrink and curl up in seats to avoid contact with strangers' while men 'spread out and take up leg room – and the arm rest'. As one respondent put it: 'I think men just feel entitled and don't notice. They are oblivious.'[7] Men's use of space includes 'manspreading' – a word entering the online Oxford dictionary in 2015 – sitting in public places knees apart, displaying dominance and occupying more than their allocated space, and sometimes justifying this in terms of 'aerating their private parts'.[8]

Toilet provision is another sore point. First, the lack of facilities was used against women's inclusion when they entered Parliament, legal chambers and other workplaces. Second, people have had to lobby for improved provision for disabled people and changing areas for mothers – and more recently fathers – with babies and young children, though facilities for fathers are still not required by UK law. Third, the increased transgender voice demands gender-neutral public toilets. And, finally, as Mary explains:

Women take longer in public toilets for several reasons – they have to sit, for much of their lives they menstruate, and they tend to do most of the work of taking young children to the toilet. I have spent many hours of my life standing in queues, watching the men whizz in and out of their toilet next door. The only time I saw this reversed was at a football match years ago, when for once I was the one blithely walking past a long line of men and sauntering in and out of the Ladies in a matter of moments. Why can't the design of public places acknowledge these facts and aim for equal experience rather than equal square footage?[9]

When it comes to public places, there is nothing more quintessentially male and British than pubs – traditionally literally Public Houses. Over the century, these have evolved. They were a white male preserve, one segregated by class with different entrances and sections – still noticeable in many of the buildings today. After the wars, women became more visible, accompanied by a male, on special events such as holidays. On their own, women continued to be frowned upon, seen to be soliciting; there were signs warning 'no unaccompanied ladies'.[10] They were particularly unwelcome by the bar, the dartboard and the pool table and were not served full pints. It was only in 1982 that the Court of Appeal repealed the law that allowed pubs to refuse to serve unaccompanied women. The pub cited was the El Vino, a Fleet Street bar, where women journalists had to use a back room, preventing conversations with male colleagues.[11]

Segregation was not just by gender. A colour bar operated in some pubs, and in the 1960s Asian men could be told to drink outside. Gradually pubs have been transformed into more inclusive places. The increased provision of food and the smoking ban introduced in 2006 in Scotland, and a year later in the rest of the country, helped them broaden the appeal. By 2017, Diane, a newly retired teacher, could say: 'I take my book and dog to the local pub every Tuesday as it's curry night. Sometimes people chat to me, sometimes I get on with my book. It makes a change from a TV dinner.'[12] Pubs are also a microcosm reflecting complex changing sexual politics with layers of contradictions. Fiona, for example, reflected:

Working behind the bar I have seen that pubs are where courtship is played out. Women get the best seats and the men spend the night playing musical chairs to ensure all the women are happy and out of the way of men barging around the bar. Some visibly go halves but sometimes women give their half of the money to the men before they go to the pub or you see through-out the night women passing money under the table to their husbands and boyfriends in an attempt to keep up the pretence that the men are buying.

I have also heard over and over again guys complaining about how much they spent on their partners for the evening and that they didn't even sleep with them. I have also been leered at and grabbed in ways that just wouldn't be acceptable the other side of the bar. The most protective managers I've had who really look out for the women behind the bar have all been gay men. The least empathetic have been women, it makes no sense to me![13]

Well beyond the example of pubs, women having a treat, with-out men at their side, was considered inappropriate at the begin-ning of the century. However, Lyons tea houses, among others, expanded opportunities for the middle and working classes, and unaccompanied women became a more common sight. Lyons also provided employment for thousands of waitresses. After a competi-tion for the public to name the waitresses, they were given the generic name of 'Nippies'. Other options had included: 'Busy Bertha', 'Speedwell' 'Dextrous Dora' and 'Sybil-at-your-service'. Nippies were short-lived because of the growth of self-service facili-ties after the Second World War.[14]

Although clubs catering exclusively to men were more common and more famous, women's clubs provided important spaces for relatively wealthy women. For instance, the University Women's Club, formerly Club for Ladies, was founded in 1883, and the Forum Club for Women's Institute members, lasted between 1919 and the 1950s, and was frequented by suffragettes. There was also the New Cavendish Club, between 1920 and 2014, and the Cowdray Club frequented by professional women, which opened in 1922 and closed in 1974.

A little aside: in 1936, Phyllis Pearsall published the first London A–Z guide, which became the indexed street map we still use today. A blue plaque commemorates her birthplace in Dulwich. As at

2016, only 13 per cent of the London blue plaques were dedicated to women; this includes one at Clarendon Road in Notting Hill for Emmeline and Christabel and one for Sylvia at Cheyne Walk in Chelsea.[15]

The concepts of space and leisure time are also gendered and interlinked. Holidays, increasingly democratised, provide opportunities to escape gendered patterns, or for them to be accentuated. Rosina wrote:

> In the 1980s, at a family party, the women cooked the food, the men ate first and then the women ate while the men went off for more drink. How we eat now means that this happens less in my family. At the time, the meal was a sit-down, bacon and spuds on a plate, whereas now it is more likely to be a BBQ, buffet or something informal. But don't get me started on men and BBQs![16]

If we turn to children's leisure, their toys and games, these are particularly telling because of how they reflect society. Since the seventeenth century, Punch and Judy shows have entertained adults and children, and on reflection the shows are so bizarre that it is worth looking at them in some detail. A puppeteer, almost always male, manipulates the central character Punch (the word adapted from the Italian without the violent connotations it has in English), who is left in charge of a baby. In the past he would beat the infant with a big stick. When his wife, Judy, appears, they would beat each other up. As if the whole story were not bad enough, Punch also had a mistress 'Pretty Polly'. Foreign characters are jeered at, pork sausages materialise to enable reference to their phallic shape and make fun of Jewish (now also Islamic) food taboos. Like fairy tales in their violence and exaggerated features and voices, the appeal lies in the mixture of a known storyline, characters and phrases, improvisation and participant engagement. One of the catchphrases that lives on is 'That's the way to do it.' Yet even parents suffused in traditional British culture are increasingly uncomfortable with the violence and storyline.

Some of the very first objects presented to children as toys are imbued with gendered implications. Girls were and continue to be given dolls and stuffed animals, boys marbles, trains, soldiers and guns. Even joint board games involve social messaging. As twelve-year-old Isabelle explained: 'I want to be a doctor. When I was younger, I automatically thought I had to be a man, since all the doctors on the card games had a picture of a male doctor.'[17]

Barbie, introduced in 1959 by Mattel, Inc., has been a symbol of the problem. She cannot stand up and is impossibly long-legged and thin; her waist would be too small to fit on clothes charts. Her boyfriend Ken was introduced in 1961. Then the equally impossibly sized first black female doll, Christie, came along in 1968. In the face of criticism and falling sales, in 2016, curvy, petite and tall Barbies, with seven skin tones, and numerous eye colours and hairstyles, were introduced. Despite the name, curvy was only scaled up to the equivalent of a UK dress size 6/8, petite a size 2, this in a context in which the average young woman in the UK is now a size 14.[18] Mattel tried to reposition the doll with a 2015 advert 'You can be anything' and another in 2017 with 'Barbie's Dad', which had a father and daughter playing together. However the company has continued to struggle. Less stereotyped dolls from other manufacturers include the British Lottie, who is normally proportioned and can be a fossil hunter, stargazer or lighthouse keeper.

In 2012 the Let Toys be Toys campaign grew out of a Mumsnet online forum, with parents frustrated at the all-pervasiveness of gender stereotyping in toys. As Jo from the campaign explained:

Play is crucial to how children develop and . . . it's recognised that children need access to a range of toys and play experiences . . . when we started our campaign many stores divided toys into separate boys' and girls' sections. Action, construction and tech-nology toys are often marketed to boys while role play and arts and crafts toys are marketed to girls. Fourteen retailers in the UK have now taken down the 'boys' and 'girls' signs but packaging, advertising and marketing still give children messages about how they ought to behave and what they can or can't aspire to. This all has an effect on life choices later on, whether it be subject choices at GCSE, being able to articulate emotions or making career choices . . . Themes of glamour and beauty mean girls worry very young about their outward appearance while the assumption reinforced in toy advertising and packaging that boys are rough, rowdy and interested only in action and violence gives boys only one dimension of how to be.[19]

The same year, 2012, Lego launched pink and pastel bricks for girls, themed around castles, hairbrushes and make-up accessories. It sparked protests and Lego seems to have seen the light, releasing a set of female scientist figures in 2013 – though with make-up – and expanding the range since then.

Computer-based toys perpetuate old gendered differences; the industry is dominated by high-earning games targeted at boys and men such as *Tomb Raider*, *Grand Theft Auto* and *Call of Duty*, based on male agency with women in skimpy clothing as love-interests or sex workers. In certain games, the aim is sometimes explicitly to chase and 'rape' women, and even in more mainstream games female characters can be 'virtually raped' by hackers, the aggressors locking other players out and verbally abusing the player through the audio link and then posting the videos on YouTube. In 2010 a female character, Lara Croft, became the most recognised female video game character.[20] She epitomises girl power, but is also a sex symbol; some fans have developed a computer 'patch' to remove her clothes. Less problematic games do exist, some created by the few women in the field, including Naomi Alderman, and groups such as Women in Games and Black Girl Gamers are supporting women in the industry and creating safe spaces for women players.

Games in new forms for the most part have continued to accentuate age-old gender hierarchies. Does the same apply when we turn to the written word of magazines and books?

Magazines

Magazines have been one of the dominant places where mass media has focused on women and girls, their lives, their interests, their stories. One of the first was the monthly *Girl's Own Paper* published from 1880 to 1956, with a number of name changes. The September 1942 edition is forty-six small pages, black and white except for the cover, a few photos on each page. It has features on life in the war-related services, on the Student Christian Movement, on life inside a secretarial bureau. A one-act comedy is set in a school dormitory and there are three serialised stories and some poetry. 'Carol's Career Corner' provides information on different occupations – in this edition on architecture – and advice is given on knitting, dressmaking and gardening. Coupons and advertisements include ones for Ovaltine and talcum powder, for a one-week shorthand course and for bicycles.[21] Another popular magazine was the *Schoolgirls' Own*, published weekly from 1921 to 1936.[22]

The publications mostly reinforced cultural and social mores, but at least they were targeted specifically at the world of girls, and provided entertainment, escapism and some practical advice. This focus on them was rare and much valued.[23]

The advice given in girls' magazines was often contradictory, reflecting the reality of more complicated lives than the fictionalised ones. Beverly remembered: 'Girls' magazines like *Jackie* were avidly read in the 1970s and were probably where most of us of that generation received our information on matters including emotional and physical relationships with boys, questions we couldn't ask our parents or peers.'[24] The girls' and teen magazine market has almost entirely vanished, with some notable exceptions such as *Girl Talk*. Girls now have a surfeit of information available to them, particularly through vloggers (discussed later in the chapter) providing a similar role, but more intimate, immediate and on a larger scale than ever before.

Magazines for adult women have an even longer history; the *Lady's Mercury* of 1693 is identified as the earliest.[25] *Vanity Fair* started in 1913, as a general 'society' magazine, *Vogue* in 1916 and *Good Housekeeping* in 1922. They were similar to girls' magazines but to higher specifications; over time these and numerous other magazines also introduced an informal, aspirational style, tips on the home, letters or agony aunt sections, gossip about the rich and famous, romances and other stories.[26]

Popular magazines were funded by big business, particularly the cosmetic industry; they perpetuated dominant values and reflected rather than anticipated or promoted change. Within the industry they often had a poor reputation, as 'catalogues' advertising products. They have also played a large role in objectifying women, perpetuating unobtainable standards of beauty, and in body-shaming. There were, of course, exceptions. These included *Ms* magazine, founded as part of the second wave of feminism in 1971 by Gloria Steinem in the United States. The magazine still had to accept advertisements, but the editors battled over editorial independence, and changed the way women were portrayed.

More radical still was *Spare Rib*, initiated in 1972 by Rosie Boycott, Marsha Rowe and others. It offered a feminist eye on the usual form – features, a fiction section, reviews, news, adverts, classifieds, and practical tips cutting across the traditional gender divide, like information on both woodwork and knitting. Feminist cartoons featured large. Journals and niche magazines also emerged linked to particular interests, such as the anarchist-socialist *Black Dwarf* and the *West Indian Gazette* founded and edited by the Trinidadian Claudia Jones who is often referred to as 'the mother of the Notting Hill Carnival'.

Overall, women's magazines have increasingly diversified and gone online. Radical ones fight for visibility among specific interest groups, while the mainstream ones continue to play an important cultural role and attract a large readership. For the most part they retain a negative aura of not quite being up to scratch, unimportant journalism, frivolous catalogues, compromised by subservience to big business. Compromised also because for the most part they feed rather than challenge the stereotypes about what it is to be a woman. There are some recent exceptions. In 2009, *Stylist* launched free to

Figure 13: Stylist *magazine, March 2017*

around 400,000 urban women on their commute. It includes as ever fashion and beauty focus, but has a feminist lens and a philosophy of not patronising, not gossiping unkindly and not printing photographs designed to show women in a negative light. Slowly, together with some others, including *Elle*, the needle is shifting.

219

Books

The whole book industry in the past was a male dominion. Writers, publishers, reviewers, editors produced information and entertainment primarily with men in mind. Even so, women have always broken through, sometimes using male pseudonyms. Novels in particular have accompanied and enriched women's lives, provided entertainment and escapism, encouraged personal development and fostered aspirations. Books have reinforced gendered traditions but, starting with children's literature, also played a critical role in changing social norms.

Children's Books

From the 1920s to 1975 Enid Blyton dominated as one of the most prolific writers ever, publishing a staggering 762 books. Blyton's female characters were presented as quieter and weaker than boys, although Georgina in *The Famous Five* insisted on being called George, and was an alternative role model for many girls. The books also presented negative attitudes towards minorities, particularly Gypsies and black people. Blyton's defenders argue that she was reflecting the prejudices of her time.

The Janet and John reading books of the 1950s and 1960s, and then the Peter and Jane series, also came with ladles of gender and social stereotyping. In later versions Jane started wearing jeans, Daddy helped in the house, and some ethnic diversity was introduced. In 2016, spoofs of the original series were published by Ladybird, using the original artwork but with altered text for grown-ups, poking fun at the typecasting they grew up with. Titles include *How it Works: The Wife, The Shed, The Mid-Life Crisis*.[27]

From the 1960s, the American *Superman* and *Marvel* comics blurred the line between magazines and books, comic strips and graphic novels. There were also the adventures of *Tintin*, first available in the UK in 1951, and *Asterix* from the 1960s. The genre often explored otherness and the central characters were on the fringes of society, yet the primary protagonists were usually male and white. Exceptions were *Wonder Woman* in the 1940s and the *Black Panther* in the 1960s. Many of the characters were regularly brought to life on TV and in films. In 2016, the UN chose Wonder Woman as its honorary ambassador for the empowerment of women and girls. The overtly sexualised, white and culturally insensitive image was a fiasco. More than 40,000 people signed a petition and Wonder Woman was sacked within two months.[28] She has, however, risen up again in the form of a successful American blockbuster film directed by a woman, Patty Jenkins, in 2017, with a sequel *Wonder Woman 1984* planned for 2020.

Girls were given princess-based stories and these continue to be ever-present. A study in 2011 of over five thousand children's books found there were 26 per cent more male main characters. Similarly, male characters featured in 37 per cent of book titles and female ones in 18 per cent.[29]

Jacqueline Wilson is one of the first pioneers of inclusive feminist children's books with realistic storylines. She started to write in 1969 and since then has published more than a hundred books with girls at their heart, often addressing troubled lives with a social and moral commentary and a valuing of resilience. She reflected: 'I always try to make my female characters strong and determined and caring – and hope that my readers feel comforted and encouraged by their example.'[30]

Singlehandedly, J. K. Rowling created a reading revolution. The story behind how the Harry Potter series was written and the adversity that the author experienced as a single mother is part of the legend around the books. Although Harry is the main protagonist, many female characters take centre stage, particularly that of Hermione, an intelligent, logical, reliable and courageous friend. Emma Watson who plays Hermione in the film versions has gone on to become a prominent feminist, fronting the UN's campaign for women's advancement through the HeForShe campaign. In the stage version, Noma Dumezweni played the part of Hermione, causing some consternation until J. K. Rowling explained that her skin colour had not been specified as white – challenging the implicit assumption.

Sally Nicholls, who in 2017 published *Things a Bright Girl Can Do*, a novel about three young suffragettes, commented:

> For many authors, children's publishing can feel like a constant battle against gendered assumptions: that boys will not read a book with a female main character, that it should be clear from the cover which gender a book is aimed at, that children's non-fiction should be predominantly 'boy' subjects like dinosaurs or space, that a thoughtful book about feelings should be marketed at girls, while an action adventure story may be aimed at both . . . Publishers argue that gendered books simply sell more copies; or that the real problems lie with a gendered society. But many authors have been quietly – or not so quietly – trying to change these assumptions.[31]

Publishers such as Letterbox Library are actively trying to increase the diversity of characters, interests and plots, and the website A Mighty Girl has also become a feminist resource for parents, with its database of over two thousand books – as well as information on toys, films, music and clothing.

Feminist Factual Writing and Women's History

If books have perpetuated social norms, they have also been at the vanguard of challenging them, and throughout the last hundred years, books by women have played a central role in communicating feminist ideas. As part of the first wave, Marie Stopes's *Married Love*, published in 1918, was groundbreaking in giving information on contraception, and Virginia Woolf's extended essay *A Room of One's Own*, first published in 1929, became a seminal feminist text about women wanting to break free.

Heralding the second wave, *The Second Sex* by Simone de Beauvoir, initially published in French in 1949, the English version appearing in 1953, laid out a feminist philosophy, highlighting the lived experience of women in history. In 1963, American Betty Freidan's *The Feminine Mystique* critiqued domestic womanhood. In the 1970s, there followed an explosion of key feminist light-bulbs, including Frances Beal's *Double Jeopardy: To Be Black and Female*, Kate Millett's *Sexual Politics*, Germaine Greer's *The Female Eunuch*, Ann Oakley's *Sex, Gender and Society* and Susie Orbach's *Fat is a Feminist Issue*. In the 1990s books spotlighting attitudes towards women's bodies – part of the third wave – included Naomi Wolf's *The Beauty Myth* and Natasha Walter's *Living Dolls*.

Bridging African and black identity in the West were the publications in the 1980s of the Americans Audre Lorde with *Zami: A New Spelling of My Name* and Angela Davis's *Women, Race and Class*. Likewise, and part of the fourth wave, the writings of Nigerian-born Chimamanda Ngozi Adichie have appealed globally and in Sweden in 2015 every sixteen-year-old received a copy of her short tract *We Should All Be Feminists*. In the UK, Caitlin Moran brought humour to her writings and quick wit to her broadcasts. Kat Banyard's *The Equality Illusion* directed attention to the differences between the theory and practice of women's lives. She, together with Laura Bates, Caroline Criado-Perez, Reni Eddo-Lodge, Lucy-Anne Holmes and Laurie Penny, are examples of a long tradition linking activism with feminist literature.

Turning to the writing of history, this has been a bastion of traditional male interests. His rather than her story. Stories almost exclusively written by men and defined by what they did, with some chinks from the beginning, as when female monarchs were the subject. Women's agency took a leap forward when women in the suffrage movement wrote memoirs and autobiographies. These built on the tradition of diary writing allowed to women and girls because it was personal and therefore permissible. Documentation of women's daily lives as a political act of reclaiming their importance included the 1931 publication of stories of women involved in the Women's Cooperative Guild entitled *Life As We Have Known It*, with an introduction by Virginia Woolf. However, the main impetus in women's history arose in the 1970s as part of 'second-wave feminism'. For example, Sheila Rowbotham's 1973 book *Hidden from History* drew attention to the need for a recalibrating of history, and Virago's first non-fiction book, *Fenwomen*, by Mary Chamberlain in 1975, was seminal as a social and oral history. History was being redefined, not in terms of the few, but of the experiences of the many – a recovery of the missing, ordinary, working-class woman. And interest in the social history of the ordinary man was also gaining currency. A recent example is Louise Raw's 2009 *Striking a Light: The Bryant and May Matchwomen and their Place in History*, which is now accompanied by an explicitly political annual Matchwomen's Festival.

The everyday experience versus the exceptional has taken on an interesting twist in the sentence 'Well behaved women seldom make history.' It tends to be assumed that the expression is exhorting women to make a noise. In fact, the American historian Laurel Thatcher Ulrich coined it to draw attention to the importance of the ordinary woman to history: 'My objective was not to lament their oppression, but to give them a history . . . I was making a commitment to help recover the lives of otherwise obscure women.'[32]

The problem is not always a missing perspective but one hidden in plain sight, as the South African Nomboniso Gasa puts it:

> Sometimes significance lies not in the absence/presence, silence/speech, but in the actual ways in which we read the historical documents, listen to the meta-narratives and pay attention to the details of history, including those which do not fit snugly into those long used, tried and apparently tested boxes that are our analytical tools.[33]

In their desire to give women significance, the enthusiasm of feminist historiography has been criticised as too protective of women.[34] Some say that women's history should not be studied in isolation, resulting in the rise of gender theory and history, for example in the *Gender & History* publication, which began in 1989.

However, even this approach is having to broaden its thinking given the challenges to the concept of gender raised by the trans movement.

Meanwhile, women historians were also writing history without a focus on gender per se and sometimes bridging the gap between historical biographies and the novel, such as the works of Hilary Mantel, Pat Barker and Alison Weir from the 1980s. The classicist Mary Beard, writing from 1985, has become an influential voice in interpreting history, without focusing on a feminist perspective, yet pointing out the sexism in historical writings. She became well known through radio and TV, popularising knowledge about Ancient Rome, and because of her visibility above the parapet, she was on the receiving end of vicious social media attacks.

The battle for a greater diversity of perspectives on history is far from won. In 2016, the A-level history syllabus hardly mentioned women and the reference to feminism was almost cut out of the politics exams, this only being prevented by a successful social media challenge led by a teenager of Nigerian descent – June Eric-Udorie.

Despite changes in formats and reach, magazines and books as a form of leisure remain largely unchanged from 100 years ago in terms of the experience they offer their reader. What then of radio and television broadcasting – to what extent have they replicated the pattern or introduced unexpected twists in the story of how central or invisible women's interests have been?

Broadcast – Radio and TV

The BBC was formed in 1922 and radio gradually entered people's homes, workplaces and schools. In 1925, educational broadcasting began, followed by the BBC Empire Service – now the BBC World Service. Women at home started to be targeted, reducing their isolation and creating a common experience.

From the 1960s pirate radio ships sailed into prominence, particularly Radio Caroline, popular for its broadcasting of music.

Political pirate stations also thrived, for example Radio Free Scotland, hosted in 1962 by Annie Knight from her front room. She was one of the few women in broadcasting, had been a suffragette and died in 2006 at the age of a hundred and eleven. Independent commercial radio stations such as LBC and Capital Radio were established in the 1970s, and specialist music stations and ethnic community stations such as London Greek Radio, Irish Spectrum, Sunrise Radio and Fever for the Asian community also flourished.

Music on the radio has been a theme in most women's lives, and shows have sometimes been introduced by women DJs including Annie Nightingale, Jo Whiley, Sara Cox and Gemma Cairney. Radio has offered companionship, entertainment and information, and generated debate. By 2016, 90 per cent of women listened to an average of twenty hours of radio a week, just marginally less than 91 per cent of men listening to twenty-three hours.[35]

The two most successful podcasts in 2017 were Radio 4's *Woman's Hour* and *The Archers*. 'Dangerously radical' yet 'laughably domestic' was how *Woman's Hour* was reviewed when it started in 1946. Initially it was scripted and presented by a man and didn't quite work. One woman commented: 'The programme is much too patronising. What women want is a programme to compensate us for being tied to our domestic chores, to help us keep in touch with the world outside, whether it's books, films, politics or other countries.'[36] Since then, *Woman's Hour* has shared women's enthusiasms, frustrations and aspirations and prided itself on covering with a mixture of fun and seriousness all aspects of women's lives: 'a unique mixture of jam, Jerusalem and genital warts'.[37] As Jane Garvey reflected:

> I'm always struck by how much our listeners are prepared to share with us, and by how unshockable they are. We are the only place where issues like the impact of pornography on relationships, or the strain of caring, or the rise in cosmetic labiaplasty, can be discussed in a radio safe place, where you know you won't be mocked or belittled.

At times, the programme's dizzying changes of mood and topic can prove challenging ... though nothing's likely to top the moment in 2010 when I moved from a live interview with then Prime Minister Gordon Brown to a conversation about whether a woman should ever go out without a bra.[38]

The presenters have felt like friends to millions of women and to a significant number of men across generations. From 2015, *Late Night Woman's Hour* was added – its intimate, frank and funny younger sister. Like all broadcast media, *Woman's Hour* has increasingly interacted with its listeners. For Jane, 'the programme's audience is its greatest asset. It's bigger than ever (nearly 4 million people listen every week) but also younger, and more diverse, than audiences of other shows on the BBC's most "establishment" radio network.'[39]

The presenters have sometimes got into trouble, as with Jenni Murray's comments about trans women,[40] or caused trouble to others, as with Emma Barnett's trenchant exposure of Jeremy Corbyn's failure to remember the cost of the childcare provision he was announcing during his election campaign in 2017.

The Archers, with its fictitious rural community of Ambridge, is another national treasure, and the world's longest-running radio soap. It started in 1951 as a way of providing farmers with information, with input from the Ministry of Agriculture. It had an audience of over 11 million in the 1950s, still has over 5 million and – having entertained generations of primarily middle-class women – remains culturally significant. For example, in 2016 it broadcast a domestic-abuse story involving coercive control, the story unfolding in parallel with new legislation on the issue. The story generated much discussion, with increased calls to helplines and donations to the charity Refuge.

Turning to TV, in 1937, a year after the first BBC broadcast, Mary Adams was employed as one of the first TV producers. Broadcasting, which initially only covered the London area, ceased during the war but was relaunched in 1946 for a few hours each day and became popular with women at home. Output was very middle-class oriented with well-spoken presenters in evening dress at all times. The first commercial channel started in 1955 with a more contemporary style. Subsequently, channels have proliferated, including with satellite and cable as well as internet-based programmes and TV on demand.

Attitudes to watching television have shifted dramatically over the period. Initially it was seen as special family time, based on a few programmes that most people watched. But it started to have more negative associations, with fears about children in particular watching too much. By the 1960s critics such as Mary Whitehouse also objected to the swearing and sexually explicit material. She campaigned against violence, pornography, feminism and gay rights. Now with different members of the family usually plugged into earphones watching different programmes, the whole family coming together and watching the same screen has become romanticised again.

Soaps and serial dramas have long attracted female audiences, including *Coronation Street* from 1959, the longest-running television soap in the UK. Set in Manchester, it centres on strong, working-class women and their men. *EastEnders*, which began in 1985, also maintains high ratings. For the most part, soaps have been predictable and stereotypical in plot and character, and slow to portray the reality of multicultural Britain. Yet they have also dealt with controversial topics including rape, murder and child abuse and have played a crucial role in furthering a normalisation of equality; for example, *Brookside* showed the first lesbian kiss in a mainstream soap pre-watershed in 1993, *Coronation Street* the first transgender character in 1998 – though the character was initially written in as a joke.[41]

Crime dramas have on occasion had women as the main protagonist, including Helen Mirren in the 1990s series *Prime Suspect* and Amanda Burton and then Emilia Fox in *Silent Witness*. Successful women drama writers also rose to fame, including Sally Wainwright, writing from the late 1980s. While there have been few inroads in the male-dominated science fiction genre, a big symbolic step was taken in 2017 when Jodie Whittaker became the thirteenth Dr Who.

Quiz and entertainment shows consistently had a sexist format from their start in the 1950s, with men the prime presenters and young, scantily clad women sidekicks, leading people on and off stage. A few women, however, presented to great success and over long periods such as Esther Rantzen from the 1970s and Anne Robinson from the 1990s. Cilla Black's *Blind Date* had a prime Saturday slot from 1985 to 2003 on ITV, reaching audiences as large as 18.2 million. Sexist undertones were never far from the surface and the genre seemed to have gone out of fashion; however, in the last few years there has been a resurgence in similar programmes, with a new series of *Blind Date* starting in 2017.

Reality TV has more recently dominated the airwaves. People are put together in unusual contexts to observe their foibles and strengths in programmes such as *Big Brother* and *Love Island*. Talent-based programmes such as *The X Factor*, *Britain's Got Talent* and *The Great British Bake Off* have launched careers. The programmes have increasingly promoted diversity and been challenged when falling short. Arlene Phillips in 2009 was deemed too old, at sixty-six, to continue as a judge on *Strictly Come Dancing* – the same show that Bruce Forsyth had hosted in his eighties. Ms Phillips's sacking sparked protest and a statement of concern in Parliament by Harriet Harman MP. In 2013 women accounted for only 18 per cent of TV presenters over the age of fifty.[42]

If we think of presenters of factual programmes, there are comparatively few female household names. Louisa commented:

I find myself watching the programmes of women historians such as Bettany Hughes, Mary Beard and Lucy Worsley, setting the record of history straight or giving voice to the often-silenced women of history, or Alice Roberts and Helen Czerski with science, Hannah Fry with maths, Kate Humble and Anita Rani with nature programmes, Charlie Dimmock and gardening,

Clare Balding on sport. Even if the subject matter is not of immediate interest – there is none of the self-importance of too many of the male presenters, and they bring in a refreshing dollop of humour and humanity. It is inspiring to see such clever women on the screen![43]

Comedies have probably been the programmes on TV with the greatest blatant sexism, with objections branded a failure of humour. Yet humour at its laziest and cruellest excludes those who are the butt of the jokes. Even so, women have started to make inroads. These have included Joyce Grenfell from the 1940s, June Whitfield from the 1950s, Carla Lane from the late 1960s, Victoria Wood from the 1980s. Since then Dawn French, Jennifer Saunders, Caroline Aherne, Jo Brand, Miranda Hart and Sandi Toksvig are but some of those drawing humour from women's lives and bringing feminism into their performances.

The Internet and Social Media

Since the late 1980s, the internet has allowed people access to information in ways that have created a massive power shift and brought the production and consumption of culture closer together. Connectivity has resulted in democratisation and a new power to influence. The benefits have been transformational, the dangers also massive, including the so-called 'echo chamber' effect – people thinking they are communicating widely but, partly because of algorithms that select the content they see, only doing so with a narrow segment of like-minded people. The diversity of views lost and the danger of metadata influencing elections has become evident and much discussed.

On a day-to-day level, the internet has been harnessed most by the young, with a resulting shift of influence. It can exclude those who have poor connectivity and some of the elderly and the disabled who may find that the world is expecting them to be able to navigate systems not always built with them in mind. From a gender perspective, despite many changes, we still see the old order exerting itself: in 2016, Wikipedia, the fifth most visited site in the world, had only 15 per cent of women as its editors and less than 17 per cent of notable profiles were of women. The BBC, as part of its annual '100 women' initiative, organised a Wikithon in 2016 to raise awareness about the sexist nature of the internet, resulting in more than four hundred entries on women being added.[44]

Facebook was founded in 2004, followed by Twitter in 2006, Tumblr in 2007 and Instagram in 2010. Together, these platforms have infiltrated almost all aspects of our lives. The benefits have been huge, but as we saw in previous chapters, so too are the problems they have generated – facilitated and fuelled by anonymity. Through a successful challenge on Facebook, Laura Bates made companies aware of reputational risks from advertisements that sometimes end up alongside violent images. As Kaitlynn Mendes, a media and communications expert, explains:

> This action was significant because there was a flourishing group of pages promoting or making light of violence against women. Despite pleas to take them off, it was only when corporations put pressure on Facebook that they listened, generating valuable lessons for how activists might get social media platforms to make changes in the future.[45]

The battle to make the internet safer is an ongoing one, driven not just by the need to tackle misogyny, racism and homophobia but, for the government, the imperative to address radicalisation.

On the more positive side, online communities have provided a place to share experiences and develop a sense of belonging. Those who have a specific concern can gain strength and support from others. For instance, typing *I'm suffering from depression, where can I seek help?* is a lot easier than the options available prior to the internet. In 2000, Mumsnet was created and developed into the UK's biggest online community for parents. By 2016 they had received over 90 million page views and over 19 million visits per month, reducing the loneliness of mothers especially, even in the middle of the night. It also spawned Gransnet, providing similar support for grandparents.

By 2017, YouTube had an estimated 1.5 billion users globally and was the second most visited site (after the search engine Google). Sixty-two per cent of the content was uploaded by men[46] and although many sites are gender neutral – music and animals figuring large – gaming and sport predominate. Material by and for women clusters around beauty and image; from around 2005 this has been dominated by young women vloggers. Examples include Zoe Elizabeth Sugg (Zoella), who teaches young girls how to use make-up and provides tips on fashion and healthy eating. By 2017 she had 664 million viewers, 11 million subscribers and also millions of followers on Twitter and Instagram. She is the writer of a book, *Girl Online*, which was the fastest-selling book in 2014 and broke the record for the highest-ever first-week sales for a debut author.

Similarly, SprinkleofGlitter, the name Louise Pentland is known by, had by her early thirties become an industry of her own. Motivated by problems at home, she started her blogs to target young women with light entertainment, beauty and fashion. Her YouTube channel had 2.5 million subscribers and 180 million views by June 2017. She identifies as a feminist, has covered political subjects and became one of a number of UN Change Ambassadors promoting in particular the UN's Sustainable Development gender equality goal.

To a large extent, the web reflects our world. It is therefore framed around reaffirmation of women's secondary position in society. The focus is on image and beauty. Yet, at the same time, opportunities have been provided to engage in cyberfeminism. Examples include: the Everyday Sexism Project, Hollaback!, the posts of the American vlogger Laci Green – named in 2016 one of the thirty most influential people on the internet[47] – and Who Needs Feminism?, a Tumblr-initiated global campaign where participants upload a photo of themselves with a sign explaining why feminism is relevant. Digital platforms such as the Standard Issue e-magazine and The Guilty Feminist and Global Pillage podcasts have also given feminists a space in which to operate. Kaitlynn Mendes reflected:

> In recent years, it is clear that girls and women are using digital platforms to challenge sexism, harassment, misogyny and rape culture . . . These sites are important for making interventions in society – for identifying street harassment as a common, yet overlooked issue; for bringing together thousands of testimonies which challenge the notion [that] we live in a post-feminist society where sexism is a thing of the past; and for showcasing a multitude of reasons why feminism continues to be necessary.[48]

The internet of things – which allows communication with physical objects – is still in its infancy but already Amazon dash buttons have simplified purchases to a click of a button positioned next to the item that is running out and 'Nest' thermostats provide smart heating of houses, simplifying domestic tasks.

The internet is not inherently transformational in terms of gender politics – but it is already pivotal in all aspects of women's lives. It is increasingly the vehicle through which we do everything – including booking theatre tickets.

Women in the Theatre

Although historically women did not go on the stage and men therefore played female roles, most notably in Shakespeare's plays, theatregoers had always included women. In 1918 actors such as Ellen Terry were household names and through the last century actresses have entertained, often weaving careers in and out of the theatre and film. However, the power in the theatre world continued to be held by men – their scripts, their production, their view of the world.

A few women playwrights did break through. Take Agatha Christie's play *The Mousetrap*, which opened in 1952 and is still running in 2018 after 27,000 performances – a world record.[49] Yet it was not until 2008 that Rebecca Lenkiewicz became the first living woman playwright to have her play performed on the Olivier stage of the Royal National Theatre. It was seen by Caroline, who remembers:

> At about the age of 32, I went to see *Her Naked Skin*. A play about two suffragettes in the early 20th century. It was like a light went on – why hadn't any of this been part of my education – how did I not understand more about the history of being a woman? What's been done, is still to be done etc. So a journey of reading and learning began.[50]

Lilian Baylis managed The Old Vic theatre from 1913 until her death in 1937. She also helped to reopen the derelict Sadler's Wells Theatre and form the English National Opera, National Theatre and Royal Ballet. In the more recent end of the last century, Phyllida Lloyd embarked on an all-female trilogy of Shakespeare plays between 2012 and 2016. These are set in a women's prison and involve a very diverse female cast. Power and gender are explored from a new angle, symbolically important given the centrality of Shakespeare's plays in British culture.

Meanwhile, during her time in office, Jude Kelly transformed the Southbank Centre into a hub of feminist activism. In 2010, she started what has now become a global movement, the Women of the World Festivals. The spotlight is on women of all backgrounds, with a common thread showcasing their work, encouraging discussion and action through performance, debate, mentoring and much else besides. Jude explained:

> When I was at university studying drama I didn't know of any women directors and my lecturer quipped, 'There are only three women directors in Britain – Joan Littlewood who's retired, Joan Knight in Scotland who's a lesbian and Buzz Goodbody who's just killed herself – which one would you like to be?' It was a hostile way of making me feel that it was a

fruitless ambition on my part. I've subsequently discovered that there were the most extraordinary women in the arts . . . As feminists, we have spoken about the wide gap between how stories by men are perceived as having world relevance and stories by women as only having relevance to women. Challenging that over and over has meant that more women are coming into the space with confidence and determination, and more men are standing aside and saying 'OK, there's a space for you here.'[51]

Women and feminism are infiltrating the large establishments; this is even more the case in small-scale productions such as those presented at the Edinburgh Fringe. For example, from 1985, the black writer, director and actor Angie Le Mar with *Funny Black Women on the Edge*; from 2004, Bridget Christie with *A Bic for Her* (and a book *A Book for Her*) showing the absurdity of misogyny. Visually impaired Maria Oshodi, has also paved a new path as a playwright and by establishing Extant, the UK's first professional theatre company of visually impaired artists.

Women in Film

By the late 1920s, going to see a film had become a recreational activity, a treat, for women of all backgrounds, many more than could even dream of going to the theatre. Matinees catered to housewives, and female audiences initially predominated. By 2014, cinema viewers were estimated to be equal and access to films had grown exponentially, taking up an ever-greater amount of people's leisure, and therefore potentially being more influential than ever.[52] In the last decade, cinema has also provided an avenue for the broadcasting of theatre productions through livestreaming, increasing access to wider audiences.

Film and theatre offer an escape to alternative worlds. Yet with some notable exceptions, what they have delivered has been reinforcement and exaggeration of gender dynamics in the real world, not surprising given that in the creation, dissemination and reviewing of films men have once again dominated.

Yet in how films are sold, women's visibility suddenly shoots up. Beautiful women have provided markers of the decades – Betty Balfour in the 1920s, Gracie Fields in the 1930s, Vivien Leigh in the 1940s, Audrey Hepburn in the 1950s, Julie Andrews in the 1960s, Glenda Jackson in the 1970s, Helen Mirren in the 1980s, Keira Knightley in the 1990s, Emma Watson and Emily Blunt in the 2000s, Emilia Clarke in the 2010s.

The Bechdel Test was developed in 1985. A film passes the test if it has a) at least two women in it, b) who talk to each other and c) about something other than a man. Despite this low bar, in April 2016, only 58 per cent of films passed all three tests.[53] As an alternative test, in 2014 the F-Rating was developed (the F for feminist) by Holly Tarquini. The rating emphasises who is telling the stories and is awarded to films directed by a woman and/or written by a woman and or/starring significant women. If a film is all three it is Triple F-Rated. The first iteration of the rating at the Bath Film Festival featured 40 per cent F-Rated titles. In 2017, the biggest film website in the world, the Internet Movie Database, IMDb, tagged over 22,000 films with the F-Rated keyword, making it possible to search for these with one key click. Holly commented:

> Highlighting and promoting F-Rated films sends a clear message to distributors, producers and funders that women can and should have more than just a supporting role within the industry. We're not saying that other films aren't good because they're not made by and about women, we're just shining a bright light on the issue and amplifying the conversation.[54]

Another spotlight has been provided by a polygraph showing how much the characters speak in 2,000 of the most famous screenplays, broken down by gender and age. Looking at the Walt Disney films, at one extreme, in the original *Jungle Book*, male characters have 98 per cent of the lines. At the other end of the spectrum is

Mulan: even though she is the lead, the male protector dragon has 50 per cent more lines than her. Likewise, in *Pocahontas*, women only have 34 per cent of the lines. Only in 22 per cent of action films do women actors speak more, and men occupy at least two of the top three roles in 82 per cent of cases.[55]

The trend, however, is positive. The 2016 remake of *The Jungle Book* has prominent female characters in it. In the earliest Disney films, *Snow White*, *Cinderella* and *Sleeping Beauty* were defined and rescued by their beauty and in many of these films the main character is orphaned or has lost their mother, adding to the invisibility of women.[56] The more recent heroines have more character, show more agency, are not always white, and the films move beyond the focus on a heterosexual love affair.

It is not just female beauty that is the attraction. It is their nudity. A study of films produced in 2014 found that 33 per cent of women were shown with some nudity, versus 11 per cent of men. This is also being challenged. As is gendered ageism. Julie Walters argued: 'Youth is not everything. Now we have all the baby-boomers in their sixties, like me, who are actively engaged in life – we're not retiring, we're not just being put out to grass once we hit 60.'[57]

As with the theatre, women remain the odd ones out. Sarah Gavron, the director of *Suffragette*, explained:

I have often felt isolated – often found myself as the only woman in a room full of men. Role models were key to my journey – it was only when I saw films directed by women that I realised it was possible to be a woman director. And it was a while after that before I dared to admit my ambition to anyone.[58]

The gender pay gap in the movie industry provides another angle to evidence of the gendered valuation at work. Generally, action movies, films with male superhero storylines and the horror genre in which, by different measures, gender inequality is greatest, can raise massive budgets. By contrast, romantic comedies, denigrated as chick flicks, dramas and documentaries, command smaller budgets. This is despite how well they can do at the box office, i.e. the logic is not financially driven but is a reflection of power balances.[59]

Actor and producer Gemma Arterton has spoken about having to confront sexism:

It's easier to conform and shut up. That's the way it's always been with women. Easier than putting yourself out there and having an opinion, to which someone might retaliate. I'm sure there are people who don't want to work with me because they think I'm difficult – 'one of those feminist girls' – but to be honest with you I don't want to work with them. And that's fine. Now.[60]

The 'now' is interesting in that Gemma can speak up because of her success moving from a role in a James Bond film – with the epitome of sexism that the franchise represents – to the musical *Made in Dagenham*, which tells the story of the equal pay strike discussed in Chapter 2. But the 'now' is also a reflection of a slowly changing landscape.

Women in Art

Caroline Criado-Perez reported in 2016 that only 3 per cent of historical, non-royal statues in the UK were of women, pointing out that: 'If you are a woman, your best chance at becoming a statue is to be a mythical or allegorical figure, a famous virgin, royal or nude.'[61] She successfully campaigned for a statue of Millicent Fawcett, made by Gillian Wearing, in Parliament Square, and statues of other political women are planned in different parts of the country.[62]

Barbara Hepworth, the most famous female sculptor of the century, hated to be called a sculptress.[63] She started exhibiting from the 1920s, her flowing abstract forms capturing a female essence. One of her triplet daughters explained that people 'thought she was mad. If you went shopping, you could hear the women in the street talking about her. "Ooh-argh, there she goes, banging away . . ." They thought she was loopy. What on earth was she doing? She should have been running the house and doing the cooking.'[64]

Prunella Clough had a long career from the 1940s, and Bridget Riley exhibited from the 1960s, becoming one of the most famous of the Optical artists. Helen Chadwick, installation artist and photographer from the 1970s, explored the relationships between image and form, surface and spectator. She used her body in odd poses, sometimes eyes closed, with imagery alongside to tell a story. Of one piece, she explained:

> I was looking for a vocabulary for desire where I was the subject and the author and the object; I felt that by directly taking all these roles, the normal situation in which the viewer operated as a kind of voyeur broke down wanting to make images of the body that would somehow circumnavigate that so-called male gaze.[65]

That male gaze surfaces again and again. Following hostile reaction to her work from some feminists who argued that she was perpetuating objectification, her work moved away from the human form to critique gender binary thinking. As early as 1991 she was lamenting: 'Why do we feel compelled to read gender, and automatically wish to sex the body before us so we can orientate our desire and thus gain pleasure or reject what we see?'[66]

In 1993, Rachel Whiteread became the first woman to win the Turner Prize. She was followed in 1999 by Tracey Emin who won the prize for *My Bed*. The installation was personal, displaying the bed in all its squalor: condoms, pants with menstrual stains, cigarette packets – an image of her own precarious mental state at the time.

Turning to art directors, Joanna Drew made her mark as the director of the Hayward Gallery from 1987, forging very strong relationships with artists and becoming a legend among curators. In

2016, Frances Morris became the director of Tate Modern. She gave me one of my favourite quotes, writing:

> There is something powerful about my generation of women who have been brought up with gender bias from birth regulating our personal and professional lives and finding – not surprisingly – that now, empowered as a result of largely our own actions, we find a different way forward, as leaders, managers and colleagues. After so long on the margins this is gratifying. The margins are the place in the forest where the great mushrooms grow, in soil that has been raked over and disturbed but often disregarded. My generation has likewise been somewhat trampled, but like the best mushrooms in the margins we are now showing our heads![67]

Maria Balshaw, who was the director of the Whitworth in Manchester, became the director of the Tate in 2017. Not only are the mushrooms in the margins showing their heads, they are creating the ecology for others to grow. In the art world, at least, a feminist 'structural overhaul' seems on the cards.[68] Here's hoping.

Women in Dance and Music

In the world of classical dance, women have throughout the last hundred years played lead roles as dancers, choreographers, teachers and directors. Russian-born Anna Pavlova moved to the UK in 1912, having become an international ballerina superstar. Polish-born Dame Marie Rambert founded the Rambert School in 1919, later the Rambert Dance Company. The Anglo-Irish Ninette de Valois established the Royal Ballet School in 1926, the Royal Ballet in 1931 and the Birmingham Ballet in 1946. Margot Fonteyn, from the 1930s, is arguably the most famous ballet dancer of all time. Turning to the more recent past, Tamara Rojo – ex-Royal Ballet – became the English National Ballet's artistic director in 2012. Despite these female giants, there were still male-dominated elements. In 2016, she programmed three female choreographers explaining she had never danced a ballet by a woman and wanted to see what this would look like. She has continued to showcase female choreographers, transforming the dance repertoire.

In classical music, by contrast, overall women have had much less influence. Few women composers have had their work commissioned, even though more than a century ago British women composers were at work. These included the suffragette Ethyl Smyth, the first female composer to be honoured as a Dame of the British Empire. In 2015, a teenage student, Jessy McCabe, challenged an A-level music syllabus, which included sixty-three composers, all male. She succeeded in getting five works by women included and an additional twelve on the recommended listening list.[69]

As players, women who have left their mark include the cellist Jacqueline du Pré with her still-much-listened-to Elgar Concertos, recorded in 1965 when she was twenty. Women violinists have also thrived, with stars such as Nicola Benedetti. From 2000 the glass ceiling has opened up to let women violinists through, with some listed as the top earners globally. What instruments women and men have played continue to carry some gender conditioning – and not surprisingly given the centrality and perceived public power of the role, there are still proportionally few female conductors.

Even when women musicians rise to the top, there is a pattern of sexualised advertising of their looks and their prowess. Nevertheless they can be heard in increasing numbers, and diversity of all kinds is being helped by blind auditioning (which is also being used in the theatre).[70] Furthermore, there are other ways in which change is happening, through a combination of individuals pushing for it and an increasing institutional acknowledgement of the need to challenge the musical status quo. For example, Edwina Wolstencroft, Editor for BBC Radio 3, commented:

> The work we have done drawing more attention to women
> composers on BBC Radio 3 began in the Autumn of 2014, when
> I decided we should start planning a whole day of music by

women composers for broadcast on International Women's Day 2015; it was time for the station to lead a cultural change around the established classical canon. We did this by celebrating women's success in the most creative and fundamental role in music – as composers, both historic and contemporary. Ever since, we've included classical music by women every day in our usual programming, for example on our Breakfast show. We continue to commission new music too, for example, to mark the centenary year of the Representation of the People's Act 1918.[71]

In pop music, diversity of colour, sexuality and socio-economic position stand more of a chance of being accepted than in most walks of life, and women and BAME singers have become as successful as their male counterparts, though they are still almost invisible as producers.[72] In the following section I gallop through the century picking out some of my favourite characters among British or UK-based female singers.

Vera Lynn became the 'Forces' sweetheart' in 1939 with her recording of 'We'll Meet Again'. She had a long career and in 2009, aged ninety-two, became the oldest living artist to reach number 1 in the British charts. In 2017, she released the album *Vera Lynn 100* to commemorate her hundredth year; it was a number 3 hit, making her the oldest recording artist in the world and the first centenarian to have an album in the charts.

Dame Shirley Bassey, the daughter of a Welsh mother and Nigerian father, rose to fame in the 1950s and began a hugely successful career lasting over sixty years, which included recording the theme tune for three Bond films. Despite great personal wealth and independence, she is no feminist. In 2015 she argued that women in her industry would never be empowered because of genetic differences that go back to the cave-days, that men need to have control and that women should not try and change this. Nor should women – 'with their periods and hormones' be pilots, firefighters, police or soldiers. She said that women were going too far, 'trying to be cleverer than men – or as clever.' Likewise she believed that men should be the breadwinners and that it was wrong for men to be house-husbands.[73]

Singer and record producer Dusty Springfield loomed large from the 1950s to the 1990s. Committed to civil rights, she did a tour in South Africa in 1964 and played to a mixed audience, despite this being barred in her contract, and was subsequently deported. She was bisexual at a time when this was almost unheard of. She subsequently reflected:

> I think my life and career would have been easier without the constant gay rumours. My sexuality has never been a problem to me but I think it has for other people. They seem to want me to be either gay or straight – they can't handle it if someone's both. How many other women entertainers can you think of who've admitted they're bisexual? Believe me, some are.[74]

Sandie Shaw was renowned for singing barefoot in the 1960s. She also recorded hit singles in Italian, French, German and Spanish, boosting her popularity in Europe. In 1967, she became the first British singer to win the Eurovision song contest, despite almost being dropped by the BBC because she had been in an adulterous relationship. Something that just would not have surfaced as a concern for a man.[75]

Marianne Faithfull also made it big from the 1960s, though her fame was accentuated by her relationship with the singer Mick Jagger, and her achievements overshadowed by their relationship with drugs. Years later she commented: 'It destroyed me. To be a male drug addict and to act like that is always enhancing and glamorizing. A woman in that situation becomes a slut and a bad mother.'[76] She became homeless and attempted suicide before turning her life around.

Folk music had its heyday in the 1960s and 1970s, with the revival of an ancient tradition. Even for an audience of the so-called sexually liberated era, the lyrics were sanitised. Historically, folk music was a counter-culture, allowing women a voice to speak of things such as unplanned pregnancy, erotic pleasure – behaviours beneath the veneer of respectable society.

Singer-songwriter Annie Lennox began her career in the early 1970s. She went on to become an award-winning icon. As a self-declared global feminist, she has championed many causes such as HIV/AIDS, gender inequality and human rights, and founded The Circle, working to support and empower women and girls around the globe. She commented:

> My profile as a musician and performer has offered an advocacy platform . . . I'm always thrilled by the potential for positive societal transformation when people connect and put truth to power. Women and men really have no excuse not to become engaged with global feminist issues.[77]

In 1996, the Spice Girls popularised the concept of Girl Power. Twenty years later they approved a remake of their hit song 'Wannabe' to publicise sustainable development goals, and the words 'What do you really, really want' were linked to quality education for all girls, equal pay for equal work, ending violence against women and ending girl marriage.

With her gravelly and distinctive contralto voice Amy Winehouse came to fame in 2003 and tragically died of alcohol poisoning at the age of twenty-seven in 2011. Her eclectic, soul-based songs broke records for the most songs by a female artist simultaneously in the UK singles chart.[78] She battled drug dependency and violence within her marriage (in which she was sometimes the aggressor) as well as depression and bulimia – the epitome of the troubled artist.

Lily Allen, a singer with influences from reggae to electropop, came to fame in 2006. She has been outspoken politically, campaigning on climate change and talking to the media about the invisibility of the socially marginalised following the Grenfell Tower fire in 2017. Lyrics from her 2013 song 'Hard Out' refer to the objectification of women. The accompanying video showed skimpily dressed black female dancers, resulting in questions about whether she was perpetuating the problem.[79]

As a singer-songwriter since 2007, Adele won numerous awards: Brit, Grammy, Golden Globe, Academy and an MBE for services to music. Her album *21* became the longest-running album by a female solo artist to stay at number 1 in the UK and US album charts. In 2017, she had more than 65 million fans on Facebook, second only to Manchester United FC. She has focused on her work, herself and her family, regularly escaping media attention and using her position to specify the terms she would perform under.[80]

Soprano Emeli Sandé, half-Zambian, half-British, came to fame in 2008. She performed in both the opening and closing ceremonies of the London Olympics and sang on CARE's March4Women event in advance of International Women's Day in 2017. She reflected:

It's very rare to find a female producer. I don't think it's due to a lack of skills but a lack of confidence and encouragement within the industry. Moving forward, I hope there will be more women venturing into production because ultimately creating everything yourself will give you more freedom, independence and creative depth.[81]

Paloma Faith's success as a soul/gospel-styled singer started in 2009. She has also been an actor and a coach on the TV show *The Voice*. She explained to me that she wouldn't be where she was without all the sacrifices and support of her mother, a single parent. Paloma has been a vocal feminist explaining: 'I think it's important that a female artist writes about something other than her heart being broken . . . We have careers, we have ideas – we're not just devoted to finding a man and having babies.'[82]

We have seen in this gallop through some of the most famous British female singers how many but not all have used their influence to highlight gender and other inequalities. In many other realms, women are fighting to be heard. Music is an exception.

Although, for the most part, it is still men who hold the power behind the scenes, women singers are centre stage.

Sport

It was because of the importance – the social visibility – of the Epsom Derby that in 1913 Emily Wilding Davison stepped in front of the king's horse, leading to her death and martyrdom. The sport has long been dominated by male jockeys. However, there are some exceptions and women are often centrally involved in looking after horses and sometimes owning them. Betting on horses – as in other forms of betting – is, however, for the most part a male pastime, and an event such as the Cheltenham Gold Cup is linked to excessive drinking, temporary lap-dancing clubs and an influx of sex workers.[83]

It was also because of the link with male privilege that suffragettes targeted golf courses – the place where men networked and women were excluded – damaging some greens. Over the century, golf courses have gradually opened their gates. Muirfield, founded in 1744, became in 2017 the last to allow women in, forced to do so to retain the right to hold the lucrative Open. Although women can now play alongside men, segregation remains, with limited playing times for women, and sometimes no voting rights. Clubs continue to be owned and run by men, with women on the fringes.

By contrast, tennis was an acceptable physical pursuit for women, and Wimbledon introduced mixed doubles as early as 1884. In 1909, Wimbledon changed its colours to green, white and purple, perhaps as a nod by some of the women on the committee to the suffragette movement, although the Wimbledon Tennis Association does not acknowledge the connection. A hundred years ago, British female tennis stars included Joan Austin and Evelyn Lucy Colyer, nicknamed 'the Babes' by the press in the 1920s. Since then there have been some notable winners, including Ann Jones, Sue Barker and Virginia Wade, and most recently Johanna Konta entered the world top ten and reached the Wimbledon semi-finals in 2017. Following campaigning by Billie Jean King, tennis has abolished gender prize differentials and now sets an example to other sports.

From before 1918, the bicycle was an important tool of the suffrage movement – a symbol of independence linked to less restricted clothing. In road and track cycling, British women have, in the last couple of decades, become particularly successful. They have including Victoria Pendleton from 2005, Laura Trott (now Kenny) from 2012, and Lizzie Armitstead from 2015. A number of the cyclists have spoken out against the continued sexism in the sport.

One of the unexpected consequences of women's entry into paid employment during the First World War was that many joined factory football teams. The most famous was Preston's Dick Kerr's Ladies FC founded in 1917. In 1920, they played on Boxing Day to 53,000 spectators with another 14,000 outside the stadium.[84] After the war, women were expected to leave the factories and stop playing football, and in 1921 the Football Association called on clubs to stop women from using their grounds.

The ban was only reversed in 1971 when women's teams started to be formed. The 2015 Women's World Cup was a watershed moment, with stars such as Steph Houghton putting their mark on the game. The 2017 Euro quarter-finals in which the British Lionesses played was watched by an estimated 4 million viewers. A number of large football clubs also now have a women's team – some progress if you close your eyes to the harassment and pay and conditions differential. But one small club is leading the way. In 2017 the community-owned Lewes FC became the first and so far only club to treat women and men equally. 'Same budget. Same stadium. Same facilities. Same support. Same everything.' It can be done.[85] However, to date there are no women's football magnates and no women's clubs own a stadium.[86] Furthermore, in the long history of the FA there has only been one woman FA board member: Heather Rabbatts, and for a long time she was the only non-white person as well.

At school, girls were rarely allowed to play football or rugby. This has been changing, spurred on by the success of the England women's rugby team in the World Cups of 1994 and 2014. By 2016 there were forty-eight professional women rugby players in England and it was estimated that more than 18,000 women and girls were playing the game, with plans to build on the momentum.[87] Players achieving fame have included Rochelle 'Rocky' Clark – playing from 2010 and with over a hundred caps for England – and Donna Kennedy, playing for Scotland.

The more common sports that girls have grown up with have been netball and hockey, which generally do not receive much public attention, although the final of the Women's Hockey at the Rio Olympics in 2016 had 9 million viewers, an exceptional moment in media coverage.

'Ladies playing cricket – absurd. Just like a man trying to knit.'[88] So said Sir Leonard Hutton, named as one of the greatest batsmen in the first half of the twentieth century. The Women's Cricket Association was, nevertheless, founded in 1926. The first women's Test series took place in 1934–5, with England winning. Myrtle Maclagan scored the first-ever century in a women's Test match in 1935. In 1973, the England team won the inaugural Women's World Cup. Rachael Heyhoe Flint, whose idea this had been, captained the team. Heyhoe Flint became the first woman inducted into the International Cricket Club's Hall of Fame in 2010. Professionalism for women cricketers started in 2014 when eighteen players were given contracts. As a sign of her influence, on the day Heyhoe Flint's death was announced, flags flew at half-mast at Lord's cricket ground and at the home of Wolverhampton Wanderers of which she was a director. Interest, visibility and success have been mutually supportive, with England winning the Cricket World Cup in 2009 and then again in 2017.

In the world of motorcycle racing, Beryl Swain (born Tolman) was racing at Brands Hatch and Snetterton in the 50cc class from the 1950s. In 1962, she became the first solo woman to complete the TT race on the Isle of Man, still considered one of the most dangerous public road races. The organisers disapproved and stopped her from riding the next year by introducing a minimum weight limit. Women did not compete again until Hilary Musson took part in 1978.

In swimming, women have long been visible. For example, Mercedes Gleitze in 1927 became the first woman to swim the English Channel and the first person to swim the Straits of Gibraltar. She used her celebrity status to raise funds for a home for unemployed mining families in Leicester, partly by advertising the new underwater Rolex watches; a pioneer both of celebrity product marketing and sports philanthropy.

In 2005 the sailor Ellen MacArthur became the fastest solo circum-navigator of the globe, contributing to attitudinal change around women's capabilities in such gruelling endeavours. She also set up her own foundation, dedicated to a sustainable reusable culture and econ-omy. Women rowers have also thrived, for example Katherine Grainger winning medals since 1997 and becoming the UK's most decorated female Olympian. In 2017, she became the chair of UK sport.

When Olympic gold-winning athlete Jessica Ennis-Hill had her first child in 2014, she faced media scrutiny about her physical and emotional state and/or changed priorities. She went on to win silver in the 2016 Olympics. In running, Paula Radcliffe is another legend of endurance, winning the women's marathon seven times in total, as well as many other shorter distances from 1997 to 2005. Kelly Holmes, previously a sergeant in the army, won Olympic golds for running the 800 and 1,500 metres at the 2004 Olympics in Athens. Tanni Grey-Thompson, a wheelchair racer, won medals until 2006, subsequently becoming a peer in the House of Lords. Other Paralympic stars have included the Scot, Isabel Newstead, who took part in seven Olympic Games from 1980, winning in a range of disciplines, and Kadeena Cox, the sprint and cycle Olympic star of Rio in 2016.

Overall, the inroads made by women in sport are substantial. In Olympic competitions in 1920, only 7 per cent of Britain's competitors were women and they were excluded from many events. This included boxing until 2012 when Nicola Adams won gold. For years beforehand, Jane Couch, 'The Fleetwood Assassin', had been fighting for women's boxing to be acknowledged. By 2016 women comprised 45 per cent of Britain's competitors at the Olympics. Yet, some gender differences remain. For example, the longest swimming race for men is 1,500 metres and for women it is 800 metres, and there were 161 men's events to 136 women's.[89]

Though still few and far between, women are also increasingly visible as coaches and as sports journalists and commentators, and not just for women's sports. Sue Barker, leading the way with tennis from the 1990s; Clare Balding started with horse-racing commentary and later played a central role in reporting on the Olympic Games; Jacqui Oatley commentates on *Match of the Day*, Alison Mitchell on *Test Match Special*, and Eniola Aluko did so for the football World Cup in 2016.

Women's Organisations

Although cultural areas and activities were male dominated, millions of women have found support through women-focused associations of various kinds. These have been formal or informal, relating to politics, work, family, self-help, sport, religion, you name it. Some have taken up large cultural spaces within British life.

Girlguiding, previously the Girl Guides, was established in 1909 in response to a group of bold girls who refused to accept that scouting was just for boys. From the beginning it sometimes reinforced sexist stereotypes, sometimes challenged them, offering girls a diverse range of activities and awarding badges in areas such as aviation, household electronics and sport. Girlguiding continues to offer a space for girls to meet and make friends, go on outdoor adventures, learn new skills and build their confidence. In the words of two of them: 'We've been fishing for bugs. It's been dirty and sticky and fun!' and: 'It's about going out in the world and exploring stuff. It's given me an opportunity to do so much.'[90]

Women leading the girls also benefit. As Karen Walker, now in her late forties, put it: 'Girlguiding is an opportunity for me to nurture others and still be a child at heart. To challenge myself and join in with everything from the singing, to the making of things with glitter and glue and the travel abroad.'[91] Julie Bentley, Girlguiding's CEO from 2012 to June 2018, reflected:

Over more than 100 years Girlguiding has shaped the lives of millions of girls and women. Whilst constantly evolving to a changing society the charity has held at its core a determination to support girls to recognise and take their rightfully equal place in the world.[92]

In 2017, Sam as a second-generation guider and the mother of two current guiders decided to develop a new 'centenary of the women's vote' challenge badge. The interest spread well beyond her local group with more than 20,000 being sold. She explained: 'Guiding is a calling and creates a sisterhood akin in spirit to that of those wonderful suffragettes and suffragists who forged a path for us all.'[93]

Just over a hundred years ago, the Women's Institute, the WI, was founded, with suffragettes and suffragists influential in the process. It emerged as an institution 'making a difference to women's lives with humour, spirit, courage, eccentricity and common sense'.[94] It was formed during the First World War to encourage women to work to a common end, in the absence of men, and to grow and preserve food. During the Second World War it worked with the Board of Education presiding over school meals, and the Ministry of Health over immunisation and venereal disease campaigns.

The first national resolution of the federation addressed 'the scandal' of poor sanitation and water provision in state-aided housing, and WI pressure resulted in improvements in utilities for rural households. Another resolution, in 1943, pointed out that gender discrimination was caused by housework not being monetised and argued that the role of women as wives and mothers should be recognised under the law as work, and compensated accordingly.

Getting the right mix between fun and purpose has not been easy, with some members feeling saddened that local resolutions have become rarer and national ones have been bogged down in a protracted process that limits activism. However, there are also many successes. In 2008, after the tragic death in custody of the son of a member, the federation – together with the Prison Reform Trust – campaigned for a 'care not custody' approach to end the inappropriate detention of people with mental health needs. Since then the government has committed significant funding to extend NHS England's liaison and diversion approach, aiming to cover 75 per cent of the population in England by 2018. Another campaign, launched in 2012, calls for an end to the shortage of midwives. The findings from its Support Overdue report were mentioned in NHS England's subsequent major review of maternity services and the National Institute for Health and Care Excellence (NICE) subsequently published its first-ever guidance on safe midwifery staffing.

Up to the millennium, like many of its sister organisations, the WI was losing members, with younger women sometimes regarding the organisation as being white, middle-class, outdated and cliquey. Since then, there seems to have been a regeneration of interest, with new WIs being formed with a more diverse membership. The success of Gary Barlow's musical *The Girls* contributed to the reversal in fortune. In 2017, there were around 225,000 members (compared with 238,000 in the 1930s) in approximately 6,300 groups.

For Christine the WI has helped her to find her feet:

> I was severely depressed, hadn't lived in the area very long and had little confidence. I happened across the details of a WI in my area, and emailed. I got a lovely email back and decided to go. I was nervous walking in, with my many tattoos, band T-shirt and brightly coloured hair, but within minutes I'd been welcomed and had a cuppa in my hand. I loved it and made wonderful friends of all ages. I was able to grow in confidence. It allowed me to regain a sense of myself. The power of a female only space can't be underestimated, and women supporting women is always amazing.[95]

Soroptimist International was founded in 1921 in order to encourage women in business and the professions to be of service to their communities locally, nationally and internationally, with a special emphasis on human rights and the status of women. The

Soroptomists have clubs operating in 121 countries with opportunities for friendship visits across the world. New clubs continue to be formed, though an ageing membership is a concern. Following in the footsteps of her suffragette great-aunt Ernestine Mills, who was a founder member of Soroptimist International in London, Irene joined in 1997. She wrote: 'The moment that inspired me to join came when a new acquaintance whose life had not been without problems exclaimed, "There have been times when I have been VERY glad I am a Soroptimist." The friendships are priceless.'[96]

The National Housewives Register, later National Women's Register, started in 1960, as a response to an article in the *Guardian* by Maureen Nicol, who wrote: 'Perhaps housebound wives with liberal interests and a desire to remain individuals could form a national register so that whenever one moves one can contact like-minded friends?'[97] The register's strapline is now 'Connecting women – interested in everything, talking about anything'. Within a few months, 2,000 women joined her register, which also spread to Australia and Canada. It linked women in a national structure, published a regular newsletter, held events and an annual conference. By 1980 it had 22,000 members in 1,000 groups across the country.[98] Jackie shared:

> I was a typical member of the early 80s. Cash-strapped, stay at home mum, no transport, husband working long hours, no family support. The register gave me a precious opportunity for intellectual stimulation and challenge, at almost no cost. I ran its house-swapping scheme enabling 100s of us to have free self-catering holidays around the UK. It is still going but typically the members are as old as me. Today's young mums have the internet, and are more often working.[99]

The Letchworth Young Wives group in Hertfordshire, begun in 1965, encouraged young mums to form a Young Wives' Club where their children could attend a crèche while they could meet, listen to speakers and plan events. Twelve women went to the initial meeting, some put in contact with each other by the social worker who had seen how lonely young mums could be. Fundamentally it was and remains about friendship and solidarity, the sharing of life's highs and lows. Fifty years after it started, Brenda reflected on how the group still serves to reduce their sense of isolation:

> We are all becoming aware of time being finite; we didn't think about it when we were twenty, but now, this is why the support becomes even more important because we know we don't like old age. You need to treat it with humour and where else are you going to get that from?[100]

The most famous young wives group was set up in Aberfan in South Wales, after the 1966 tragedy of a coal spoil tip engulfing a junior school, killing 116 children, 4 teachers and 23 local people. A group of around sixty young mothers came together to support each other, initially without broaching the subject of the disaster itself. They have continued to meet weekly and go out together occasionally, the bond growing over the years, many unwilling to leave the place where their loved ones are buried. The members now aged between sixty and over ninety dropped the 'young' from the name of the group.

One final and different example, this time more informal, is that of knitting groups. These had national visibility for their contributions to the war effort; interest waned in the 1980s, but has revived, linked in part to internet communication. For some feminists, getting together with other women and reclaiming the skills has been important and part of pushing back against the undervaluing of women's interests. One of the websites has 246 groups, 97 per cent of the participants are women and 76 per cent of them are over forty-five. They meet in local libraries or pubs and bars, some formal with a charge for attending, others very informal.[101] As Juliet explained:

We have supported each other through bereavements, births, divorces, problems with kids, operations, mental illness – all the usual trials of life. There is no pressure to produce or achieve anything. Because we all have different abilities, there hasn't been a knitting or crochet problem yet that one of us hasn't been able to solve.[102]

Finally, the rituals of our culutre have also been framed by the most dominant of all structures, namely organised religion.

Religion

When heckled about what God would make of her antics, Emmeline Pankhurst is reported to have responded, 'I'm sure she would approve.' Though spirituality per se is not necessarily gendered, in most religions the sacred texts have almost exclusively been written, translated and interpreted by men in patriarchal societies. Not surprising, then, that God is usually male and the scriptures perpetuate unequal gender norms.[103] There are exceptions: Lakshmi and Kali are female Hindu goddesses, Sophia is the figure of wisdom in Greek mythology, and Quakers don't necessarily envisage God as male. The three Marys[104] play subsidiary but critical roles within Christian texts, and likewise for the wives of the Prophet Muhammad, particularly his first wife Khadija, in Islam.

Gloucester Cathedral was initially an abbey founded in c.679 as a combined monastery for both monks and nuns. It was run by three generations of abbesses before being taken over by priests, and much later converted by Henry VIII into a cathedral. It was not until 2015, after years of campaigning to allow women to be appointed bishops in the Anglican Church, including by the suffragist Maud Royden,[105] that Gloucester's first female bishop, Rachel Treweek, was appointed to lead the establishment once again.[106] Across most faiths there has been in the attitudes to gender – and continues to be – a tug of war between conservative and reformist interpretations of the 'essence of the faith', as there is regarding all radically progressive aspects of religion.[107]

Globally, women are more likely to report having a religious belief, taking part in religious observances, and valuing the role of religion in their lives.[108] In the UK in 2015 there was a 12 per cent difference in reporting religious affiliation by women compared with men.[109]

However, British society has secularised and the influence of Christianity has declined steeply since the 1960s.[110] By 2016, the figures were 53 per cent of no affiliation, 41 per cent Christian – 15 per cent of them Church of England – and 6 per cent other religions.[111] Nevertheless, Christianity still permeates culture and society. Church and Crown are linked, and Christianity – and to a lesser but growing degree, other religions – provides a moral compass and cultural underpinning to society. People refer to and swear on religious texts such as the Bible, the Koran or the Torah for jury service and for other legal transactions. Religion also continues to figure large in life-cycle events including marriage and death, and it remains pivotal in how communities define themselves.

The influence of religion is also maintained through education in faith-based schools. These have often been sought after because of the high standards, parents even attending religious services to obtain entry for their children. Religion, health and social care have also long been linked. This weakened with the NHS taking over church-affiliated institutions after 1948, although the relationship remains because of the support that continues to be provided by faith-based women's organisations such as the Mothers' Union and Muslim Women's Network UK. Faith and community have also been behind women's engagement in philanthropic work through organisations such as Christian Aid, World Vision, Muslim Hands and World Jewish Relief.

The social glue provided by religion has often taken the form of an enforcement of patriarchal morality, traditionally imagining women in domestic roles, expected to 'speak softly' and stay in the background. Religions have tended to censure cohabitation and childbirth outside marriage, to denounce equal rights to divorce and remarriage, abortion, the use of modern contraception, gay rights, and so on. However, religions have often preached radical departures from the cultural mores dominant at the time and see themselves as progressive. Over the last century, in some faiths and some denominations, a door has been opened for women in a leadership role. For example, The Right Reverend Libby Lane explained:

Being the first woman bishop in the Church of England is an extraordinary privilege, and (mostly) a great pleasure. I am very conscious of the debt of gratitude I owe to countless women and men who prayed and worked for decades, centuries, for such an appointment to happen. A call to ordained ministry is always a gift not a right, and my ministry is deeply rooted in gratitude to God that my response to Jesus' call to follow him has led me to this role. I have been joined very swiftly by other women appointed to be bishops (10 more in two and a half years), and I rejoice if my circumstances have contributed to their gifts being recognised.[112]

The relationship between women leaders and their male colleagues and their religious establishments can be difficult, however. As Faeeza puts it, in the context of Islam:

Patriarchal cultural norms appear to have plagued the development of the Islamic legal tradition, silencing the voices of Muslim women, and thus coming to be the source of the many injustices faced by Muslim women in their daily lives . . . While many Muslims proudly declare that 'Islam gave women their rights' denying Muslim women access to advanced religious knowledge and accepting them as authorities is rarely considered a denial of rights.[113]

The trends are far from being unidirectional. The global context in 2018 is both one of increased liberalism and of growing fundamentalism. Faith-based organisations have long been the location of significant support to women; however, religious spaces are no different from other areas of women's lives in being based on social hierarchies where women have had to fight for visibility and influence.

Conclusion

This chapter has covered cultural spaces and activities, taking us on numerous journeys through an eclectic set of topics. These have ranged from playgrounds to pubs, from magazines to feminist literature, from dance to sport, from women's organisations to religion – all critical areas in defining the place women occupy within society and having significant impacts on their lives.

There are numerous examples and stories even from early on in the century of women pushing through in all these areas. They are increasingly occupying cultural spaces and transforming them – representing feminism in action. However, in most parts of mainstream culture women have persistently been trying to catch up and to be allowed in. At the same time, they have always found ways of coming together formally and informally to provided support to each other, develop friendships and skills – adding a sprinkle of magic to their lives.

Culture: how did we do?

My score for the progress of women in culture
is 3.5 out of 5. What would yours be?

6

POWER

'Hope is a belief that what we do might matter, an understanding that the future is not yet written.' (Rebecca Solnit, American writer and activist)[1]

Power, the way women have fought to gain it in order to shape their own future and that of society more generally, is an underlying theme of this book. Bringing it all together in this last chapter, what factors do we need to look at, across sectors, to continue the march towards gender equality?

To answer this question the first point to put centre stage is the need for a clear understanding of the heterogeneity of women's experiences – another subtheme of this book. Women's experience is influenced by space and time, by age, health, family structure and reproductive status, sexuality, ethnicity and relative economic position, i.e. by intersectionality. Every individual experience is informed by and informs more structural systems of power and privilege.[2]

As can be seen in the spider diagram (Figure 14) I have developed, an individual's position in society is made up of many different axes of power or capital (which increase the further you go along the axis). The shaded area represents the self-assessed power basis of a hypothetical woman. The position of a person on a particular axis can be fixed for their lives – their colour for example – but most can change in their lifetime. Furthermore, many can be mutually reinforcing, for example education and wealth. There is no single unifying causal logic to all these axes; instead different power bases are at play perpetuating spheres of influence.

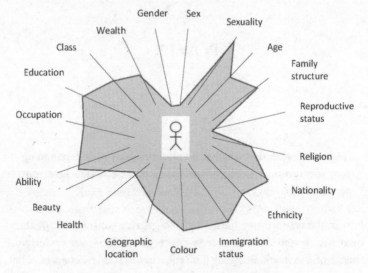

Figure 14: Privilege or personal capital map

A formative writer who tackled the subject of multiple discriminations was the black American feminist lesbian Audre Lorde, who wrote in 1980:

> Somewhere on the edge of consciousness, there is what I call a *mythical norm*, which each one of us within our hearts knows 'that is not me'. In America, [as in the UK,] this norm is usually defined as white, thin, male, young, heterosexual, Christian and financially secure. It is with this mythical norm that the trappings of power reside within this society. Those of us who stand outside that power often identify one way in which we are different, and we assume that to be the primary cause of all oppression, forgetting other distortions around difference, some of which we ourselves may be practising. By and large within the women's movement today, white women focus upon their oppression as women and ignore differences of race, sexual preference, class, and age. There is a pretence to a

homogeneity of experience covered by the word sisterhood that does not in fact exist. [. . .] Refusing to recognise difference makes it impossible to see the different problems and pitfalls facing us as women.[4]

Faeeza shared with me:

When I first moved to this country, I used to get asked at school by other Asian children, 'What are you?' I'd say I'm South African. They'd say, 'No – but what are your parents . . .?' I'd say, they're South African. Then they'd say, 'No, no – what language do you speak at home?' I'd say English. Eventually . . . we'd conclude with, 'Oh, so your grandparent was from India – you're Indian!' Yet I now also consider myself a Brummie [from Birmingham]. I believe that this tendency to categorise people in singular norms is our biggest hindrance to accepting diversity. Even the Queen of England has another national heritage, and she is the pinnacle of 'Britishness'.[5]

An intersectionality lens requires the negotiation of difference and an acknowledgement of relational thinking. It also requires a valuation of all that it is to be human – with its variations, fluidity and beauty and shows how no one axis is necessarily and immutably more important as a determining factor in experiences of power or powerlessness than others.

Does that mean that in my focus on women I have been wasting my time writing this book, and that you have been wasting yours reading it? Clearly, I think not. But we must understand how that one axis relates to others and therefore bring out not just the common factors but also the differences between women's lives. What the intersectional approach also highlights is that when we are looking to reduce discrimination, we need to think about how some sources of power or oppression are more visible than others and how they can change over time. More fundamentally still, it calls for alliances across oppressions, because of our understanding of the costs of any type of discrimination, and the value we place on diversity.

Recognising intersections but focused on the common experiences of women, we must consolidate and keep moving forward. Mitch offers a particularly vivid warning:

> Change can sometimes be of the elastic band kind. You take the strain and stretch forward for progress. You begin to see real change, new motivations, a future. And then you ease the pressure – you tire, you're moved to a new post, vital funding is cut. And the elastic band does what it does best, snaps back to its original shape. You just can't let up the pressure, can't relax, can't ever believe the job is done. And that's the mistake feminists and feminist institutions make, believing that an issue is solved, and it's OK to take your eye off the ball.[6]

As I write this book it feels like the band is snapping back. There are threats to progress, the shrinking of support to women funded by the welfare state, and a worrying global context emerging. Fundamentalism is on the rise, a force that is by definition a threat to intersectional feminism. Many of the gains of the modern world, including the internet, are also expanding vulnerabilities.

To continue to push the feminist agenda, despite the setbacks, we need to reflect on how change happens. A simple conceptual framework I have borrowed from my work at CARE International involves thinking about three strands that need to be woven together as tightly as possible. These are first, institutional or structural aspects, second, the actions of individuals, i.e. individual and collective agency and, third, what is happening to social norms, that is the views of society as a whole. I will argue that it is the last of these that, at this point in time, needs the most attention.[7]

Institutional/Structural Change

Structural or institutional change, although pivotal, does not happen on its own. Laws and policies are hewn by individuals who negotiate them within their organisations and in the context of the dominant views around them. In Chapter 1 we saw how the political structures in our democracy generally provide brakes rather than engines to feminist transformation. Overall, the problem has been that the caretakers of structural change have been traditionalists who reflect rather than challenge privilege. Nevertheless, structures and institutions have played a critical role in protecting gender equality, and now and again they have been ahead of the game. Without, for example, legislative safeguards to protect the rights gained so far, progress would be fragile at best.

Agency and Feminism

Individuals, or groups of individuals, provide the source from which change has always sprung. Yet at its core the whole problem of gender inequality has stemmed from the fact that society has quashed women's agency and prescribed where it should be directed. As Pauline put it:

> When we were young, 50 years ago, we got married, had children, that's just what happened, we didn't look into the future, we didn't have personal aspirations or expectations about what we would do for ourselves, our only role was support to our husbands and our children.[8]

Most women in the UK today have much more freedom to shape their own lives. This freedom is the result of feminist activism in the public sphere but also at home. Ann Feloy reflected:

> I have always been a feminist, although probably not consciously until the age of about 15. I have no doubt this was because of my

mother and grandmother, for both of whom the words 'fearless' and 'undaunted' spring to mind. It never occurred to me that women couldn't do anything they wanted to do or be anything they wanted to be.[9]

Women's agency is what feminism is all about. That is why we should refuse to let the F-word be hijacked as a negative one – just as the WSPU members refused the belittling implied by the suffragette label, and embraced the term as a badge of honour. Moreover, we must not 'rarefy' the badge and make it an impossible standard to live up to, or one that cultivates a puritanical hierarchy. Instead we need to value our diversity and our very different histories and experiences, accepting that we do not have the same view on everything, that we all carry paradoxes within us because we are formed by and reflect the society we live in. As Professor Mary Evans put it: 'We are all porous.'[10] For Helena Kennedy, QC:

> I maintained a visceral pleasure in dressing up. I loved lipstick and mascara, high heels and push-up bras, nail polish and scent. No political movement was going to inhibit my desire to make life glamorous, or my sensuous enjoyment of things that felt good, even if produced by corporate capitalism. Contradictions were the stuff of life.[11]

In my case, my heritage had a dominant influence, seeping through my veins and colouring all aspects of my persona and my life. However, I am as full of contradictions as any other woman. Irony of ironies, I hate confrontation – despite a consciousness of how little would change without these – and I am very partial to rom-coms, knowing how problematic the storylines are yet happy to enjoy them nonetheless.

Feminism has to be more welcoming of all our contradictions, a home for those on the left or the right or those more comfortable in alternative politics, and for those not interested in political feminism at all, but more in the feminism of personal and working lives and in the challenge to culture norms. It also needs to be relevant to and embrace the young and old, the privileged and the marginalised.[12] And, crucially, it must be open to men as well as to women.

In 2015, CARE Norway produced a short YouTube video that went viral entitled *Dear Daddy* in which an unborn girl tells her father about the dangers she is going to experience, not from lions or wild animals, but from boys and men no different from himself and his friends. It highlights the insidious nature of seemingly harmful 'locker room banter' and its impact on our wider culture. Progress across all aspects of women's rights will continue to falter without men's agency in challenging sexism and identifying as feminists.

Current influential British role models include the tennis player Andy Murray, speaking up for women and challenging conscious and unconscious sexism, time and time, and time again, and Sadiq Khan, the Mayor of London from 2016, who declared:

> As Mayor, I have vowed to be a proud feminist at City Hall, and I will do all I can to remove any barriers to women. Equal rights is not just a fight for women – all of us need to stand in solidarity with our mothers, sisters, daughters and friends to say that discrimination, in all shapes and forms, will not be tolerated.[13]

These words have been backed up with action, including the first-ever pay audit of City Hall, bans on body-shaming advertisements, and involvement in activism to help change attitudes.

Activism and agency have a ripple effect – creating visibility, leadership and collective power. Globally, more than 5 million people are thought to have marched on 21 January 2017, the day after American President Donald Trump was inaugurated. An estimated 100,000 joined the London Women's March, with many other events up and down the country.[14] In Edinburgh, it was a sixteen-year-old girl who organised the event; in London, three women who had never organised a campaign before. The story of feet on the ground, marching as of old, was repeated in over 130 countries.

Banners, placards and other products encapsulated the argument. They included 'Women's Rights are Human Rights', 'I cannot believe we still have to fight this shit', 'Different century same problem', 'Trump is what happens when people would rather believe the worst rumours about a woman than the worst facts about a man', and 'Hands off my human rights and my pussy for that matter'. Some wore pink woollen hats with small ears, so-called pussy power hats – already preserved for history in the V&A collection – in defiant reference to Donald Trump bragging about his sexual conquests and his infamous 'grab them by the pussy' comment. The diversity of those marching was in evidence, as was the backlash, with insults and comments such as 'go back into the kitchen'.[15]

Social Norms

Social norms are the third aspect of the change framework and the one I feel we need to focus on most. They are the expected behaviours, the shared beliefs about others that influence us, the invisible power at a societal level that maps out how people think, speak and behave. Norms are steered by individuals and groups who maintain them by sanctioning those that stray and approving of those that comply. These may be family, friends, neighbours and colleagues, as well as more distant powerful figures. Theorists have argued that social norms can be 'sticky', in that they don't change easily, but can 'bend' and 'relax'. Norms are not natural and timeless but situational, they occur within contexts that sustain them but can also be challenged and are subject to tipping points.[16] In the struggle between continuity and change what happens is that more radical ideas and counter-norms, if successful, *become* the customary way.

The battle can be seen when we look at attitudes towards masculine and feminine identities. For the most part, society has adopted a simple masculine and feminine polarity. However, in his study of psychoanalysis, Sigmund Freud was already a century and a half ago identifying contradictions and layers cross-cutting the simple male / female polarity – though with a value-laden approach that was anything but positive about the feminine.

Since then, the concepts of femininity and masculinity have evolved, with a growing recognition of the toxicity of some forms of extreme masculinity associated with showing-off, risk-taking behaviour, fighting, alcohol and promiscuity, a laddish subculture of doing things 'just for a laugh'.[17]

The costs to men of the current framing of dichotomised identities, the crisis of masculinity, has involved violence by men, including on other men and boys, getting into trouble with the police, the pattern of few men having close friends they can turn to, the difficulties they have expressing their feelings, the disproportionately high rates of male suicide, concerns about boys switching off from school.[18] The idea that 'patriarchy hurts men too' is growing.[19]

Although there is no talk of a 'crisis of femininity' to parallel men's, maybe there should be given the unrelenting and dangerous sexualisation of young girls and the image-focused valuing of women.

Extremes of femininity and masculinity are still very current, but the middle ground is expanding. Moreover, the LGBTQIA movement is forcing a rethink not just about masculinity and femininity but also the relationships between biology, gender and sexuality. Evolutionary biology, hormone behaviour science, neuroscience and psychology all increasingly point to individuals operating within a spectrum rather than discrete boxes.[20]

Similarly, ethnicity, race and religion are increasingly blended by intermarriage; families are constituted and reconstituted in more varied formats. Age itself is understood differently over time, given that the age of puberty has been changing and people's longevity is redefining the customary phases in life. Although the gap between the poorest and richest has increased rather than narrowed, in many contexts class as a social construct is no longer as rigid and self-defining. In summary, social norms are shifting, there are no longer simple patterns of socially expected behaviours linked to simple identities, and hierarchical absolutes are being challenged by increasing fluidity.

Case Studies

I have argued that institutional structures, agency and social norms are at work and need to move forward the feminist agenda. But how do these three relate to each other? To explore this question I have looked at five very different examples.

Case 1. Female Crime Writers and War Correspondents

Isn't it slightly odd, from everything discussed so far, that women have featured so centrally in the genre of crime writing? It is not an obvious niche, and yet we have had the literature of the golden age of the 'Queens of Crime'. The best-selling author of all time, Agatha Christie, wrote eighty-five books and sold over 2 billion worldwide.[21] Other household names are Dorothy L. Sayers, Margery Allingham, P. D. James, Ruth Rendell, Martina Cole and Kate Atkinson. More recently, Paula Hawkins wrote the very successful *Girl on the Train*, which epitomises the development of complex, sometimes flawed, central female characters in domestic dramas. Explanations for their popularity include the suggestion that women writers are good at narrating complex emotions because of their socialisation in emotional intelligence, and that dark and violent worlds are ones that they have experience or fear of as women. The large female readership of gory crime novels has also been explained in terms of women feeling safe in the hands of female crime writers who – unlike in real life – will ensure retribution and closure.[22]

A similarly unexpected niche is in war journalism. The 'scoop of the century' was the name given to Clare Hollingworth's report on the build-up of German tanks on the Polish border in 1939 at the beginning of the Second World War. According to John Simpson, Hollingworth was the first and the last person to interview the Shah of Iran for British newspapers, being 'the only person he wanted to speak to'.[23] She was followed by many other foreign correspondents known for reporting in war zones, such as Martha Gellhorn, daughter of an American suffragist, whose husband Ernest Hemingway famously enquired, 'Are you a war correspondent, or wife in my bed?'[24] Gellhorn was followed by Audrey Russell, the first accredited war reporter, Kate Adie, Christina Lamb, Orla Guerin, Maggie O'Kane, Alex Crawford, Lindsey Hilsum and Lyse Doucet, among others.

Despite the obvious dangers involved – the military context that would traditionally exclude women – the concept of women war correspondents has become normalised. In 2009, the *Sunday Times* war correspondent Marie Colvin wrote a blog about women in journalism entitled 'Courage Knows No Gender'. In it she reflected:

> Women, I think, tend to try harder to understand what is really happening to people on the ground. They are less inclined to settle for writing an analysis of a situation and leaving it at that . . . This is a huge generalisation, and by no means always true, but writing about the 'big picture' seems to carry a certain prestige that, to me, often misses the point of journalism.
>
> I remember talking to a male colleague after writing a story about a man whose wife and five young children had been executed by the Serbs. It didn't seem enough for me to simply report on his loss. I sat for hours with him, by their grave on a river bank, staring at a bloody and bullet-ridden romper suit, listening to his memories and his guilt.
>
> My colleague mused that he simply would not have stopped. 'There would have been other things to do that day, a briefing, whatever, more important or not. I would have written down his details and moved on.'

Why? That's hard to work out. From experience, I know men think differently from women, but since I've never been able to figure out their behaviour in other walks of life, I find it just as impossible to explain why they think differently in wars . . . Gellhorn said it best describing her 40 years of reporting wars. 'Beware of the Big Picture,' she wrote. 'The Big Picture always exists. And I seem to have spent my life observing how desperately the Big Picture affects the "little people" who did not devise it and have no control over it.'

There is probably a darker side to all this. Fewer women than men become foreign correspondents, and even fewer cover wars. Those of us who do are probably more driven than most, simply because it is harder to succeed. Maybe we feel the need to test ourselves more, to see how much we can take and survive.[25]

Marie Colvin's article presents someone grappling with the ideas around difference – in outlook and motivation, differences that are not necessarily universal and fixed, but that are relevant nonetheless. She had been injured and lost an eye in Sri Lanka in 2001, but carried on with her work and was subsequently killed in Syria in 2012.[26] Despite the odds, individual war correspondents have created a norm, and at least from the outside it appears as if the institutions they work for have accepted that women bring a useful perspective even to the most brutish male dominated of terrains.

Case 2. Work and Care

We saw in Chapter 2 how government policies *vis-à-vis* care have been erratic over time, but also how there is a growing realisation of the need for better institutional engagement to support families, and at the same time a need for attitudinal change. As Fiona reflected:

Now I'm in my thirties, I see my female friends being divided into those who choose to have a family and those who choose a career, and they look down on each other for their decisions. I also work with women who are under so much pressure to do both, 'to do it all' but no one has defined what 'it all' is and how to do it. To a certain extent, I feel it's a discrimination we have created ourselves, so it's up to us to tear it down. My hope for the future is that people – men and women – will stop judging each other and start supporting each other in whatever they decide.[27]

The associative link between women and care and men paid to do 'important work' is an underlying factor behind ongoing inequality. Breaking the link would be transformative. For a number of reasons, now is a conducive time to do this. First, most women are now in paid employment, so the demand for better childcare and more flexible work is greater than ever before. Second, female and male employment are increasingly precarious, resulting in a need to renegotiate who does what. Third, social norms about who can parent, and how that links to masculinity, are shifting. Fourth, increased connectivity in work and care makes the juggling easier. Finally, and most importantly, there is a better understanding of the economic and social costs of the current situation – to individuals, families, employers and society in general. Some families are managing the balance better than before; others are sinking, from poverty, stress and/or unfulfilled potential. The pace of change is much too slow and needs intensified feminist activism.

Case 3. Heels, Make-up and Clothes at Work

Nicola Thorp, aged twenty-seven, signed up to work as a temporary receptionist through an agency in 2016. When she got to the agency they told her to go back home and change her shoes from flats to 2- to 4-inch heels. She explained:

If they could give me a reason why wearing flats would impair me to do my job, then fair enough, but they couldn't. I was just expected to do a nine-hour shift on my feet escorting clients to meeting rooms. I said I just won't be able to do that in heels and was laughed at for challenging the policy and sent home without pay.[28]

She decided to set up a petition – to see whether others would share her sense of indignation. The petition stated:

It's still legal in the UK for a company to require female members of staff to wear high heels at work against their will. Dress code laws should be changed so that women have the option to wear flat formal shoes at work, if they wish. Current formal work dress codes are out-dated and sexist.[29]

The petition was an immediate hit, with more than 69,000 signatures within three days and more than 150,000 in a few months.[30] The government's response included the statement that:

Employers should not be discriminating against women in what they require them to wear. The Government takes this issue very seriously and will continue to work hard to ensure women are not discriminated against in the workplace by outdated attitudes and practices.[31]

Under the law, as at 2017, legal redress was possible because having to wear high heels could be claimed as unfair and therefore a form of indirect discrimination. However, it was found that companies could argue that women wearing heels is reasonably justified in pursuit of a legitimate aim, and quite what this aim was did not need to be defined in practice. The joint Petitions and Women and Equalities Committee therefore concluded that the Equality Act 2010 was not yet fully effective in protecting workers and advised a review of the law. It recommended that the government introduce guidance targeted at employers, workers and students, to improve understanding of the law and workers' rights.[32] The committee has, for now, stopped short of enforcing any legal change.

The anecdotes provided during the hearings provide a glimpse of the social norm around high heels and, connected to this, obligations to wear make-up at work and the cost to women. Chloe reported:

> At an iconic Knightsbridge luxury department store it is in the company handbook that women must wear high heels and makeup . . . it wasn't unheard of for girls to be found crying on the shop floor after being insulted by management for not wearing enough makeup or scolded for trying to sneak flat shoes on behind their counters. It was expected that we would wear high heels whilst taking trips to the sub-basement to bring up pushchairs and small items of furniture for customers as well as whilst demonstrating the pushchairs.[33]

Jasmine explained:

> I came in one morning and my manager [female] was cracking down on uniform and informed me that I had to look 'sexy', which entailed wearing heels. I was 20 at the time and quite uncomfortable with this requirement; smart or sophisticated I could understand but 'sexy' seemed pretty inappropriate.[34]

Rationally, it seems unbelievable that in the twenty-first century women's comfort and well-being is not considered to be as important as their decorative value at work. However, as we saw in Chapter 3, the situation is complicated by the fact that almost all women find themselves complicit in accepting some elements of pain for the sake of beauty.

Case 4. 'No More Page 3' and Giving Lads' Mags the Boot

'No More Page 3', run by Lucy-Anne Holmes between 2012 and 2015, was a petition to stop the *Sun* newspaper displaying topless women in provocative poses, something it had been doing daily since 1970. It was partially successful in that page 3 women now wear a bikini top. The campaign built on previous initiatives, including by Clare Short MP in the 1980s. It gained nearly 250,000 signatures and endorsement from over sixty organisations and numerous celebrities. The Green MP Caroline Lucas wore a 'No More Page Three' T-shirt in Parliament, until told to cover it because of protocol, which she did, but not before pointing out the irony of her T-shirt being inappropriate yet it being considered acceptable to be able to buy the *Sun* in eight places in the Palace of Westminster. Lucy-Anne reflected:

> If I think about the two and a half years I spent working on the No More Page 3 campaign . . . I realize that an awful lot of that time was spent with an 'I'm on the edge of my comfort zone' knot in the belly.
>
> . . . Yet despite all this it will always be one of the most wonderful and remarkable times in my life . . . We were doing it really for the women coming after us: we wanted a society for them that was a little bit safer, kinder and more respectful than it had been for us. Our belief in what we were doing united and fuelled us, and there was such magic in that, and in the silliness, the creativity, the confidence we gave each other and the vulnerability we shared.[35]

Another campaign, in 2013, involved Object and UK Feminista against the supermarkets' sale of pornographic 'lads' mags' *Nuts* and *Zoo*, including to young boys. On the one hand was the right to produce, advertise, sell and buy magazines; on the other a desire by feminists to challenge society – to reject the normalisation of such material. The campaign involved demonstrations, for example at

Tesco supermarkets selling the magazines. Tesco shareholders were targeted at their AGM and top executives lobbied through the Twitter handle #losetheladsmags. I wrote a blog for the *Huffington Post*, arguing:

> The fact that Tesco currently stocks misogynistic lads' mags sends out the deeply dangerous message that it is normal and acceptable to treat women like dehumanised sex objects. But it would be so easy to change this. Tesco's eleven Board members – only 3 of whom are women – and seventeen Executive Committee members – also only 3 of whom are women – can demonstrate that the firm's claim to be a 'responsible corporate citizen' aren't just hollow words: that they do in fact care about the safety of their female customers. They can do this by announcing that Tesco is going to lose the lads' mags.[36]

Within days of the campaign's launch, Tesco met the organisers and, in a few months, they introduced a minimum age for buying the magazines. Meanwhile, the Co-op decided to stop selling the publications in all its 4,000 stores. After a couple of years the magazines went out of business, heralding the end of 'lads' mags'.[37]

Although the success needs to be celebrated, female objectification is still around. The more upmarket, more institutionally powerful American *Playboy* magazine continues to be sold in the UK. It had pledged to stop showing nude female images but reversed the decision in February 2017, emboldened perhaps by the low tide of Donald Trump's election, and it thrives underground and online. Increasingly realistic sex dolls – reflecting for the most part idealised female images – have also taken the objectification to a new level. They might well serve a purpose in relieving loneliness and sexual frustration, but the global interest in the dolls within the existing unequal and exploitative context is disturbing.

There is a danger in feeling that the 'Lose the Lads' Mags' and the

'No More Page 3' campaigns won the battle, but lost the war, given the proliferation of images degrading women and paving the way for abuse in the sex industry. As Kat Banyard puts it:

> Attitude shift . . . society collectively drawing a line in the sand that says to men and boys: when you have sex with someone, they should want to have sex with you. It's not a lofty ask, but a rock bottom requirement. It's simply not good enough that she wants a drug fix – which you are effectively willing to finance if she agrees to have sex with you. It's not good enough that she is in debt to her trafficker or that she feels she has few other options. Handing over cash in order to get someone to agree to your sexual demands is sexual exploitation and society won't stand by idly while you do it, much less license commercial venues dedicated to facilitating this abuse.[38]

The line in the sand still needs to be drawn.

Case 5. The Tampon Tax

The final example concerns the social media campaign against taxation of menstrual hygiene products – a tax on being a woman. The argument is that these products are a necessity, and should be tax-exempt like other necessities, such as incontinence products and even a rather bizarre set of products including crocodile meat, razors and Jaffa Cakes.[39] Tampons began to be taxed in the UK in 1973 when the UK joined the EU and adopted a common approach to taxes. After years of campaigning, the rate of taxation for these products was dropped to 5 per cent in 2001 but campaigners wanted it at zero. In 2015, Charlie Edge and Ruth Howarth wore stained white trousers in front of the Houses of Parliament and a Change.org petition set up by Laura Coryton was signed by 320,000 people forcing a debate in Parliament, which was narrowly lost.[40] However, in an attempt to mollify protestors, the Chancellor agreed to allocate the tax revenue, some £15 million a year, to support women's aid programmes.

The British government then raised the matter at the EU where, in 2016, member states made an unprecedented and unanimous decision to grant tampon taxation flexibility. The UK subsequently axed the tax and it is expected that this will also happen in other countries.[41] Throughout, the campaign was subjected to ridicule and hate messaging.

What is intriguing is that it was not the overall cost of the menstrual hygiene products themselves and the manufacturers that were the target of the campaign – although the costs and the practical burden are significant, particularly for vulnerable poor girls and women.[42] Menstrual products are therefore increasingly added to food banks. The economic impact of the tax itself on individual women is relatively small – an estimated £5.72 a year.[43] However, the tampon-tax campaign touched a collective nerve – the aggregated injustice of having to pay a tax to the government for being a woman. It also showed a willingness to bring to public attention something that is a taboo – millions of women's regular unspoken pain, which they are expected to bear, and pay for, in silence. It has triggered other initiatives, including, in 2018, legislation towards free menstrual products in schools, colleges and universities across Scotland.[44]

A Pathway

The task ahead is for all of us to keep chipping away, addressing the different layers and locations of discrimination. I offer up ten suggestions of how to go about affecting change.

1 Strengthen links between institutional change, agency and social norms. For example, through launching government petitions together with other activism to exert targeted pressure for legal and other forms of institutional change. It is by looking at how campaigns can consider all three elements and build links between them that we can foster a powerful, growing and resilient feminist ecosystem.

2 Be a feminist. A feminist in words and deeds. Role model the change you want to see. Support the actions of others but also initiate your own. This could be through Cyberfeminism. Globally, over 700,000 women have started petitions on Change.org; 61 per cent of shares and 56 per cent of comments come from women. In 2016, they accounted for seven of the ten largest petitions and received over 1.5 million signatures.[45] Change.org's UK director, Brie Rogers Lowery, reflected:

Millions of women and girls use Change.org to start bold campaigns calling for social change . . . Even where they are not yet represented adequately in traditional power chambers, they are able to get their voice heard and deliver results . . . people power is challenging not only the emerging women's rights issues today, but [maintaining] the importance of women's achievements throughout history.[46]

The website provides useful information about how to develop campaigns. Lucy-Anne Holmes's booklet *How to Start a Revolution* also has brilliant tips.[47]

3 Get the data to tell the story. Information is still and will always be a powerful catalyst for change, despite the so-called post-truth era. For example, the WHO in 2013 called violence against women a 'global health problem of epidemic proportions'. Caroline Criado-Perez points out:

Epidemic is not a term that the WHO uses lightly. Governments have established procedures for dealing with epidemics . . . with the first step being the methodological gathering and analysis of data. If this were any other kind of epidemic, we'd have found a cure by now – If this were any other kind of epidemic, we'd at least have started counting.[48]

4 Build alliances and check our privileges. Alliances should not just be with the like-minded – the more unlikely the ally, the more powerful the alliance. Adapting the spider diagram from page 260 could be a useful way to reflect on likely biases, individually and collectively.

5 Make the invisible visible, the undervalued valued and the implicit explicit. This includes changing the lens through which we view the world, by making visible the hard graft in the domestic sphere, reassessing the valuation of different types of paid work, in general calling out biases and not accepting an injustice because it has always been thus. And nothing is too small to be dismissed; call out discrimination whenever and wherever it pops up.

6 Engage with the mainstream and disinterested and not just the converted who might be on the margins. Problematic traditions are sometimes sustained by default, not by intent, by those who quietly go along rather than stand up against them. This is not to say that there is no 'patriarchal dividend',[49] rather that addressing gender inequality is not a zero-sum game and that the 'patriarchal cost' of the status quo is not yet articulated strongly enough. The crushing of women is often not done for a gain, but is done nevertheless. Getting buy-in from all those who want to be on the right side of history is part of the battle.

7 Strategy is key as is being adaptable and opportunistic. Any feminist initiative needs a vision, a change objective as well as answers to questions about the campaign such as why, what, when, who, how, where and how much. Of all of these, often the most powerful question comes from drilling down repeatedly with 'why' – to keep delving deeper and deeper and thereby strengthen the thinking around the campaign.

8 The media and social media need to be at the heart of initiatives because they are part of the solution as well as part of the problem. We increasingly live in a world in which images, slogans, short messages and the endorsement of celebrities are gold dust. Communication through the media and social media is therefore increasingly pivotal – it is the connector between institutions, agency and norm change. However, media and social-media attention are not sufficient for change to happen and, if not managed, can detract and divert rather than amplify a cause.

9 Increasingly we have the power of numbers. As feminists, we are numerically and proportionally a greater potential force than ever before. We are everywhere, tackling discrimination in millions of different ways. Let's enjoy that sense of community and purpose, full of dynamism and, yes, difference of opinion. Let's appreciate and learn from those who campaigned to get us to this point, and from the youngsters ready to take up the baton.

10 Bring persistence, courage and lateral thinking to the table. There is an Ethiopian proverb that goes 'slowly, slowly, the egg walks', meaning that with patience and perseverance, amazing things happen.

It is time gender inequality is acknowledged as the harmful, wasteful practice it is. A practice well past its sell-by date, and which should be prevented from continuing to damage society. The American historian and activist Rebecca Solnit wrote that giving up hope is not an option:

> . . . I use the term hope because it navigates a way forward between the false certainties of optimism and of pessimism, and the complacency or passivity that goes with both. Optimism assumes that all will go well without our effort; pessimism assumes it's all irredeemable . . . Hope for me has meant a sense that the future is unpredictable, and that we

don't actually know what will happen, but know we may be able to write it ourselves.

Hope is a belief that what we do might matter, an understanding that the future is not yet written. It's informed, astute open-mindedness about what can happen and what role we may play in it. Hope looks forward, but it draws its energies from the past, from knowing histories, including our victories, and their complexities and imperfections.[50]

I hope and believe that the solidarity and fearless optimism of the suffragettes will keep driving us on; that sooner rather than later, discrimination against women will be consigned to the history books. We have work to do.

Figure 15: Hebe Gumbleton and Scarlett Haniffa at CARE's
International Women's Day March 2015, © CARE International

HOW DID WE DO?

'My grandmother was a lady
My mother was one of the girls
I am a woman
My daughter is a doctor'
(Doreen Thakoordin)[1]

Writing about the experiences of half the population of Great Britain over a century in a few hundred pages has been fascinating but also painful – in no small part because I had to exclude so many voices and themes, in the interest of keeping the book to an almost acceptable length. The distillation needed to conclude is even tougher.

We can say, unequivocally, that social, economic, political, cultural and technological changes have all contributed to a society in which women's lives are generally better than those of our mothers, grandmothers or great-grandmothers. For most women, it's a kinder, less cruel world.

However, on the centenary of what was only a partial right for women to vote, the assessment is that we have made important but incomplete gains since then. Moreover, this is not a simple trajectory of progress or of stasis, but of constant evolution, reversals and change experienced differently for a multitude of reasons. In every substantive area there is more to be done.

The main trends include a greater variation in the arc of women's lives, reduced formality and greater diversity. Ailish's street in a small town in Hertfordshire might be unusual, but it is a microcosm of twenty-first-century reality. As she explained:

Sandra and I are a white same sex couple, myself Irish born and my civil partner born in England with Scottish and Italian parents. We are in our fifties and have a young Kenyan-British man with dreadlocks living with us at the moment. Next door a very conservative Christian, across the road a Thai woman with a child from a previous marriage and her British partner. Next to them is someone transitioning to a woman and on the other side a very traditional British woman, who has lived in the street since the 1960s. Initially hesitantly but increasingly with gusto, she is adapting to all the diversity around her. On hearing of a new arrival, she bakes them scones and turns up to greet them, making friends of newcomers to the street, whatever their background.[2]

Politically we have gone from the first time women could vote to almost within touching distance of a representation that counts as critical mass. Furthermore, this applies to most of the institutions of our democracy. Yet the sense that women are usurpers of the public sphere still lurks in the shadows. Minister for International Development, Penny Mordaunt, for example, has argued that there are still people who struggle to comprehend the notion of a woman being in charge: 'I do believe, though, that society at large regards such views as outmoded, and in the case of abuse directed at female MPs and others, deserving of censure.'[3]

Nevertheless, obstacles for the political woman abound and feminist policies are far from being embedded in the establishment. In the conclusion to Chapter 1 on politics I opted for 3 out of 5 as a fair summary. Going forward, Justine Greening, Minister for Women and Equalities, reflected:

As we celebrate the centenary of women's suffrage, this is our opportunity to reignite the campaign for equality fought 100 years ago. Our Parliament is most effective when it reflects the society it has been elected to represent. We cannot just wait for equality to happen, we need to push for a 50:50 Parliament. Our society and democracy will be richer for it.[4]

Women's economic opportunities have expanded massively, creating ripples of power and visibility. Women now make up almost half the paid workforce and income differences have narrowed. However, poverty still wears a female face and female employment is particularly precarious. Furthermore, women's potential economic power has been restricted by other forms of inequality – particularly by the structures and expectations within the family, with employers and the state perpetuating women's secondary status. Overall, I scored Chapter 2 on economics another 3 out of 5.

The widening in women's autonomy and control over their fertility and sexuality has transformed women's lives. For most, their domestic roles still dominate, but women have much more control over who and when to marry and whether or not to have children. The trans movement is also shaking up simple gender and sexual binaries. However, the obsession with how a woman looks still continues to diminish her horizons. Health and wellbeing are gendered and women's concerns too often swept under the carpet. Chapter 3 on women's personal lives I initially scored a generous 4 out of 5, however, based on thousands of conversations throughout 2018, I took this right back to a 2.5.

Violence against women is still omnipresent. Although covered in Chapter 4 of this book, it has seeped into every other chapter. The legal framework to address violence has become more responsive, yet almost all women at one point or another experience abuse, and for some it is a prison they cannot escape from. The intrusion of sexual images, the threat of misogynistic abuse and the objectification of women fuelled by the sex industry has greater impact than ever before. Meanwhile conflict on a larger scale, with all the testosterone-driven rhetoric and practice, has a habit of flaring up and a feminist alternative vision barely exists. For Chapter 4 on violence, I could only give 1 out of 5.

Jude Kelly reflected:

> If women's life stories are seen to be purely domestic, purely romantic, they cannot be seen to contribute to world thinking, even though the domestic and romantic are world thinking too – so when a man writes about love it's an existential examination; when a woman writes about love it's a personal, romantic, sentimental journey. This is one example of a pattern in the way we value men and women differently. Yet the experiences that women have, including their knowledge of inequality, is one that can make the world a much better one for all. We need to get to a place where women can bring that knowledge of systemic injustice and a different perspective into the centre of our society – into the centre of influence.[5]

The cultural and social spaces women occupy and their engagement in the written and physical world has a very chequered story and yet one where there is clearly a pattern of women's visibility increasing significantly. Furthermore, social media has, over the last two decades, exponentially increased access to cultural spaces and contributed to the age of transparency but at great cost in flaming opportunities for aggression. Meanwhile, women have always found ways of fostering their own networks and interests, and continue to do so. Chapter 5 I gave 3.5 out of 5 for progress.

Adding up the scores for the five main thematic chapters, we end up with an average of 2.6 out of 5: progress indeed, but a suggestion that we are only just past the half-way mark, not a result to be particularly proud of and that is without even considering whether our expectations should not be much, much higher, given the hundred year timeframe. Although some of the more overt and blatant biases have gone, the drip drip of gender bias continues to infiltrate our lives in a cumulative way, creating an all-pervasive and relentless culture of inequality and socialised sexism. Some women might occasionally escape the worst of this, depending on particular privileges and even luck; they might be under the illusion they are treated equally, but fortunate indeed are those untouched by gender discrimination over the course of their lives.

This is also why, decade after decade, what we have seen is the continuity, the similarity in women's lives. The need for resilience and the central role of family, of friendships and health. The desire for a political voice, for economic and personal security, for cultural spaces and social value.

In terms of the feminist trinity of objectives, progress has been primarily in terms of equality and to a lesser extent acknowledgement of difference, with fewer examples of women being given the space to transform the agenda for society as a whole.

Turning to the future, in Chapter 6 we saw how we need to strengthen the ecosystem by looking at the links between institutions, agency and social norms, paying particular attention to the last of these. At the same time, we need to be more sensitive to the structural basis of power and privilege and the need for individual and collective defiance of discriminatory traditions that weigh society down.

Although this book focused on the UK looking at women's lives framed in terms of a British Act in 1918, feminism does not start or stop on our shores. We are interlinked through migration and family ties, and face many of the same opportunities and risks in terms of cultural influences and our social norms. Our experiences are also very similar, as I found out during discussions about the findings of the book in a number of other countries including Ireland, France, Germany, Vietnam, Ethiopia and the United States.

The title of this book is the suffragette slogan *Deeds Not Words*, and their legacy has been a golden thread running through the book. There are those who dislike the saying, arguing that what was required then and still today is both deeds and words – that the two are intertwined. This is true but the expression draws attention to the need for activism – that words on their own are not enough. We must walk the talk.

There is a great yearning for deeds that will create fairness. As twelve-year-old Olivia explained: 'I'm on our School Council and help to make decisions about what's best. I would not be happy if only the boys could be on the Council and not the girls. The boys don't always think about what the girls want, so it would not be fair.'[6] Olivia is taking her first few important steps as an activist, clear in her mind that she has a role in ensuring that fairness prevails. With her generation in mind, and before the Epilogue, I would like to end this conclusion with a few words from the South African author Olive Schreiner. They may be familiar to you, from the film *Suffragette*:

And she stood far off on the bank of the river. And she said, 'For what do I go to this far land which no one has ever reached? Oh, I am alone! I am utterly alone!'

And Reason, [. . .] said to her, 'Silence! What do you hear?'

And she listened intently, and she said, 'I hear a sound of feet, a thousand times ten thousand and thousands of thousands, and they beat this way!'

[. . .] 'They are the feet of those that shall follow you. Lead on!'[7]

TO 2028 AND BEYOND

If the last hundred years have taught us anything, it is that there is no silver bullet. The goal of equality and social transformation still lies before us. We can expect some sliding backwards and it could well be that the second half of the journey will be particularly difficult. Many feminists were galvanised by centenary celebrations in 2018. We must build on the networks and the initiatives created rather than let the momentum slip away in the years to come. I would like to end with hopes and aspirations of women and girls over a ten-year horizon, to 2028, the centenary of equal franchise, when women were granted the right to vote on the same grounds as men.

Politics

The Isle of Man was the first country where women were given the vote. Having served in the island's parliament for over 30 years, my hope for 2028 is that country by country the appalling democratic deficit which is experienced by women and girls shrinks under the global spotlight. (Clare Christian, Manx politician who has had a range of roles including President of Tynwald)[1]

In 2018 and going forward we want to recognise the suffrage movement but also raise awareness that the work is not yet done – that equal representation in public life is still overdue and that we need to continue to knock down the barriers holding talented women back from fulfilling their potential, whether that be in

Parliament, in a boardroom or in a classroom. (Hilary Spencer, Director, Government Equalities Office)[2]

By 2028 I would like politics to be made for and by women and for this to be normal because all of our institutions understand that feminism is an essential bedrock of our democracy. I would like to see black and disabled and LGBT+ and older and young and refugee and working-class women in Parliament and the devolved governments and city regions and local councils, as MPs and mayors and council leaders, in equal numbers to men. And so, by 2028 voter turnout would be at record highs because finally we will be creating legislation and doing politics in a way that understands and represents the entire population instead of half of it. (Sophie Walker, Leader of the Women's Equality Party)[3]

As an elected MLA in the Northern Ireland Assembly I am very aware that legislative change happens slowly. By 2028 women will no longer be plagued by the 1861 law on forced pregnancy and birth and they will have full access to opportunities in all aspects of life that are so freely afforded to men. (Clare Bailey, Member of the Legislative Assembly in Northern Ireland, Deputy Leader, Green Party Northern Ireland)[4]

While great strides have been made since the battles fought by the suffragettes, our politics still do not reflect our society as a whole. No matter how daunting and impossible it looks, I urge every woman with an interest in politics to get involved; only with a wider engagement will our politics and our society flourish. Do something. Anything. Get involved. (Leanne Wood, AM, Leader of Plaid Cymru and Assembly Member for the Rhondda)[5]

By 2028 I would like to see much more transparency by political parties in who is being nominated, selected and put forward including for winnable seats. Greater transparency through enacting Section 106 of the Equality Act 2010, which sets this out, would provide necessary scrutiny and lead to increased diversity, and after 100 years this is well overdue. (Helene Reardon-Bond, OBE, former head of Gender Equality Policy and Inclusion at Government Equalities Office)[6]

Given the democratic deficit, I hope that compulsory voting is legislated for in the UK. I think that if the suffragettes were alive today that is what they would focus on with ever more engaging forms of direct action. (Philippa Bilton, Spokesperson and relative of Emily Wilding Davison)[7]

By 2028 I want to see a level playing field for women in political life. It is very often women who stand up to injustice first, then they bring others with them onto the front line to organise for more progressive social and economic change. Women will continue to empower other women. (Michelle O'Neill, Leader of Sinn Féin in the Northern Ireland Assembly)[8]

By 2028, I would like to see a Diplomatic Service that was truly representative and empathetic to all parts of British society that visibly contributed to the national and international debate with a strong interface with universities, business, media and the UK's regions and cities as well as having a strong international profile. I also hope that women UK Ambassadors will have been appointed to the most influential locations, including the US, the United Nations, France and Germany. (Dame Judith Macgregor, DCMG LVO diplomat, previously High Commissioner to South Africa)[9]

By 2028, I'd like to see a balance, even more women as current affairs and lobby journalists and more men in lifestyle journalism and for presenters to be of different ages (including old age), and colour. I'm also looking forward to the BBC appointing its first female Director General. (Victoria Derbyshire, journalist and broadcaster)[10]

By 2028 I would like to see the majority of world leaders and policy makers on issues affecting our global welfare be grandmothers, instead of grandfathers. (Anohni, transgender singer)[11]

I am the first Emily ever to be elected to the House of Commons. I hope that by 2028 there will be many more. I also hope that within Parliament a statue is erected to my namesake Emily Wilding Davison and to many other of the women's rights campaigners who have pushed open the gates, for us to follow through. (Emily Thornberry, Labour MP Member for Islington South and Finsbury and Shadow Foreign Secretary)[12]

Money

By 2028, I would like to see wide-ranging and successful attempts within the education system to nurture the potential of more marginalised girls, including working-class girls, girls from ethnic minority backgrounds, and Muslim girls. This kind of inclusive, intersectional approach will allow us to tap into the amazing power of all girls, building a fairer, more compassionate and more visionary society. (Dr Vanessa Ogden, CEO of Mulberry Schools Trust and headteacher of Mulberry School for Girls)[13]

By 2028, the Syrian crisis will be something of the past. I hope that the refugee girls who have made their home in the UK will have succeeded in their education. I also hope that, by then, refugee women and girls will be participating actively in British society, bringing out the best of British and Syrian cultures. The sum of these is greater than the parts and this will be more widely recognised than it is now. (Muzoon Almellehan, Syrian activist and refugee resettled in the UK)[14]

We won't think of a job as a male or a female job. (Fiona Martin, heritage officer, Luton Irish Forum)[15]

We will no longer have men doing high-quality jobs and women doing low-quality jobs; all genders should be able to do what they want when they get older. (Amber Lewis, aged twelve)[16]

My 2028 aspiration is universal income for all; that may encourage more men to also take up and share the parenting role. (Donna Basquille, part-time university administrator and grandmother)[17]

By 2028 I hope that employers will have stopped considering parenting as a woman's issue. That means we will have created family-friendly workplace environments that enable all parents to thrive at work and play their full part in the upbringing of their children. (Cherie Blair, barrister and QC)[18]

By 2028, we need to have changed the societal norm of women being the first call for a sick child. (Rosina, writer)[19]

Because of Brexit, well before we get to 2028, women need to get organised and strengthen networks across civil society and trade unions, both in the UK and across the EU, to keep an eye on legislative changes that will have a direct and indirect impact on women's rights in the UK. The rights of part-time workers and [those on] precarious contracts are especially at risk. In addition, proposed new European legislation to extend paternity, parental and carer's leave entitlements will not apply to the UK post Brexit. Future generations stand to lose out on these extended rights. As for women in the rest of the EU and EU nationals in the UK, these are also areas where we need to see activism so that women's rights in 2028 have significantly improved rather than stagnated or been curtailed. (Joanna Maycock, Secretary General of the European Women's Lobby)[20]

I would like to see some huge life-changing things invented by women engineers. Women definitely have the brains to invent things if they are given the opportunity. (Rhea Basra, aged twelve)[21]

I would like to see women participating equally in employee share plans and for companies to publish the take-up figures. (Janet Cooper, OBE, for Services to Equality, Women's Empowerment and Employee Share Ownership)[22]

I don't think anything illustrates the gender pay gap problem better than the BBC *Woman's Hour* presenters working on a programme designed to celebrate and promote women, their stories and their achievements. They were routinely paid less than the presenters of less successful but apparently more important shows. I sincerely hope this has been rectified by 2028! And: the women at the top of big organisations. Why do they adopt the stance of the patriarchy when they get there?? Is it because there aren't enough of them, and if there are more in a decade's time, will that have changed? Here's hoping. (Jane Garvey, radio presenter, currently of BBC Radio 4's *Woman's Hour*)[23]

Identity

I love being a woman and sometimes the concept of feminism can be misconstrued. By 2028 women will be celebrated for their differences and not exploited because of them. (Lesley Covington, full-time wife and mother and part-time Olympic suffragette)[24]

By 2028 I hope that women in politics are judged on their capabilities and positive contributions to society, and the days of being scrutinised and judged because of what we wear, what we weigh, and our personal circumstances are gone. (Nichola Mallon, Member of the Legislative Assembly in Northern Ireland, SDLP)[25]

All photo-shopped images should have a warning label as cigarettes do. (Jo Broughton, Press Officer, CARE International, #*March4Women* organiser)[26]

I long to see 'feminine hygiene' renamed in the supermarket aisles to stop reinforcing the idea that our bodies are naturally unhygienic. I long for an unshaven leg to be viewed in the same regard as a man's choice to have a beard. By 2028 I long for the day when we <u>all</u> ask ourselves, 'would I do or say this differently to a man?' (Helen Petrovna, actor)[27]

By 2028 I hope we break the stigma and social isolation for women suffering from postpartum psychosis by raising awareness and allowing their choice of recovery to be a pathway that makes them feel understood in society. I hope also that we will have closed the gap on pregnancy and banished maternity discrimination. (Marica Wainner, Mental Health Development & Wellbeing Worker in East London)[28]

By 2028, I would like to see *all* women in Britain – whoever we are and irrespective of all our diversities and our specific vulnerabilities, including those of us living with HIV – feel happy, healthy and safe, at home, in our communities, at work, and supported by a reinvigorated National Health Service, free at the point of care, valued, cherished, respected and funded by a fairer tax system. (Alice Welbourn, founding director of the Salamander Trust)[29]

I hope that by 2028 my daughter and her daughters, should they have illnesses such as endometriosis, or chronic fatigue syndrome or urinary tract infections, will be taken seriously and will receive expert treatment, rather than being trapped by assumptions that their problems are psychological. (Dr Kate Middleton, psychologist)[30]

Violence

By 2028, I hope that the casual dismissal of women's voices and experiences will have diminished. I hope that the normalisation of everyday sexism will have been eroded, so that people no longer ignore it when a woman is being harassed, turn the other way when they witness workplace discrimination, or dismiss a rape survivor's account with 'She was asking for it.' (Laura Bates, founder of the Everyday Sexism Project)[31]

Media sexism isn't funny. How people and groups of people are represented in the media goes a long way to determining how they are treated in the real world. By 2028 we want to see violence against women taken seriously in the press as crimes, not romps. We want perpetrators of violence against women and girls tried in the courts, not their victims objectified, and judged in the media. (Jo Harrison, No More Page 3 and Shape Your Culture)[32]

I would like to see police, health agencies and NGOs working even more closely together to provide safe places for victims of personal crimes to tell their story once, to provide forensic, health and counselling services, and to support them and their families with practical help. If we were really serious about this, we could keep many vulnerable women safe and substantially reduce – even eliminate – so-called 'domestic' murders by 2028. That really would be something to celebrate. (Judith Gillespie, CBE former Deputy Chief Constable of the Police Service of Northern Ireland)[33]

By 2028 I hope that we will have ended the practice of FGM both in the UK and globally. To do this we will have maintained a clear focus and had the necessary honest discussions about FGM in the wider context of the control over women's sexuality and their oppression. (Leyla Hussein, anti-FGM activist, co-founder of Daughters of Eve)[34]

By 2028 I hope that the Legal System, the Criminal Justice System and statutory support services will be totally aware of the lack of choice and control that women that are exploited have over their lives and life choices. That women who work in the sex industry are not seen as criminals and that they have the same rights as everyone else in society. (Claire Holcombe, Exit worker)[35]

By 2028 I would like to see the UK adopt an abolitionist law – which works to end the exploitation of women and girls through the sex trade. This law would criminalise paying for sex, decriminalise selling sex, and provide support and exiting services for people exploited through prostitution. By passing this law, we can send the message to a new generation that sexual consent cannot be bought, and create a world in which women and men can live as equals. (Kat Banyard, feminist campaigner and writer)[36]

By 2028 I suspect we will not have had the imagination to abolish prisons. Maybe the 'powers that be' will have digested the fact that our prisons are not fit for purpose: the purpose being to reduce the likelihood of re-offending by offering hope, opportunity and support to those who have 'served their time'. However, will we have managed to reduce the number of women in prison? Will we have abolished imprisonment for minor offences, and encouraged the use of suspended sentences or community-based penalties for others? Without strong political leadership, I fear not, I fear that we will still be keeping women in under-resourced prisons which exacerbate inequality and disadvantage. I hope I'm wrong. (Nicola Padfield, professor in Criminal and Penal Justice, University of Cambridge)[37]

I dream that by 2028 all women everywhere will be exercising all their rights. I fear this is unlikely, so I hope that, at the very least, governments and international agencies will have implemented the raft of women's rights commitments they have already agreed to: for women here in the UK, for women making their way to safety on perilous journeys, and for women living in abject poverty and conflict. (Hannah Bond, director of Gender Action for Peace and Security (GAPS))[38]

We face crises that threaten the very possibility of life on our planet and so it is difficult to be optimistic both about women's, and all humanity's, future. However, when looking ahead, the context will require recognition and support for the kinds of leadership that women within the environmental and peace movements have always shown. I hope therefore that by 2028 women will be continuing to do what they have always done – leading the environmental and peace movements – but more urgently and with more recognition than ever before. (Tamsin Omond, author, environmental activist and journalist)[39]

Culture

By 2028 I would dearly love the term 'manel' to be consigned to history's dustbin. The 'manel' or 'man panel', with no female representation, is sadly too prevalent in politics, academia, finance, media and the judiciary. Platforms of power ought to be fully representative and inclusive. Manel – eurch . . . it's such a stupid-sounding word for such a daft concept. (Anita Anand, radio and television presenter and journalist)[40]

Until the queues outside public toilets are the same for women and men there is no gender equality. I hope that by 2028, the problem will have been resolved – it's a simple enough indicator of whether women are welcome in society. (Elaine De Fries, Independent Domestic Violence Advocate and mother)[41]

By 2028, we would love to see the toy and children's media industry completely restructured. Retailers, manufacturers, licensors, publishers, TV programme makers and advertisers will have woken up to realising that boys and girls are not just one-dimensional gender stereotypes. Job roles such as 'girls' buyers' and 'boys' buyers' or concepts of 'boy-skewing' TV programmes or 'girl only' toys will be quaint and extinct. (Olivia Dickinson, Let Toys be Toys)[42]

I'd like to see a magazine market which acknowledges and celebrates the full breadth of women's and girls' interests and activities, instead of focusing on the narrow, stereotypical and limiting topics we see in most of them today. Will we get there by 2028? I hope so. (Elizabeth Lovegrove, tutor Oxford Brooks University)[43]

By 2028 I'd like to see every girl grow up considering herself the equal to any boy in every way and that the books available to young girls and boys increasingly provide positive and not stereo-typical role models. (Jacqueline Wilson, children's author)[44]

By 2028 I hope girls will not just dream of being princesses and mermaids, but will dream of being astronauts, scientists and superheroes . . . and that women heroes in graphic novels won't have such skimpy costumes whilst saving the world from the bad guys. (Siofra Mawdsley, aged eleven)[45]

By 2028, I hope that my daughter and all the other young girls in Britain have the same opportunities as and consider themselves equal to their brothers. I also hope that they combine an interest in beauty, fashion and light entertainment with a greater interest in women's rights internationally because in the internet world, we are increasingly interconnected. (SprinkleOfGlitter, Louise Pentland, British fashion and beauty vlogger, Youtuber and author)[46]

By 2028 I hope that women actors are no longer put out to grass once at 60, that they are as visible as older men, that films and plays no longer fixate on youth and beauty, and instead reflect the real world – in all its wonderful complexity. (Dame Julie Walters, actress and writer)[47]

By 2028, globally, we will have roughly equal numbers of women and men rating films and plays. We will have done this by calling out inequality where it exists, and by many more women coming forward as critics to redress the existing bias. (Meryl Streep, who plays Emmeline Pankhurst in the film *Suffragette*, American actress and philanthropist)[48]

By 2028 no woman will feel insecure about their body or their looks because the days will have long gone where women are judged by or commented on or referred to by their appearance. Every woman will be judged on what they do and who they are and every body shape will be acknowledged as uniquely beautiful. No woman will feel less than any other, but will be accepting of their unique beauty. (Miranda Hart, actress and comedian)[49]

I hope that one day soon female musicians, performers as well as composers, are represented as widely in music education as their male counterparts and that female representation in music education inspires young women to pursue careers in all aspects of music making. (Rachel Duckhouse, music teacher)[50]

By 2028 I hope to see more female artists with ownership of their own music working with women in senior roles in the industry. I hope the stereotype of what a female artist should be has completely disappeared, that ever more confident and unique female artists are out there doing their own thing and being truly inspirational. (Emeli Sandé, recording artist and songwriter)[51]

Women's football is becoming one of the most popular sports in the United Kingdom. I hope that the inclusivity of football will continue to develop and improve, with girls being given the chance to play the game I love at all schools around the country. As the women's game continues to grow, I hope that I and my teammates can inspire and influence the next generation of girls whilst breaking through boundaries and stereotypes. (Steph Houghton, footballer, captain of Manchester City and the England women's national football team)[52]

I hope that by 2028 there will no longer be gender discrimination on sports boards, that it is not even talked about as an issue, and that on the ground, in all sports, women have as many opportunities to grow and excel as their male counterparts. (Dame Kelly Holmes, retired British middle-distance athlete)[53]

By 2028 I'd love sport to be considered, promoted and celebrated as something for everyone, especially by parents, and for women's sport to be so visible that when perusing the sports pages, all male sports teams will need to be followed by the word 'men', and women will no longer feel second-rate. I'd also like to see elite female sports people judged, promoted and criticised for their skills and playing ability and not for anything else. (Helen Richardson-Walsh, Olympic field hockey player)[54]

By 2028 I would like to see official gender quotas for the sports news broadcast – there's nothing fair about the current imbalance in broadcasting outside the Olympics. High visibility once every four years isn't good enough. (Louisa Orr)[55]

My prayer is that by 2028 gender will not determine anyone's value. I hope that all will be honoured as made in the image of God and reflecting God's glory, and so women will have freedom of opportunity and achievement. Therefore, it will be as likely that the Governor of the Bank of England or the highest-paid sports star would be a woman as a man, and that girls are as likely to become plumbers or physicists as their male peers. I also hope, of course, that men and boys are as free to choose what to do and be, without similarly being determined by their gender. (Right Reverend Libby Lane, first woman appointed in the Church of England, Bishop of Stockport)[56]

For this world to have a fighting chance of progress by 2028, I'd like to see Muslim women not defined by their gender, race, religion or dress code. So rather than being judged by what's on their heads,

I'd like the focus to be on what's **in** their heads and hearts! (Faeeza Vaid, Executive Director, Muslim Women's Network UK)[57]

By 2028, I hope we aren't still debating whether or not we live in a patriarchal society and whether feminism is or isn't an incredibly important part of addressing a historic injustice and cultural imbalance that makes our world worse – less dignified, less just, less equal. I hope that we are even more sure-footedly on a path to where the role women play in society will be VALUED. Deeply. Truly. Meaningfully. EQUALLY. Without judgement. By 2028, I hope that no one questions any more whether gender equality is something that can be achieved and is within our reach. And that we appreciate and honour the women that came before us and fought for us and the rights that we enjoy today. (Emma Watson, actress and activist)[58]

Power

By 2028 I'd love for every little girl growing up to know that she can pursue any career she wants, and achieve everything she sets her mind to, rather than what she feels society wants her to do. (Zoella, fashion and beauty vlogger, YouTuber and author)[59]

I hope that by 2028 no girl child will hear the words 'girls can't . . .', and no woman will hear the words 'as a woman you cannot expect to . . .' (Vivienne Abbott, engineer)[60]

In all situations, doing something 'like a girl' will be synonymous with showing independence, positivity and empowerment. (Rhiannon Broome, secondary teacher and Olympic suffragette)[61]

For decades, women have been told what to wear. Whether explicitly in the workplace, by law or religion, or implicitly, by the media, advertising and the need to conform to social 'norms'. Women feel the pressure to sexualise their appearance for the benefit of the opposite sex, or are even pitted against each other to see 'who wore it best'. But they are seldom given permission to dress for themselves. I would hope that by 2028, women are fashionably autonomous. (Nicola Thorp, actress and high heels campaigner)[62]

By 2028, I'll be out of a job because the tampon tax will be well and truly axed. Women will be winning as fearless campaigners and issues that affect women will be tackled as well and taken as seriously as those that affect men. Our work will be far from over. But my story of the Chancellor saying the word 'tampon' in Parliament will pale in comparison to the many other milestones that will have been made by many other women. (Laura Coryton, campaigner and activist)[63]

We will have eliminated the invisible barriers that result in women losing custody of their ambition. Amongst other things, this involves women reflecting on the social contract they have with those around them, to ensure that, individually and collectively, they play leading roles in their own lives, finally confining to the history books the poisonous presumption that they are worth less than men. (Emma Barnett, broadcaster)[64]

Women live in a hand-me-down world. The medicine we are prescribed; the infrastructure governments build; the tools we use: all are designed around male bodies and male needs, leaving women at a huge but hidden disadvantage in almost every area of life. There is a chronic global data gap when it comes to women: partly because we forget women, and partly because we think women can make do and mend. The evidence of the cost and consequence of this one-size-fits-men approach is mounting. My vision for the world is that by 2028, we will have stopped forgetting women and started making them count. (Caroline Criado-Perez, feminist activist, journalist and writer)[65]

A whole new generation of people that are proud to call themselves feminists have emerged and by 2028 they will be the ones in the driving seat. With the increasing speed of technological change and the power of the internet they will be righting wrongs more easily and effectively than ever before. We will look back on the transformations brought about by gender equality, thinking we should've done them sooner. (Brie Rogers, UK Director, Change.org)[66]

What I'd like to see happen is that all human beings start to make their true connections. That we start to understand that we are very alike, men and women, and that making a hierarchy of our shared qualities e.g. strong: good, yielding: bad hasn't worked for us. In fact, that the obsession with patriarchy in all its forms has led us to the brink of destruction. That men need to come to women and learn from them. That it's not always about women making their way into the man's world. For most people, the man's world isn't working. We need to change, make a great leap within ourselves not only for the sake of future generations but for the sake of the planet which will not continue to give us house room if we go on like this. (Emma Thompson, actress and screenwriter)[67]

I hope in 2028 that I am talking about cake and spending sunny days with my friends and family. That I have put my marching shoes away and that the world is a better place. The good thing is in 2028 the young people of 2018 will be blossoming into the wonderful activists I see developing. I am sure that some of them will smash through the glass ceiling but mainly I hope that for most women the floor beneath them does not continue to collapse. (Sandi Toksvig, comedian, writer, presenter, founder of the Women's Equality Party)[68]

My advice to young women as we go forward to 2028 is to remember that friction is necessary to keep moving forward. Always embrace challenge as it serves to strengthen rather than deter. (Claire Sugden, Member of the Legislative Assembly in Northern Ireland, Independent)[69]

My hope for 2028 is that women in the UK have made use of the lessons and confidence they have gained in the past 100 years to inspire and support the struggles of women elsewhere. Internationally, women face similar problems and we can both help and be helped by others around the world. (Marion Kelly, consultant in International Health and Development)[70]

It is great how girls like me have so many opportunities today in the UK and that we aren't condemned or frowned upon and if anything, we are thought to be even smarter than boys. But I can see that not all families encourage their daughters. Religious and cultural practices sometimes still limit what they can do and how they think. Exposure to such different views makes me realise that we still have a long way to go, to not only help the young girls in other parts of the world like Africa and Afghanistan, but also bridge the gap between girls from different backgrounds in London itself. (Adya Ranjan, twelve-year-old student)[71]

And young Adya's comments bring me to the generation that we will be handing over to. What are some of the aspirations of those who will be young adults in 2028?

At Gordon Primary School, in the rural town of Huntly in Aberdeenshire, the girls wanted to become Olympic gymnasts, dance and sing, be a scientist that makes a cure for cancer, save animals that are endangered and swim with sharks. Some of their hopes included those of Chloe and Alexis, that there would be nobody homeless and that everyone would have a house with heating in it. Elsie looked forward to being in cars that float in mid-air, and, possibly even more aspirational, Lilia and Leah hoped that politicians would be nice to each other and that there would no longer be any bombs.[72]

At Pentrepoeth Primary School in Newport, Wales, Carenza wanted to become a tennis player, Elise to be a teacher, Nia an actor, Ellie to be able to travel the world, experience new things and have freedom. Arianwen wanted to be able to do the same things as boys and Millie to have the freedom to follow her dreams. They felt that all over the world, girls and women should believe in themselves and be proud of who they are without worrying about their gender.[73]

Girls at St Christopher's Church of England School in Oxford had gloriously eclectic answers to the question on what they wanted for their future: archaeologist, artist, chef, doctor/nurse, fashion designer, poet, a South Korean singer, teacher/writer, YouTuber, vet and women's rights campaigner. Helen commented, 'I would like everyone to be whatever they want, however they want, whenever they want.' Laiba suggested it would be good if 'everyone any age can vote', while Elinor wanted to 'explore the world, have children, get married, and climb a mountain (a big one)'.[74]

At Hitchin Girls in Hertfordshire, Jessica, Anya and Rhea wanted to be lawyers, Sabrina a doctor, Sophie a speech therapist, Sofia an interior designer or architect, Fiona a film-maker. Eden P. wanted to find a cure for cancer because 'life can be cruel to kind caring people and I believe that has to change'. Amber explained: 'When I get older, I want to design aircraft, satellites and helicopters.' Eden G. wanted to be 'a zoologist, an artist or a cyclist', Lucy to be a famous Olympian. Layla explained, 'My dream job is to be a visual effects technician because I like computers and TV. I would also love to travel the world (even though I'm afraid of planes) and have a family.'

A number of others mentioned motherhood. Anabel wanted to be a mother and teach young children at primary school; Amy commented, 'I would like to have a family, but not before I've seen the things in the world that I want to, and accomplished some of my goals.'

Alisha and Mimi hoped people would stop catcalling or for it to be illegal, and for people not to be judged based on their looks. Rosie, for women to be seen as people: 'not homeworkers, not assistants, not there for the pleasure of men – women to be seen as equals and nothing less.' Evie wanted to see herself 'as a young woman who can stand up for myself'. I leave the last word to Mia, who hopefully defines the next generation in planning to become 'a strong, independent woman who will try to make a positive impact on the world'.[75]

ACKNOWLEDGEMENTS

Reflections and anecdotes from innumerable people have provided the oxygen and life-blood to this book. My thanks to all of you who contributed – family and friends, groups at meetings and events, individuals who I reached out to and who became friends and pulled even more people into the process. Apologies to those whose suggestions had to be trimmed or were, in the end, omitted. Many thanks also to the team at Hodder and Sceptre who helped with the magic of transforming it all into a manageable-sized book.

Figure 16: Statue of Emmeline Pankhurst sculpted by Hazel Reeves unveiled at St Peter's Square in Manchester, 14 December 2018. © Our Emmeline.

PICTURE ACKNOWLEDGEMENTS

The publisher would like to thank the following for their kind permission to reproduce their photographs. Every attempt has been made to contact the copyright holders, however in the case of any omissions please contact the publishers and we will rectify any errors at the earliest opportunity.

In some instances we were unable to trace the owners of the copyright material and we would appreciate any information that would enable us to do so.

Picture Research by Jane Smith

Page Opener: People's History Museum
Page 24: GBPhotos.com
Page 80: U.S. National Archives and Records Administration
Page 96: Museum of London
Page 116: IWM/Getty Image /Contributor
Page 169: Domestic Abuse Intervention Programs, Duluth, MN, 55802
Page 178: Jennifer Robinson in 2003
Page 200: 'Madame Pankhurst...', *New Times and Ethiopia News*, 7 September 1940 (print) / British Library, London, UK / Bridgeman Images
Page 219: *Stylist* magazine
Page 282: GBPhotos.com /CARE
Page 308: Our Emmeline

NOTES

Where do we start?

1 Including the Isle of Man because of the constitutional links, the similarities in women's lives and the family links. Many of the official statistics are for England and Wales only.

2 Kate Millett, *Sexual Politics*, 2000.

3 The wave metaphor, usually thought of as water rather than electromagnetic, is useful. However, the reality has been difficult to plot onto these waves. The concept allows for the fact that the pace and nature of change is not uniform, but experiences have not been synchronised across the UK, let alone globally. Eastern European feminists in particular have been hostile to this metaphor and there have been attempts to popularise others, such as Karen Offen's volcano – feminism the fluid discontent that keeps erupting to challenge the patriarchal crust. Jo Reger, *Different Wavelengths: Studies of the Contemporary Women's Movement*. New York: Routledge, 2005 and Karen Offen, *European Feminisms, 1700–1950: A Political History*, pp. 25–6. Stanford, CA: Stanford UP, 2000.

4 For more on the history of the myth see history.howstuffworks.com/history-vs-myth/women-burn-bras-in-70s.htm and footage on app.nimia.com/video/104946/1960s-bra-burning.

5 Shelley Budgeon, *Third Wave Feminism and the Politics of Gender in Late Modernity*, 2011; Stacy Gillis et al., *Third Wave Feminism: A Critical Exploration*, 2007.

6 Imelda Whelehan, *Modern Feminist Thought: From the Second Wave to Post-Feminism*, 2005.

7 Kira Cochrane, *All the Rebel Women: The Rise of the Fourth Wave of Feminism*, Guardian Books, 2013.

8 Patricia Hill Collins and Sirma Bilge, *Intersectionality*, Cambridge, 2016.

9 Roxane Gay, *Bad Feminist: Essays*, Corsair, 2014. See also www.ted.com/ talks/roxane_gay_confessions_of_a_bad_feminist.

10 Sylvia Walby, *The Future of Feminism*, 2011, p.81.

Prologue: 'women, imbeciles and criminals'

1 See quote below, from Audrey Rees Webbe, aged ninety-eight, interview by Philippa Bilton, recorded 20 March 1985.

2 Namely householders, wives over the age of thirty, occupiers of property with an annual rent of £5 or more and graduates of British universities.

3 The document is recorded as having 1,499 names; however, a subsequent counting of the document found an additional twenty-two signatures: www.parliament.uk/business/committees/committees-a-z/commons-select/petitions-committee/petition-of-the-month/votes-for-women-the-1866-suffrage-petition/.

4 https://www.parliament.uk/business/committees/committees-a-z/commons-select/petitions-committee/petition-of-the-month/votes-for-women-the-1866-suffrage-petition/.

5 Melissa A. Butler and Jacqueline Templeton, 'The Isle of Man and the First Votes for Women', *Women & Politics*, 1 June 1984, Vol.4 (2), p.38.

6 *Daily Herald*, 6 June 1910, p.4 (with thanks to Frances Bedford and Steven Anderson).

7 Leonard W. Matters, *Australasians Who Count in London and Who Counts in Western Australia*, Truscott & Son Ltd, 1913, pp.161–2. (with thanks to Frances Bedford and Steven Anderson).

8 Krista Cowman, email to author, 21 August 2016.

9 In addition to Emmeline Pankhurst, one of the leading WSPU members and the treasurer was Emmeline Pethick-Lawrence.

10 Autobiographies and biographies include Margaret Haig, Viscountess Rhondda, *This Was My World*, 1933; Emmeline Pethick-Lawrence, *My Part in a Changing World*, 1938; Mary Gawthorpe, *Up Hill to Holloway*, 1962; David Rubinstein, *A Different World for Women: The Life of Millicent Garrett Fawcett*, 1991; Audrey Kelly, *Lydia Becker and the Cause*, 1992; Richard Whitmore, *Alice Hawkins: And the Suffragette Movement*, 2012; Nina Boyd, *From Suffragette to Fascist: The Many Lives of Mary Sophia Allen*, 2013; Anita Anand, *Sophia: Princess, Suffragette, Revolutionary*, 2015; Lyndsey Jenkins, *Lady Constance Lytton: Aristocrat, Suffragette, Martyr*,

2015; Simon Butler and Olive Hockin, *Land Girl Suffragette: The Extraordinary Story of Olive Hockin*, 2016; Lyndsey Jenkins' PhD on the Kenney sisters and the Kenney Papers archive at the University of East Anglia. Also for the books by or about the Pankhursts, see Katherine Connelly, Mary Davis, Sheila Harrison, Rachel Holmes, June Purvis and Pankhurst in the bibliography.

11 Beverley Cook, email to author, 12 June 2017.

12 www.thepankhurstcentre.org.uk.

13 Jane W. Grant, *In the Steps of Exceptional Women*, 2016.

14 Sam Smethers, email to author, 13 March 2017.

15 Emmeline Pankhurst, preface in Sylvia Pankhurst's *The Suffragette*, 1911.

16 Photocopies of letter sent to me by Diana Dollery, Myra Sadd Brown's great granddaughter, from LSE Library collection, 9/20/105.

17 Audrey Rees Webbe, aged ninety-eight, interview by Philippa Bilton, recorded 20 March 1985.

18 June Purvis, email to author, 14 August 2016.

19 Dee Collins, email to author, 6 October 2016.

20 Annie Lennox, email to author, 10 February 2017.

21 Alexandra Thacker, Manchester High School for Girls, via Lex Taylor, email to author, 1 March 2017.

22 Noor Al-Saffar, Manchester High School for Girls, via Lex Taylor, email to author, 1 March 2017.

23 Jill Liddington and Elizabeth Crawford, *Vanishing for the Vote: Suffrage, Citizenship and the Battle for the Census*, 2014.

24 Margaret Haig, Viscountess Rhondda, *This Was My World*, 1933, pp.299–300.

25 Nicoletta F. Gullace, 'White feathers and wounded men: female patriotism and the memory of the Great War', *The Journal of British Studies*, 36(2) (1997).

26 Nicoletta F. Gullace, 'Christabel Pankhurst and the Smethwick Election: right-wing feminism, the Great War and the ideology of consumption', *Women's History Review* 23, no.3.

27 June Purvis, 'Emmeline Pankhurst in the aftermath of suffrage, 1918–1928', in *The Aftermath of Suffrage: Women, Gender and Politics in Britain 1918–1945*, edited by Julie V. Gottlieb and Richard Toye, 2013, p.33.

28 For example, *Time* magazine, 1999. http://content.time.com/time/magazine/article/0,9171,26473,00.html; ListVerse 2011, listverse.com/2011/08/30/top-10-women-of-the-20th-century/.

29 There is some controversy over her birth date, which on her birth certificate has 15 July but Emmeline always claimed she was born on the 14th,
which might be correct but might also be because of her desire for the
date to coincide with revolutionary Bastille Day in France.

30 The shortlist included Emmeline Pankhurst, and also Victorian novelist
Elizabeth Gaskell, anti-racism campaigner Louise da-Cocodia, Manchester's
first female councillor Margaret Ashton, Elizabeth Raffald, eighteenth-
century entrepreneur; and Ellen Wilkinson, Labour Cabinet minister and
leader of the Jarrow March.

31 Susan Hogan, email to author, 18 September 2017.

32 Mary Davis, email to author, 25 October 2016.

33 Shirley Harrison, email to author, 7 November 2016.

34 Dr Kate Cook and Professor Julia Rouse, email to author, 12 October 2016.

35 Aceil Haddad, email to author, 27 February 2016.

36 Lesley Covington, email to author, 27 February 2016.

1. Politics

1 Earl Ferrers, House of Lords Debates, 3 December 1957, vol. CCVI, col.
709-10m quoted in *Commons and Lords*, p.24.

2 Words generally attributed to Elizabeth I including by Antonia Fraser, *The
Warrior Queens: Boadicea's Chariot*, Arrow, 1999, p.249. However, also chal-
lenged, e.g. by Felix Barker, in 'If Parma Had Landed', *History Today*, 1
May 1988, Vol. 38(5), p.34.

3 www.bl.uk/learning/histcitizen/21cc/struggle/suffrage1/suffragists.html.

4 www.historyofwomen.org/suffrage.html.

5 Emma Barnett, 'The Queen is My Feminist Icon and She Should Be Yours
Too', *Telegraph*, 9 September 2015, accessed 6 November 2017.

6 Paula Bartley, *Votes for Women 1860–1928*, 1998; Sandra Stanley Holton,
*Feminism and Democracy: Women's Suffrage and Reform Politics in Britain,
1900–1918*, 2002.

7 Claire Eustance, email to author, 14 October 2016.

8 Dawn Langan Teel, 'Ordinary Democratization: The Electoral Strategy
that Won British Women the Vote', *Politics & Society*, December 2014, Vol.
42, no. 4, pp.537–61.

9 Mari Takayanagi, article for *Parliamentary History* 37:1, 2018, special issue
on the Representation of the People Act 1918, ed. Stuart Ball.

10   Patricia M. Thane, 'What Difference Did the Vote Make? Women in Public and Private Life in Britain since 1918', *Historical Research* 76, no.192 (2003) 268–85. Also Mari Takayanagi kclpure.kcl.ac.uk/portal/en/theses/parliament-and-women-c19001945%2834708cef-2efd-4389-9382-5e847fd50189%29.html.

11   researchbriefings.files.parliament.uk/documents/SN01467/SN01467.pdf. The Women's Library Collection at LSE library has the Pass the Bill archive.

12   www.ipsos-mori.com/researchpublications/researcharchive/3575/How-Britain-voted-in-2015.aspx. See also www.britishelectionstudy.com/bes-resources/following-the-pink-battle-bus-where-are-the-women-voters-in-2015-by-dr-rosie-campbell/#.WJDeobGw3LZ.

13   researchbriefings.files.parliament.uk/documents/SN01467/SN01467.pdf.

14   https://yougov.co.uk/news/2017/06/13/how-britain-voted-2017-general-election/.

15   Ann Goulden, email to author, 5 July 2016.

16   www.bbc.co.uk/news/magazine-32154443.

17   www.thetimes.co.uk/tto/news/politics/article4392397.ece.

18   www.telegraph.co.uk/women/womens-life/11583845/Helen-Pankhurst-My-grandmother-fought-for-vote-dont-let-her-down.html.

19   Rosie Campbell. The gender gap is calculated as the difference between the Con–Lab lead for women and men. Gallup polls 1945–59. Rosie Campbell. 'What do we really know about women voters? Gender, elections and public opinion', *Political Quarterly* 83(4), pp.703–10, 2012.

20   Harold L. Smith, 'The Women's Movement, Politics and Citizenship, 1960s–2000', in Ina Zweiniger-Bargielowska, *Women in Twentieth-Century Britain*, p.285.

21   Mona Morgan-Collins, 'First women at the polls: examination of women's early voting behaviour', etheses.lse.ac.uk/3320/; Nathalie Giger, 'Towards a modern gender gap in Europe? A comparative analysis of voting behavior in 12 countries', *The Social Science Journal*, Vol. 36, Issue 3, September 2009, pp.474–92.

22   Tim Immerzeel et al., 'Explaining the gender gap in radical right voting: A cross-national investigation in 12 Western European countries', *Comparative European Politics*, 13.2 (February 2015), pp.263–85; Robert Ford and Matthew Goodwin (2014), *Revolt on the Right: Explaining Support for the Radical Right in Britain*, Routledge.

23   Krista Cowman, *Women in British Politics, c.1689–1979*, 2010, p.143.

24 www.ted.com/talks/sandi_toksvig_a_political_party_for_women_s_
    equality#t-498056.

25 https://researchbriefings.parliament.uk/ResearchBriefing/Summary/
    SN05125.

26 Quoted by Senia Paseta, Irish Nationalist Women 1900–1918, p.264.

27 https://thehistoryofparliament.wordpress.com/2015/12/14/the-eligibil-
    ity-of-constance-markievicz/.

28 Nancy Astor, p.10 HC Deb, 24 February 1920, quoted in Women in
    Parliament: Key Speeches: Past and Present, Houses of Parliament, www.
    parliament.uk/vote100.

29 Martin Pugh, 'Nancy Witcher Astor, Viscountess Astor (1879–1964)',
    Oxford Dictionary of National Biography, Oxford University Press, 2004;
    online edn; thehistoryofparliament.wordpress.com/2014/05/02/nancy-
    astor-the-first-female-mp-in-the-house-of-commons/.

30 Athol, Working Partnership, p.139. Quoted in Krista Cowman, The Political
    Autobiographies of Early Women MPs, c.1918–1964, p.211.

31 Helen Jones, Women in British Public Life, 1914–1950, p.118.

32 Philip Williamson, 'Bondfield, Margaret Grace (1873–1953)', Oxford
    Dictionary of National Biography, Oxford University Press, 2004; online edn,
    January 2011, www.oxforddnb.com/view/article/31955.

33 Brian Harrison, 'Wilkinson, Ellen Cicely (1891–1947)', Oxford Dictionary of
    National Biography, Oxford University Press, 2004.

34 researchbriefings.parliament.uk/ResearchBriefing/Summary/SN01250.

35 www.gov.uk/government/ministers.

36 www.ipu.org/wmn-e/classif.htm.

37 www.parliament.uk/mps-lords-and-offices/lords/composition-of-the-
    lords/.

38 As at 1 May 2017, www.ipu.org/wmn-e/world.htm.

39 https://www.parliament.uk/business/committees/committees-a-z/
    other-committees/speakers-conference-on-parliamentary-representation/
    news/final-report-published/.

40 Harold L. Smith, 'The Women's Movement, Politics and Citizenship,
    1960s-2000', in Ina Zweiniger-Bargielowska, Women in Twentieth-Century
    Britain, p.288.

41 news.bbc.co.uk/1/hi/uk_politics/1564419.stm.

42 www.theguardian.com/politics/2001/sep/27/uk.houseofcommons.

43 www.bbc.co.uk/news/election-2017-40192060.

44 www.telegraph.co.uk/news/politics/7265221/David-Cameron-I-will-impose-all-women-shortlists.html.

45 www.bbc.co.uk/news/election-2017-40192060.

46 Maria Miller, email to author via Anastasia Starostina, 4 October 2017.

47 www.quotaproject.org/country.cfm.

48 www.bristol.ac.uk/media-library/sites/news/2016/july/20%20Jul%20Prof%20Sarah%20Childs%20The%20Good%20Parliament%20report.pdf.

49 hansard.millbanksystems.com/lords/1917/dec/11/representation-of-the-people-bill.

50 Valerie Ellis, 'Current trade union attempts to remove occupational segregation in the employment of women', in Sylvia Walby, *Gender Segregation at Work*, p.138.

51 strongerunions.org/2012/04/26/2011-trade-union-membership-figures-released/.

52 Jane Hannam, 'Women and Politics', in June Purvis (ed.), *Women's History: Britain 1850–1945*, p.236.

53 www.theguardian.com/commentisfree/2016/jan/07/misogyny-feminism-stop-the-war-jeremy-corbyn.

54 www.eveshamjournal.co.uk/news/12864809._quot_Sexist_twaddle__quot____Worcester_parliamentary_candidate_in_Facebook_storm_over_pink_bus_campaign/.

55 www.bbc.co.uk/news/uk-politics-13211577.

56 Jane Hannam, 'Women and politics', in *Women's History: Britain 1850–1945*, ed. June Purvis, p.237.

57 Harriet Harman, *A Woman's Work*, p.134.

58 Maguire, G. E., *Conservative Women: A History of Women and the Conservative Party, 1874–1997*, 2000.

59 Harold L. Smith, 'The Women's Movement, Politics and Citizenship, 1960s–2000', in Ina Zweiniger-Bargielowska, *Women in Twentieth-Century Britain*, p.281.

60 Rosie Campbell and Sarah Childs, ' "What the coalition did for women": A new gender consensus, coalition division and gendered austerity', in *The Coalition Effect, 2010–2015*, ed. Anthony Seldon et al., p.399.

61 Helen Jones, *Women in British Public Life, 1914–1950*, 2000, pp.137, 161; Krista Cowman, *Women in British Politics, c.1689–1979*, 2010, p.148.

62 Nicky Morgan, email to author via Lee Davis, 2 February 2017.

63 Nirmal Puwar, www.bloomsbury.com/uk/space-invaders-9781859736593/.

64 Sue Bruley, *Women in Britain Since 1900*, p.108.

65 Mari Takayanagi, email to author, 13 February 2017.

66 news.bbc.co.uk/2/hi/uk_news/politics/4074877.stm; www.telegraph.co.uk /news/2016/04/01/male-mps-accused-of-not-listening-to-women-and-telling-them-to-s/.

67 Harriet Harman, *A Woman's Work*, pp.92–3.

68 Diane Abbott p.33, HC Deb, 11 June 2008, c368, quoted in Women in Parliament: Key Speeches: Past and Present, Houses of Parliament, www.parliament.uk/vote100.

69 Emma Crewe, email to author, 19 January 2017.

70 www.theguardian.com/commentisfree/video/2016/mar/17/mhairi-black-owen-jones-video-interview.

71 Jess Phillips, *Everywoman: One Woman's Truth about Speaking the Truth*, 2017, p.126.

72 www.democraticaudit.com/2014/01/22/select-committees-are-becoming-increasingly-significant-but-show-an-enormous-gender-bias-in-their-choice-of-witnesses; Crew, *The House of Commons*, p.214.

73 Rosie Campbell and Sarah Childs, 'Parents in Parliament: "Where's Mum?"', *Political Quarterly*, vol. 85, issue 4, pp.487–92.

74 www.youtube.com/watch?v=PQ8csgPS-QI.

75 House of Commons Briefing Paper: Hours Sat & Late Sittings, SN02226.pdf, July 2015.

76 Nicky Morgan, email to author via Lee Davis, 3 February 2017.

77 www.bristol.ac.uk/media-library/sites/news/2016/july/20%20Jul%20Prof%20Sarah%20Childs%20The%20Good%20Parliament%20report.pdf.

78 Jess Phillips, email to author, 14 September 2016.

79 Sarah Champion, email to author, 10 September 2016.

80 Anna Turley, email to author, 24 August 2017.

81 Helen Jones, *Women in British Public Life, 1914–1950*, p.138.

82 Emma Crewe, *The House of Commons*, 2015.

83 Mentioned by Margaret Hodge at a discussion in Parliament on InternationalWomen'sDay2016m.youtube.com/watch?v=TLDjhjhNLW8 and also Sarah Champion.

84 Emma Crewe, email to author, 13 January 2017.

85 Mari Takayanagi in Julie V. Gottlieb and Richard Toye, *The Aftermath of Suffrage: Women, Gender, and Politics in Britain, 1918–1945*.

86 John Stewart, 'Summerskill, Edith Clara, Baroness Summerskill (1901–1980)', *Oxford Dictionary of National Biography*, Oxford University Press, 2004.

87 www.theguardian.com / politics / 2008 / may / 08 / labour. gwynethdunwoody.

88 Emma Crewe, email to author, 19 January 2017.

89 www.itv.com / news / 2016-07-06 / what-theresa-may-said-about-being-a-bloody-difficult-woman /.

90 Catherine Mayer, *Attack of the 50 Ft. Women: How Gender Equality Can Save the World!*, HQ, 2017, p.79.

91 MP Nicky Morgan, email to author, 3 February 2017.

92 Emma Crewe, email to author, 13 January 2017.

93 Susan Pedersen, 'Rathbone, Eleanor Florence (1872–1946)', *Oxford Dictionary of National Biography*, Oxford University Press, 2004.

94 Jane Hannam, 'Women and politics', in *Women's History: Britain 1850–1945*, ed. June Purvis, p.237.

95 www.margaretthatcher.org / document / 101374.

96 www.telegraph.co.uk / news / politics / margaret-thatcher / 9979922 / Margaret-Thatcher-a-pioneering-woman-with-no-time-for-feminists.html.

97 www.telegraph.co.uk / news / politics / margaret-thatcher / 9979399 / Margaret-Thatcher-A-life-in-words.html.

98 Prime Minister Theresa May, letter to author, 11 September 2017.

99 E.g. Joni Lovenduski and Pippa Norris (2003), Westminster Women: The Politics of Presence. *Political Studies*, 51: 84–102. doi:10.1111/1467-9248.00414. Also, regarding 1881 Isle of Man elections, Melissa A. Butler and Jacqueline Templeton, 'The Isle of Man and the First Votes for Women', *Women & Politics*, 1 June 1984, Vol. 4(2), p.45 of pp.33–47.

100 Pippa Norris and Joni Lovenduski, 'Blair's Babes: Critical Mass Theory, Gender, and Legislative Life', KSG Faculty Research Working Paper Series RWP01-039, September 2001. SSRN: https://ssrn.com/abstract=288548 or http://dx.doi.org/10.2139/ssrn.288548; also Sylvia Walby, *The Future of Feminism*, p.71.

101 Conservative MP Margot James, email to author via Lee Davis, 9 March 2017.

102 Emily Thornberry, discussion with author, 4 September 2017.

103 Maria Miller, email to author via Anastasia Starostina, 4 October 2017.

104 https:// / www.gov.uk / government / uploads / system / uploads / attachment_data / file / 467910 / 20151014_Percentage_of_New_Public_Appointments_made_to_Women_in_2014_2015.csv / preview.

105 Six Point Group Archives are held in The Women's Library collection at the LSE Library.

106 House of Lords Debates, 3 December, 1957, vol. CCVI, col. 709–10m quoted in *Commons and Lords*, p.24.

107 Emma Crewe, *Commons and Lords*, p.25.

108 Baroness Deech, email to author, 1 February 2017.

109 Baroness Jane Campbell, email to author, 10 March 2017.

110 Baroness Bakewell, email to author, 10 January 2017.

111 Associated Press (28 July 1920), 'FIRST WOMEN APPEAR ON JURIES IN ENGLAND', *New York Times*, Retrieved 6 November 2017. Women had served on forms of juries to discover if a guilty woman was pregnant or not, but not in actually deciding if they were guilty or not. (Kevin Crosby, first100years.org.uk/1481-2/)

112 Shamena Anwar, Patrick Bayer and Randi Hjalmarsson, 'A Jury of Her Peers: The Impact of the First Female Jurors on Criminal Convictions', *NBER Working Paper* No. 21960, 2016, www.nber.org/papers/w21960.

113 First100years.org.uk/timeline/, also personal communication Katie Broomfield.

114 Interview with Helena Normanton in *Ladies' Pictorial*, March 1918. Helena Normanton's archives are held in The Women's Library collection, at the LSE Library.

115 www.google.com/?client=safari#q=2014+gender+in+the+Law& gfe_rd=cr.

116 Erika Rackley, 'Women, Judging and the Judiciary' xiii, 2013, p.18.

117 European Commission, 'More Women in Senior Positions: Key to Economic Stability and Growth, Directorate-General for Employment, Social Affairs and Equal Opportunities Unit GI, January 2010, p.66; quoted in Erika Rackley, 'Women, Judging and the Judiciary', 2013.

118 www.barstandardsboard.org.uk/media-centre/research-and-statistics/statistics/practising-barrister-statistics/.
www.judiciary.gov.uk/wp-content/uploads/2016/07/judicial-diversity-statistics-2december.pdf www.chambersstudent.co.uk/where-to-start/newsletter/women-in-law-firms.
www.lawsociety.org.uk/law-careers/becoming-a-solicitor/entry-trends/.
www.gov.uk/government/uploads/system/uploads/attachment_data/file/31480/11-745-women-on-boards.pdf.

119 Jayne Croft, email to author, 7 October 2016.

120 Margaret Owen, email to author, 23 November 2016.

121 *Joan Heals Book of Careers* (1955), quoted in Patrick Polden, 'Portia's progress: women at the Bar in England, 1919–1939', in *International Journal of the Legal Profession*, 2005, Vol. 12(3), pp.312–319.

122 Lady Brenda Hale, 'A minority opinion?', p.331, quoted in Erika Rackley, *Women, Judging and the Judiciary*, 2013, p.23.

123 Erika Rackley, *Women, Judging and the Judiciary*, 2013, p.23.

124 www.fawcettsociety.org.uk/does-local-government-work-for-women-final-report-of-the-local-government-commission.

125 www.local.gov.uk/research-pay-and-workforce/-/journal_content/56/10180/6202579/ARTICLE.

126 Cathy Bakewell, email to author, 10 January 2017.

127 Sarah Judge, email to author, 2 December 2016.

128 www.theguardian.com/world/2003/may/09/gender.uk.

129 http://researchbriefings.files.parliament.uk/documents/SN01250/SN01250.pdf.

130 peterross.scot/articles/nicola-sturgeon-on-the-brink/.

131 www.newstatesman.com/politics/uk/2016/05/ruth-davidson-new-type-tory-21st-century.

132 Shared by Louisa Orr, In conversation with Monica McWilliams and George Mitchell, Queen's University Belfast, 10 February 2017.

133 journal-iostudies.org/sites/journal-iostudies.org/files/JIOSEisenberg2013-4-2.pdf.

134 www.mfa.org/exhibitions/amalia-pica/transcript-womens-rights-are-human-rights.

135 With some reservations and the Holy See, Iran, Somalia, Sudan and Tonga that did not sign the treaty; Sue Bruley, *Women in Britain Since 1900*, p.161.

136 www.womenlobby.org/Brexit-Women-s-Rights?lang=en European Parliament, Results of the 2014 European elections, europarl.europa.eu.

137 Joanna Haycock, email to author, 6 September 2017.

138 www.mirror.co.uk/news/uk-news/who-voted-brexit-how-eu-8277077.

139 www.mumsnet.com/Talk/guest_posts/2666109-EU-referendum-guest-post-Helen-Pankhurst-The-EU-gives-us-the-best-of-both-worlds.

140 www.parliament.uk/business/committees/committees-a-z/commons-select/women-and-equalities-committee/news-parliament-2015/equalities-legislation-brexit-report-published-16-17/.

141 Mala Htun and Laurel Weldon. 'When do governments promote women's

rights? A framework for the comparative analysis of sex equality policy', *Perspectives on Politics* 8, no. 1 (2010): 207. doi:10.1017/s1537592709992787.

142 Sian Evans, *Queen Bees*, Two Roads, 2016.

143 Lesley Abdela, email to author, 10 January 2017. Women for Westminster and 300 Group archives are held in The Women's Library collection at the LSE Library.

144 Frances Scott, email to author, 8 June 2017.

145 'Women Activist of East London: A study of radical female history in Tower Hamlets, Hackney and Waltham Forest', Share UK, 2016, pp.10–13.

146 https://www.bl.uk/sisterhood/articles/womens-liberation-a-national-movement; Sue Bruley, *Women in Britain since 1900*, p.149.

147 Pat Thane, 'The Impact of mass democracy on British political culture, 1918–1939', p.61, in Julie V. Gottlieb and Richard Toye, *The Aftermath of Suffrage: Women, Gender, and Politics in Britain, 1918–1945*, Palgrave Macmillan, 2013.

148 wnc.equalities.gov.uk/component/content/article/343-womens-national-commission-legacy-document.html.

149 downloads.bbc.co.uk/historyofthebbc/board_of_governors.pdf.

150 news.bbc.co.uk/1/hi/programmes/newsnight/newsnight25/4227695.stm; www.bbc.com/news/magazine-36129328.

151 http://www.telegraph.co.uk/culture/tvandradio/bbc/8265982/Angela-Rippon-BBC-boss-Lord-Birt-told-me-Id-had-my-day-at-50.html.

152 www.inter-media.co.uk/uk-newspapers-reveal-readership-demo-graphics/.

153 Andrew Sparrow, *Obscure Scribblers: A History of Parliamentary Journalism*.

154 Harriet Harman, *A Woman's Work*, p.82.

155 www.bristol.ac.uk/media-library/sites/news/2016/july/20%20Jul%20Prof%20Sarah%20Childs%20The%20Good%20Parliament%20report.pdf, Table 2, p.13.

156 www.theguardian.com/news/2002/sep/18/guardianobituaries.gender.

157 www.independent.co.uk/news/people/theresa-may-s-995-trousers-sparked-debate-but-david-cameron-s-suits-cost-much-more-a7462891.html.

158 Jo Swinson, 'The media's reporting of the childs review sums up why we're still light years from equality', *The Huffington Post*, 21 July 2016, accessed 19 August 2016; www.huffingtonpost.co.uk/jo-swinson/childs-review-breastfeeding_b_11111012.html.

159 Meg Luxon, *More than a Labour of Love*, p.207, quoted by Sheila Rowbotham, *The Past is Before Us*, 1989, p.57.

160 Susanna Moorhead, email to author, 16 June 2017.

2. Money

1 Elaine Lister, email to author, 1 May 2017.

2 Linda McDowell, *Migrant Women's Voices*, pp.1–2.

3 Richard Pankhurst, personal communication, 2 September 2016.

4 www.theguardian.com/football/2012/jun/24/euro-2012-bedford-italians.

5 Rita Pankhurst, personal communication, 2 September 2016.

6 Linda McDowell, *Migrant Women's Voices*, p.53; Bressey and Dwyer, *New Geographies of Race and Racism*, Routledge: 2008, p.57.

7 Sue Bruley, *Women in Britain Since 1900*, p.118.

8 Christine Low, email to author, 6 July 2016.

9 Cecilia Drayton, email to author, 1 June 2017.

10 Azmara, personal communication, 27 July 2017.

11 www.gov.uk/government/uploads/system/uploads/attachment_data/file/267913/britnatsummary.pdf.

12 As explained to me by Mari Takayanagi, senior archivist, parliamentary archives, email to author, 14 February 2017. See also, M. Page Baldwin, 'Subject to Empire: married women and the British nationality and status of Aliens Act', *Journal of British Studies*, Vol. 40, No. 4.

13 Annie Phizacklea, 'Gender, racism and occupational segregation', in Sylvia Walby, *Gender Segregation at Work*, p.45.

14 Wendy Webster, '"Race", Ethnicity and National Identity', in Ina Zweiniger-Bargielowska, *Women in Twentieth-Century Britain*, p.296.

15 www.gov.uk/government/uploads/system/uploads/attachment_data/file/486107/Shortage_Occupation_List_-_November_2015.pdf. Similarly, as of 2012, there was also a lower threshold of £18,600 for UK citizens and settled residents to bring in a spouse or partner from outside the European Union, the threshold increasing with number of children. www.migrationobservatory.ox.ac.uk/resources/reports/the-minimum-income-requirement-for-non-eea-family-members-in-the-uk-2/.

16 Carol Dyhouse, *Girl Trouble*, Zed Books, p.26.

17 Liz Chamberlain, email to author, 14 August 2016.

18 Maxine, email to author, 21 September 2016.

19 http://webarchive.nationalarchives.gov.uk/20090108131525/http:/dcsf. gov.uk/research/data/uploadfiles/rtp01-07.pdfwww.gov.uk/government /uploads/system/uploads/attachment_data/file/399005/SFR06_2015_ Text.pdf.

20 https://www.bbc.co.uk/news/education-40952125; www.telegraph.co.uk/ education/secondaryeducation/11813571/GCSE-results-2015-Boys-catching-up-with-girls-as-pupils-opt-for-more-digital-based-courses.html; https://assets. publishing.service.gov.uk/government/uploads/system/uploads/attach-ment_data/file/399005/SFR06_2015_Text.pdf; https://www.suttontrust.com/ research-paper/missing-talent-disadvantaged-pupil-attainment/

21 Dame Ann Dowling, mentioned Bristol University, BBC Radio 4, *Woman's Hour*, 23 June 2015.

22 Helena Kiff, email to author, 8 November 2016.

23 Jacqueline Roberts, email to author, 31 May 2017.

24 Paul Bolton, Education Historical Statistic, Social and General Statistic, 2012, www.parliament.uk/briefing-papers/SN04252.pdf.

25 http://reports.weforum.org/global-gender-gap-report-2015/report-highlights/.

26 Gail Braybon, *Women Workers in the First World War*, p.49.

27 Sue Bruley, *Women in Britain Since 1900*, p.61.

28 Penny Summerfield, 'Women and war in the twentieth century', in J. Purvis (ed.), *Women's History: Britain 1850–1945*, p.324.

29 Sue Bruley, *Women in Britain Since 1900*, p.62.

30 Sue Bruley, *Women in Britain Since 1900*, p.65.

31 Sue Bruley, *Women in Britain Since 1900*, p.94.

32 Ina Zweiniger-Bargielowska, *Women in Twentieth-Century Britain*, p.269.

33 Sue Bruley, *Women in Britain Since 1900*, p.96.

34 Penny Summerfield, 'Women and war in the twentieth century', in J. Purvis (ed.), *Women's History: Britain 1850–1945*, p.324.

35 Penny Tinkler, 'Girlhood and Growing up', in Ina Zweiniger-Bargielowska, *Women in Twentieth-Century Britain*, p.43.

36 http://hansard.millbanksystems.com/commons/1927/apr/29/married-women-employment-bill.

37 Shani D'Cruze, 'Women and the Family', in ed. J. Purvis, *Women's History: Britain 1850–1945*, p.74.

38 Angela Holdsworth, *Out of the Doll's House*, pp.71, 74. www.bbc.com/ news/magazine-36129328.

39 Judy Page, email to author, 7 May 2016.

40 www.thisismoney.co.uk / money / news / article-1536997 / Your-say-Marriage-perk-fiasco.html, also Helen Jones, *Women in British Public Life, 1914–1950*, p.226.

41 Jackie Sayers, email to author, 5 May 2016.

42 www.mylearning.org/museums/peoples-history-museum/.

43 J. Howard Miller, artist employed by Westinghouse, poster used by the War Production Co-ordinating Committee.

44 Sue Bruley, *Women in Britain Since 1900*, p.42. /https://libcom.org/history/london-transport-women-workers-strike-1918.

45 including the NUSEC, the Women's Freedom League, the Open Door Council, the Women's Co-operative Guild and the Women's section of the Labour Party; Caitriona Beaumont, 'The women's movement: politics and citizenship 1918–1950', in Ina Zweiniger-Bargielowska, *Women in Twentieth-Century Britain*, p.270. Penny Summerfield, 'Women and war in the twentieth century' in J. Purvis (ed.), *Women's History: Britain 1850–1945*, p.318.

46 www.airtransportaux.com/history.html.

47 Including the Women's Co-operative Guild; Sue Bruley, *Women in Britain Since 1900*, p.140.

48 www.historymatters.group.shef.ac.uk/the-men-turned-me-winston-churchill-gender-politics-1945-election/.

49 Sue Bruley, *Women in Britain Since 1900*, p.119.

50 Sylvia Walby, *The Future of Feminism*, p.65.

51 Equal Opportunities Commission was incorporated within the Equality and Human Rights Commission in 2007.

52 Mary Hunter, *The Women's Centenary*, p.144.

53 Mary Hunter, *The Women's Centenary*, pp.141–3.

54 http://news.bbc.co.uk/1/hi/business/8044720.stm.

55 Harold L. Smith, 'The women's movement, politics and citizenship, 1960s–2000', in Ina Zweiniger-Bargielowska, *Women in Twentieth-Century Britain*, p.284.

56 www.gov.uk/government/collections/trade-union-statistics.

57 www.permanentrevolution.net/entry/3245.

58 www.publications.parliament.uk/pa/cm200910/cmselect/cmtreasy/482/482.pdf.

59 https://www.ons.gov.uk/employmentandlabourmarket/peopleinwork/earningsandworkinghours/bulletins/genderpaygapintheuk/2018.

60 Diane Perrons, talk at the LSE on 11 January 2017.

61 www.mckinsey.com/global-themes/women-matter/the-power-of-parity-advancing-womens-equality-in-the-united-kingdom.

62 www2.deloitte.com/uk/en/pages/growth/articles/technology-career-pathways-gender-pay-gap.html.

63 Sarah Hurley, email to author, 9 September 2016.

64 www.standard.co.uk/news/london/first-woman-takes-over-at-london-fire-brigade-as-chief-retires-after-almost-a-decade-a3425826.html. There was one other female chief fire officer, Rebecca Bryant of the Staffordshire Fire and Rescue Service.

65 Jane Lewis, *Women in Britain Since 1945*, p.81.

66 www.hesa.ac.uk/data-and-analysis/publications/staff-2015-16.

67 Marianne R. Huison, email to author, 18 October 2016.

68 Judith Gillespie, email to author, 31 August 2016.

69 www.theguardian.com/uk-news/2016/aug/09/northumbria-police-dismiss-ex-chiefs-sue-sim-sexist-boys-club-claim.

70 http://schooloflaw.academicblogs.co.uk/2015/06/17/baroness-scotland-of-asthal-lld/.

71 Jayne Croft, email to author, 7 October 2016.

72 Jackie Longworth, email to author, 10 September 2016.

73 Quoted by Jane Lewis, *Women in Britain since 1945*, p.86, from Rosemary Crompton and Key Sanderson, *Gendered Jobs and Social Change* (1990).

74 Ken Roberts, D. Richardson and S. Dench, 'Sex discrimination in youth labour markets and employers' interests', in Sylvia Walby, *Gender Segregation at Work*, pp.100–13.

75 Sylvia Walby, *Gender Segregation at Work*, p.2; The American Actor Geena Davis among others addresses this in www.seejane.org; Patricia M. Thane, 'What difference did the vote make? Women in public and private life in Britain since 1918', *Historical Research* 76, no.192 (2003): 268–85.

76 Elaine Lister, email to author, 1 May 2017.

77 Elizabeth Stanko, 'Keeping women in and out of line: sexual harassment and occupational segregation', in Sylvia Walby, *Gender Segregation at Work*, pp.91–9.

78 Dr Lucy Bowyer, email to author, 22 March 2017.

79 www.barstandardsboard.org.uk/media/1597662/biennial_survey_report_2013.pdf.

80 Jayne Croft, email to author, 7 October 2016.

81 Janet Fordham, Manchester High School for Girls, via Lex Taylor email to author, 20 March 2017.

82 Caitriona Beaumont, 'The women's movement: Politics and citizenship 1918–1950', in Ina Zweiniger-Bargielowska, *Women in Twentieth-Century Britain*, p.273.

83 Juliet, email to author, 23 May 2016.

84 www.telegraph.co.uk/men/fatherhood/paternity-leave-how-britain-compares-with-the-rest-of-the-world/.

85 www.telegraph.co.uk/women/mother-tongue/10241815/Number-of-stay-at-home-mothers-falls-to-new-record-low.html.

86 http://icelandmonitor.mbl.is/news/politics_and_society/2015/10/22/plans_to_extend_paid_parental_leave/.

87 www.equalityhumanrights.com/en/managing-pregnancy-and-maternity-workplace/pregnancy-and-maternity-discrimination-research-findings.

88 www.publications.parliament.uk/pa/cm201617/cmselect/cmwomeq/90/9008.htm.

89 Joeli Brearly, email to author, 23 March 2017.

90 www.equalityhumanrights.com/en/managing-pregnancy-and-maternity-workplace/pregnancy-and-maternity-discrimination-research-findings.

91 Kate, email to author, 10 June 2017.

92 Sue Bruley, *Women in Britain Since 1900*, p.97.

93 Angela Holdsworth, *Out of the Dolls House*, p.124.

94 Baroness Deech, email to author, 1 February 2017.

95 Madeleine, email to author, 17 March 2017.

96 www.businessinsider.com/sheryl-sandberg-career-advice-to-women-2011-12?IR=T.

97 Institute of Fiscal Studies www.ifs.org.uk/uploads/publications/bns/bn186.pdf, p. 12. Individuals in the bottom two and top one percentiles of the gender- and year-specific hourly wage distributions are excluded. Source: BHPS 1991–2008.

98 Institute of Fiscal Studies www.ifs.org.uk/uploads/publications/bns/bn186.pdf, p.12.

99 www.theguardian.com/money/2016/oct/14/gender-pay-gap-widest-during-50s-analysis.

100 www.thisismoney.co.uk/money/pensions/article-3720211/Pension-gap-endures-women-retire-27-men-2016.html.

101 Pat Thane, 'Ageing – older women', in Ina Zweiniger-Bargielowska, *Women in Twentieth-Century Britain*, p.107.

102 www.carersuk.org.

103 www.ilcuk.org.uk / index.php / publications / publication_details / moved_to_care.

104 Katharine Whitehorne, on *Late Night Woman's Hour*, 26 February 2016.

105 By 2012/13 in Northern Ireland, for example, 54 per cent of businesses had an additional off-farm income; this was broken down in terms of 5 per cent of male farmers who had off-farm employment, while the spouse of the male farmer had off-farm employment on 23 per cent of farms. Sally Shortall, 'Farming, identity and well-being: Managing changing gender roles within Western European farm families', *Anthropological Notebooks*, 20.3 (2014).

106 Sally Shortall, 'Farming, identity and well-being', p.79.

107 Linda McDowell, *Migrant Women's Voices*, p.56.

108 Calculated from Olive Robinson, 'The changing labour market: growth of part-time employment and labour market segmentation in Britain', in Sylvia Walby, *Gender Segregation at Work*, p.116.

109 www.ons.gov.uk/employmentandlabourmarket/peopleinwork/earnings andworkinghours / bulletins / annualsurveyofhoursandearnings / 2015provisionalresults#gender-pay-differences.

110 Sylvia Walby, *Gender Segregation at Work*, p.6.

111 www.lawgazette.co.uk/news/women-solicitors-believe-flexible-working-damages-career/54728.article.

112 www.theguardian.com/uk-news/2016/sep/08/uk-workers-zero-hours-contracts-rise-tuc; www.ons.gov.uk/employmentandlabourmarket/peoplein work/earningsandworkinghours/articles/contractsthatdonotguaranteeam inimumnumberofhours/march2016.

113 http: / / wbg.org.uk / analysis / afs-2016-full-response-from-the-womens-budget-group/.

114 Mary Hunter, *The Women's Centenary*, p.144.

115 Sheryl Sandberg, *Lean In*, p.63.

116 http://30percentclub.org; www.catalyst.org/knowledge/statistical-over-view-women-workforce.

117 www.ft.com/content/43177e48-8eaf-11e5-8be4-3506bf20cc2b.

118 Vanessa Vallely, *Heels of Steel*, 2013, p.39.

119 www.thewomensorganisation.org.uk/about-us/our-mission.

120 www.hbr.org/2007/09/women-and-the-labyrinth-of-leadership;
Northouse, 2015.

121 www.theguardian.com/science/2004/sep/07/psychology.

122 www.telegraph.co.uk/culture/music/opera/11922705/Cressida-Pollock-
Im-no-opera-buff-but-Im-the-right-woman-for-the-job.html.

123 www.mckinsey.com/business-functions/organization/our-insights/why-
diversity-matters.

124 wwwhbr.org/2011/06/defend-your-research-what-makes-a-team-
smarter-more-women.

125 Baroness McGregor-Smith, via email from Lee Davis, 21 June 2017.

126 Mary Turner, *The Women's Century*, p.121.

127 https://www.theguardian.com/small-business-network/2017/mar/
08/dame-stephanie-shirley-flexible-remote-working-glass-ceiling;
www.steveshirley.com.

128 Jacqueline Gold, CEO of Ann Summers, *Woman's Hour*, 5 July 2016.

129 www.thisismoney.co.uk/money/smallbusiness/article-3599179/
Jacqueline-Gold-Ann-Summers-multi-million-pound-brand.html.

130 www.huffingtonpost.co.uk/news/michelle-mone/.

131 www.thetimes.co.uk/article/the-sunday-times-rich-list-2017-boom-time-
for-billionaires-pzbkrfbv2.

132 Susan, personal communication, 25 February 2017.

133 Dinah Scudder, email to author, 4 July 2016.

134 https://www.theguardian.com/lifeandstyle/2009/sep/19/divorce-law
-history.

135 Jean Vincent, personal communication, 25 February 2017.

136 Ann Goulden, email to author, 4 July 2016.

137 www.rbs.com/heritage/subjects/women-in-banking/women-in-bank-
ing--customers.html.

138 www.bbc.co.uk/news/magazine-36662872.

139 http://fortune.com/2016/01/05/wall-street-women-financial-crisis/.

140 Louise Drake, care of Janet Cooper, email to author, 10 July 2017.

141 Janet Cooper, email to author, 10 July 2017.

142 http://techcrunch.com/2016/04/19/the-first-comprehensive-study-on-
women-in-venture-capital/.

143 Stephen Dowell, *History of Taxation and Taxes in England*, Vols 1–4; Martin
Daunton, *Just Taxes: The Politics of Taxation in Britain 1914–1979*.

144 Annie Harrison, email to author, 20 April 2017.

145 Dinah Scudder, email to author, 4 July 2016.

146 See 'Taxation and Marriage', House of Commons Library Research Paper 95/87, 13 July 1995.

147 www.gov.uk/marriage-allowance/how-it-works; www.conservativehome. com/thinktankcentral/2010/01/csj-recommends-600m-transferable-tax-allowance-for-married-couples-with-very-young-children.html.

148 Rosie Campbell and Sarah Childs, ' "What the coalition did for women": A new gender consensus, coalition division and gendered austerity', in Anthony Seldon and Mike Finn (eds), *The Coalition Effect, 2010–2015*, p.419.

149 *Sunday Post*, 16 April 1950, p.7.

150 http://africasacountry.com/2016/09/corporate-tax-is-a-feminist-matter/

151 Margaret Casely-Heyford, email to author, 16 June 2017.

152 'A Fair Deal for Women' involved a collaborative campaign of 13 organisations, http://womenspeakout.wrc.org.uk/wp-content/uploads/2015/08/Fair-Deal-for-Women-Report-1-Women-Speak-Out-on-Work-and-Family-life-.pdf.

153 By the Women's Budget Group and the think tank Runnymede Trust http://wbg.org.uk/news/new-research-shows-poverty-ethnicity-gender-magnify-impact-austerity-bme-women/.

154 Ruth Pearson and Diane Elson (2015), 'Transcending the impact of the financial crisis in the United Kingdom: Towards plan F—a feminist economic strategy', *Feminist Review*, 109(1), pp.8–30.

155 www.equalitytrust.org.uk/how-has-inequality-changed.

156 www.equalitytrust.org.uk/sites/default/files/research-digest-trends-measures-final.pdf.

157 www.ifs.org.uk/publications/9539.

158 '10% Pay Rise? That'll Do Nicely', High Pay Centre, 8 August 2016, accessed 6 November 2017, http://highpaycentre.org/pubs/10-pay-rise-thatll-do-nicely.

159 www.lse.ac.uk/InternationalInequalities/pdf/III-Working-Paper-5---Atkinson.pdf.

160 www.equalitytrust.org.uk/how-has-inequality-changed.

161 www.jrf.org.uk/report/monitoring-poverty-and-social-exclusion-2016; http://www.crisis.org.uk/pages/homeless-diff-groups.html.

162 Sarah Fox, email to author, 20 December 2016.

3. Identity

1 Naomi Wolf, *The Beauty Myth*, Vintage, 1991, p.83.

2 Annie Harrison, email to author, 20 April 2017.

3 Sylvia Walby, *The Future of Feminism*, pp.70–1.

4 Point made by Dr Veitch Clark, the medical officer of health for Manchester, quoted in Sylvia Pankhurst, *Save the Mothers*, p.16.

5 Dr Comyns Berkeley, quoted in Sylvia Pankhurst, *Save the Mothers*, p.46.

6 Helen Jones, *Women in British Public Life, 1914–1950*, pp.93–100.

7 'Statistical Bulletin: National Life Tables, United Kingdom: 2012–2014', National Life Tables, United Kingdom – Office for National Statistics, 23 September 2015, accessed 11 August 2016; www.ons.gov.uk/people-populationandcommunity/birthsdeathsandmarriages/lifeexpectancies/bulletins/nationallifetablesunitedkingdom/2015-09-23.

8 Susan, email to author, 25 February 2017.

9 Figures range from 1 to 2 million, www.military-history.org/articles/world-war-2/blitz-ww2.htm.

10 Ina Zweiniger-Bargielowska, 'Housewifery', in Ina Zweiniger-Bargielowska, *Women in Twentieth-Century Britain*, p.159.

11 www.lancaster.ac.uk/fass/projects/esf/freezers.htm.

12 Shani D'Cruze, 'Women and the family', in J. Purvis (ed.), *Women's History: Britain 1850–1945*, p.67; Ina Zweiniger-Bargielowska, 'House-wifery', in Ina Zweiniger-Bargielowska (ed.), *Women in Twentieth-Century Britain*, p.159.

13 Dinah Scudder, email to author, 4 July 2016.

14 www.telegraph.co.uk/motoring/news/9717065/Number-of-women-drivers-soar.html.

15 Mari Takayanagi, email to author, 19 June 2017; kclpure.kcl.ac.uk/portal/en/theses/parliament-and-women-c19001945%2834708cef-2efd-4389-9382-5e847fd50189%29.html.

16 Ann Feloy, email to author, 22 June 2016.

17 Clare, email to author, 8 October 2016.

18 Ursula, personal communication, 12 September 2016.

19 Jean Martin, email to author, 22 April 2017.

20 Ann Goulden, email to author, 5 July 2016.

21 Andrea Shore, personal communication, 5 July 2016.

22 www.theguardian.com/lifeandstyle/2014/jun/15/fathers-spend-more-time-with-children-than-in-1970s.

23 https://stats.oecd.org/index.aspx?queryid=54757.

24 www.huffingtonpost.co.uk/ashley-beolens/babysitting-your-own-kids_b_6694518.html.

25 Jackie Sayers, email to author, 11 April 2017.

26 Ursula, personal communication, 12 September 2016.

27 Anu, personal communication, 13 October 2016.

28 www.independent.co.uk/life-style/health-and-families/features/we-need-to-talk-about-periods-9638267.html.

29 Lesley Covington, email to author, 21 June 2016.

30 www.pocket-lint.com/news/131704-apple-s-health-app-won-t-let-women-track-reproductive-health-but-there-are-workarounds.

31 www.theguardian.com/lifeandstyle/2011/aug/08/truth-period-pain.

32 Lesley Hall, 'Sexuality', in Ina Zweiniger-Bargielowska, *Women in Twentieth-Century Britain*, p.58.

33 Lesley Hall, 'Sexuality', in Ina Zweiniger-Bargielowska, *Women in Twentieth-Century Britain*, p.56.

34 Sue Bruley, *Women in Britain Since 1900*, p.75.

35 During the First World War it had been on the word of one man, a position built on the Contagious Diseases Acts, which had been repealed in 1886 after an outcry.

36 Sue Bruley, *Women in Britain Since 1900*, pp.114–16.

37 Jane Lewis, 'Marriage', in Ina Zweiniger-Bargielowska, *Women in Twentieth-Century Britain*, p.75.

38 www.open.edu/openlearn/body-mind/health/health-studies/brief-history-sex-education.

39 wwww.subzin.com/quotes/M214514593/Mean+Girls/Don%27t+have+sex+in+the+missionary+position%2C.

40 www.theguardian.com/education/2015/mar/24/personal-social-health-education-compulsory-schools-estelle-morris.

41 Laura and Maggie, communication in person, 28 April 2017.

42 Louisa Orr, email to author, 20 April 2017.

43 www.independent.co.uk/news/education/education-news/compulsory-sex-education-schools-mps-vote-against-commons-a7524381.html?cmpid=facebook-post.

44 https://www.schoolsweek.co.uk/Relationships-and-sex-education-what-should-schools-do.

45 Emily Hamer, *Britannia's Glory: A History of Twentieth-century Lesbians*, London: New York, 1996, p.74.

46 www.glbtqarchive.com/ssh/united_kingdom_02_S.pdf; http://hansard.millbanksystems.com/lords/1921/aug/15/commons-amendment-2.

47 Radclyffe Hall, Havelock Ellis and Morris L. Ernst, *The Well of Loneliness*, Covici Friede, 1929.

48 Although Radclyffe Hall's book is usually quoted as the first British book addressing lesbian love, less well known and less controversial was Welshwoman Amy Dillwyn's 1884 book, *Jill*, republished by Honno in 2013, which was never banned. She had a romantic attachment to another woman and became a member of the NUWSS. www.swansea.ac.uk/riah/research-projects/thelifeandfictionofamy-dillwyn/.

49 pinkuk.com/events/gay-pride-2016.

50 Sarah, email to author, 29 August 2016.

51 E.g. in Mexico (the *Muxe*), by indigenous North Americans (*berdache*, or two spirit), the Philippines (*bakla* or *bading*), in Thailand (*kathoeys*), Indonesia (*Waria*), Oman and the Arabian Peninsula (*khanith*) and the Balkans (*burrnesha*).

52 yougov.co.uk/news/2015/08/16/half-young-not-heterosexual/.

53 www.bbc.co.uk/news/uk-36010664.

54 www.theguardian.com/society/2016/jul/10/transgender-clinic-waiting-times-patient-numbers-soar-gender-identity-services.

55 Andrea, email to author, 9 October 2017.

56 www.telegraph.co.uk/technology/facebook/10930654/Facebooks-71-gender-options-come-to-UK-users.html.

57 Susan, personal communication, 25 February 2017.

58 Miss Sara Burstall in article entitled 'Should clever girls marry?', *Manchester Evening News*, 2 November 1923.

59 Sue Bruley, *Women in Britain Since 1900*, p.135.

60 www.telegraph.co.uk/women/sex/online-dating/10107800/Why-online-love-is-more-likely-to-last.html.

61 Jane Lewis, 'Marriage', in Ina Zweiniger-Bargielowska, *Women in Twentieth-Century Britain*, p.71.

62 www.ons.gov.uk/peoplepopulationandcommunity/birthsdeathsandmarriages/marriagecohabitationandcivilpartnerships/bulletins/marriagesinenglandandwalesprovisional/2014.

63 Máire Ní Bhrolcháin, 'The age difference at marriage in England and Wales: A century of patterns and trends', *Population Trends* 120, 2005, pt120agedifference_tcm77-160774-3.pdf.

64 www.bbc.co.uk/news/magazine-29804450.

65 Kate Richardson-Walsh, email to author via Lisa Norman, 5 September 2017.

66 www.telegraph.co.uk/women/womens-life/11921140/Suffragette-Pankhurst-family-tree-has-a-woman-problem.html.

67 Caroline Pankhurst, email to author, 19 March 2017.

68 Jill Haves, Manchester High School for Girls, email to author via Lex Taylor, 20 March 2017.

69 Vivienne Abbott, email to author, 27 June 2017.

70 www.telegraph.co.uk/news/2017/04/17/baronet-70-interviewing-hard-young-bride-not-past-sell-by-date/.

71 Samantha, email to author, 19 September 2016.

72 Coral Lomax, personal communication, 11 October 2016.

73 Jo Couldry, personal communication, 12 August 2017.

74 Anna Ashmole, email to author, 30 April 2017.

75 Manchester High School for Girls questionnaire (Lex Taylor), 15 May 2017.

76 www.ons.gov.uk/peoplepopulationandcommunity/birthsdeathsandmarriages/divorce/bulletins/divorceinenglandandwales/2016.

77 www.gingerbread.org.uk/content/2297/Missing-maintenance.

78 Emma Crewe, *The House of Commons*, pp.183–210; hansard.parliament.uk/commons/2016-09-15/debates/34FB8AA3-6931-4A38-B1E22D5AE13B1F84/DomesticAbuseVictimsInFamilyLawCourts.

79 Denise Chilton, email to author, 30 April 2017, referring to *Suddenly Single*, Fernlea Publishing House, 2017.

80 Abortionrights.org.uk.

81 Sue Bruley, *Women in Britain Since 1900*, p.137; Barbara Harrison, 'Women and health', in J. Purvis (ed.), *Women's History: Britain 1850–1945*, p.173.

82 Sue Bruley, *Women in Britain Since 1900*, p.152; Harold L. Smith, 'The women's movement, politics and citizenship, 1960s–2000', in Ina Zweiniger-Bargielowska, *Women in Twentieth-Century Britain*, p.280.

83 According to the Royal College of Obstetricians and Gynaecologists.

84 Sue Bruley, *Women in Britain Since 1900*, p.137.

85 www.cancerresearchuk.org/about-cancer/causes-of-cancer/hormones-and-cancer.

86 www.womansday.com/relationships/family-friends/g1783/pregnancy-superstitions/?slide=1.

87 www.theguardian.com/lifeandstyle/2015/jul/15/teenage-pregnancies-uk-drops-lowest-level-70-years.

88 www.demographic-research.org/volumes/vol2/default.htm.

89 Data for England and Wales, webarchive.nationalarchives.gov.uk/20160105160709/www.ons.gov.uk/ons/dcp171778_410897.pdf.

90 Helen Jones, 'Health and reproduction', in Ina Zweiniger-Bargielowska (ed.), *Women in Twentieth Century Britain*, p.96.

91 Dr Lucy Bower, email to author, 22 March 2017.

92 www.huffingtonpost.co.uk/entry/free-the-nipple-protest-brighton-beach-censorship-social-media_uk_575949ede4b041514369549f, see also Jennifer Reich, 'Public mothers and private practices: Breastfeeding as transgression', in Chris Bobel and Samantha Kwan (eds), *Embodied Resistance*, pp.130–42.

93 https://www.theguardian.com/society/2016/nov/04/more-than-250000-uk-babies-born-ivf.

94 www.theguardian.com/society/2014/nov/23/whats-next-for-worlds-5-million-ivf-babies.

95 Baroness Deech, email to author, 2 February 2017.

96 Helen Walmsley-Johnson, *The Invisible Woman: Taking on the Vintage Years*, London: Icon, 2016, p.91.

97 Clare Holmes, personal communication, 19 July 2016.

98 Sue Bruley, *Women in Britain Since 1900*, p.115.

99 Ann, personal communication, 11 October 2016.

100 Nikki B., personal communication, 20 April 2017.

101 Ursula, personal communication, 12 September 2016.

102 Margaret Casely-Hayford, email to author, 16 June 2017.

103 www.theguardian.com/society/2014/dec/03/why-no-advertising-targeted-over-50s.

104 www.grandparentsplus.org.uk/news/childcare-poll2017.

105 Nan Watson, email to author, 20 September 2016.

106 Gill, personal communication, 26 September 2016.

107 Ina Zweiniger-Bargielowska, 'The body and consumer culture', in Ina Zweiniger-Bargielowska, *Women in Twentieth-Century Britain*, p.188.

108 Joan Martin, email to author, 19 April 2017.

109 Naomi Wolf, *The Beauty Myth*, Vintage, 1991, p.187.

110 Naomi Wolf, *The Beauty Myth,* Vintage, 1991, p.83.

111 www.theguardian.com/fashion/2016/sep/12/why-do-women-paint-their-nails-clue-it-has-nothing-to-do-with-men.

112 Maggie Ashmole, personal communication, 27 April 2017.

113 Madeleine Bowyer, email to author, 30 March 2017.

114 Lynn, email to author, 20 April 2017.

115 Jo B. Paoletti, *Pink and Blue: Telling the Boys from the Girls in America,* Bloomington: Indiana UP, 2012; www.todayifoundout.com/index.php/2014/10/pink-used-common-color-boys-blue-girls/.

116 Claire, email to author, 14 August 2017.

117 www.waisttrain.uk/pages/why-use-a-waist-trainer.

118 Lesley Covington, email to author, 21 June 2016.

119 Elaine De Fries, Manchester Women's Aid, 19 July 2016.

120 Nicola Thorp, email to author, 14 March 2107.

121 www.youtube.com/watch?v=wb7neUBxEhc.

122 www.thinkbox.tv/Creative/Insight/10-from-50-Women-in-advertising.

123 http://www.bbc.co.uk/news/business-40638343.

124 Sarah Chaney, *Psyche on the Skin: A History of Self-harm,* 2017. www.pulse-project.org/sites/default/files/ThepEmp%20-%2010%20-%20Sarah%20Chaney%20-%20mp4.mp4.

125 Penni Blythe, personal communication, 14 October 2016.

126 Dr Kate Middleton, personal communication and email to author, 21 December 2016.

127 www.britishfashioncouncil.co.uk/About#RL?rl_playlist=playlistReports&rl_id=8.

128 Amy Drayton, email to author, 27 March 2017.

129 www.hellomagazine.com/healthandbeauty/skincare-and-fragrances/2015102327855/kate-winslet-will-no-longer-let-adverts-be-retouched/.

130 Izzy, personal communication, 13 December 2016.

131 www.b-eat.co.uk/latest/4370.

132 www.eatingdisorderhope.com/information/anorexia/anorexia-nervosa-highest-mortality-rate-of-any-mental-disorder-why.

133 Izzy, personal communication, 13 December 2016.

134 http://healthpsych.psy.vanderbilt.edu/HealthPsych/feminist.htm.

135 www.diabetes.org.uk/Guide-to-diabetes/Life-with-diabetes/Diabulimia/.

136 www.bbc.co.uk/newsbeat/article/27509051/self-harm-rate-triples

-among-teenagers-in-england; www.theguardian.com/society/2016/dec/09/self-harm-children-rises-steeply-england-wales.

137 https://www.childrenssociety.org.uk/sites/default/files/good_childhood_summary_2018.pdf.

138 www.bbc.co.uk/newsbeat/article/35500951/figures-reveal-rise-in-self-poisoning-with-teenage-girls-most-at-risk; www.bbc.co.uk/newsbeat/article/36302758/rise-in-poor-female-teens-poisoning-themselves.

139 www.bbc.co.uk/newsbeat/article/25711600/higher-suicide-risk-for-young-gay-and-lesbian-people.

140 'Obesity Statistics', House of Commons Library Briefing Paper Number 3336, 20 January 2017.

141 www.netdoctor.co.uk/conditions/pregnancy-and-family/a9293/antenatal-depression/.

142 Juliet Webster, email to author, 19 January 2017, based on Keith Randle, J. Webster, and K. Randle (eds), *Virtual Workers and the Global Labour Market*, 2016.

143 M. I. Husain, W. Waheed and Nusrat Husain, 'Self-harm in British South Asian Women: Psychosocial Correlates and Strategies for Prevention', Annals of General Psychiatry, 22 May 2006; https://doi.org/10.1186/1744-859X-5-7.

144 www.gov.uk/government/uploads/system/uploads/attachment_data/file/401662/2014_PHE_HIV_annual_report_draft_Final_07-01-2015.pdf.

145 www.who.int/hac/techguidance/pht/InfoBulletinIntimatePartnerViolenceFinal.pdf.

146 Alice Welbourn, email to author, 27 July 2017.

147 www.theguardian.com/commentisfree/2016/sep/27/me-affects-four-times-women-men-chronic-fatigue-syndrome.

148 Discussions and correspondence with Dr Kate Middleton, 21 December 2016, see also: blogs.bmj.com/medical-ethics/2016/12/06/mind-the-gap-ethical-failures-in-the-treatment-of-chronic-fatigue-syndrome/.

149 www.theguardian.com/science/2017/apr/28/uti-test-used-by-gps-gives-wrong-results-in-at-least-a-fifth-of-cases-study-claims.

150 www.migrainebuddy.com/understanding-migraines-the-gender-divide/.

151 www.theguardian.com/commentisfree/2016/sep/27/me-affects-four-times-women-men-chronic-fatigue-syndrome.

152 Rita Pankhurst, personal communication, 4 September 2016.

153 Elizabeth, email to author, 27 July 2017.

154 www.macmillan.org.uk/information-and-support/treating/surgery/having-breast-reconstruction.

155 Elizabeth, email to author, 27 July 2017.

4. Violence

1 Mitch Egan CB, email to author, 29 June 2016.

2 WHO, the World Health Organisation, MSC and LSHTM, 2013.

3 Susan Brownmiller, *Against Our Will: Men, Women and Rape,* Simon & Schuster, 1975; Jill Radford, and Diana E. H. Russell, *Femicide: The Politics of Woman Killing,* Twayne, 1992.

4 www.gov.uk/government/statistics/historical-crime-data.

5 www.cps.gov.uk/sites/default/files/documents/publications/cps_vawg_report_2018.pdf.

6 Angela Preston, email to author, 27 April 2017.

7 Penni, email to author, 18 October 2016.

8 Domestic abuse defined as 'partner / ex-partner abuse (non-sexual), family abuse (non-sexual) and sexual assault or stalking carried out by a current or former partner or other family member'. Stats from webarchive.nationalarchives.gov.uk/20160105160709/www.ons.gov.uk/ons/dcp171776_394500.pdf.

9 www.cps.gov.uk/sites/default/files/documents/publications/cps_vawg_report_2018.pdf.

10 Office for National Statistics, *Crime Statistics, Focus on Violent Crime and Sexual Offences, Year Ending March 2016, Chapter 2: 'Homicide'.*

11 Lynn, email to author, 19 March 2017.

12 www.gov.uk/government/news/new-definition-of-domestic-violence-and-abuse-to-include-16-and-17-year-olds.

13 www.judiciary.gov.uk/publications/president-of-family-division-circular-practice-direction-pd12j-domestic-abuse/.

14 Article 5 of the Human Rights Act protects our right to liberty and security. See Scottish Women's Aid, 'Coercive Control', 2013.

15 https://www.theduluthmodel.org/wheel-gallery/.

16 www.cps.gov.uk/legal/a_to_c/controlling_or_coercive_behaviour/; https://www.theguardian.com/commentisfree/2015/dec/28/domestic-violence-law-coercive-control-abuse-partners-courts.

17 www.womensaid.org.uk/matter-life-death-proposed-one-size-fits

-funding-model-supported-housing-threatens-refuges-warns-womens-aid/.

18 Labour Councillor Sarah Judge, email to author, 30 September 2016.

19 Professor Catherine Donovan, Dr Rebecca Barnes and Dr Catherine Nixon, University of Sunderland and University of Leicester, 'The Coral Project: Exploring Abusive Behaviours in Lesbian, Gay, Bisexual and/or Transgender Relationships', p.42.

20 https://www.refuge.org.uk/our-story/our-history/

21 www.sistersuncut.org/2016/06/08/we-are-the-suffragettes-sisters-uncut-chain-themselves-to-parliament-at-government-art-launch/.

22 https://www.gov.uk/government/uploads/system/uploads/attach-ment_data/file/420963/APVA.pdf.

23 www.communitycare.co.uk/2016/10/20/child-parent-abuse-social-workers-dont-know/.

24 http://www.adfam.org.uk/docs/dv_prelease.pdf.

25 www.gov.uk/government/uploads/system/uploads/attachment_data/file/505827/Forced_Marriage_Unit_statistics_2015.pdf.

26 https://www.cps.gov.uk/sites/default/files/documents/publications/cps-vawg-report-2018.pdf.

27 www.cps.gov.uk/publications/docs/cps_vawg_report_2016.pdf.

28 www.unfpa.org/resources/female-genital-mutilation-fgm-frequently-asked-questions#practice_origins.

29 www.gov.uk/government/uploads/system/uploads/attachment_data/file/469448/FGM-Mandatory-Reporting-procedural-info-FINAL.pdf.

30 Shakira Hussein and Camille Nurkam 'Entitled to be free: exposing the limits of choice', in *The Beauty Myth*, in Miranda Kiraly and Meagan Tyler (eds), *Freedom Fallacy*, pp.89–90.

31 Carolyn Pedwell, *Feminism, Culture and Embodied Practice: The Rhetorics of Comparison*, p.1.

32 http://www.bbc.co.uk/news/health-40410459. http://www.bbc.co.uk/news/health-24942981.

33 Catherine Mayer, *Attack of the 50 Ft. Women: How Gender Equality Can Save the World!* HQ, 2017, p.13.

34 Ipsos MORI interview of 1,000 British adults aged 18+ by telephone, February 2016 for WOW Southbank Centre.

35 http://everydaysexism.com; https://ldn.ihollaback.org/about/ .

36 Shani D'Cruze, 'Crime', in Ina Zweiniger-Bargielowska, *Women in Twentieth-Century Britain*, p.209.

37 Harold L. Smith, 'The women's movement, politics and citizenship, 1960s–2000', in Ina Zweiniger-Bargielowska, *Women in Twentieth-Century Britain*, p.281.

38 *House of Commons Briefing Paper*, No. 6261, 19 May 2016, 'Stalking Criminal Offences'.

39 https://www.cps.gov.uk/sites/default/files/documents/publications/cps-vawg-report-2018.pdf.

40 www.suzylamplugh.org/news/homicide-research.

41 www.youtube.com/watch?v=pZwvrxVavnQ.

42 'Women activists of East London: A study of radical female history in Tower Hamlets, Hackney and Waltham Forest', Share UK, p.18.

43 oro.open.ac.uk/10655/1/download.pdf.

44 Shani D'Cruze, 'Crime', in Ina Zweiniger-Bargielowska, *Women in Twentieth-Century Britain*, p.209.

45 https://www.cps.gov.uk/sites/default/files/documents/publications/cps-vawg-report-2018.pdf.

46 www.theguardian.com/society/2017/dec/14/sexual-history-sometimes-revealed-rape-cases-moj.

47 Sarah Silverman, verified account @SarahKSilverman, 20 March 2015.

48 www.telegraph.co.uk/news/2017/03/10/women-get-drunk-must-protect-against-rapists-judge-says/.

49 www.theguardian.com/society/2016/sep/10/misogyny-hate-crime-nottingham-police-crackdown.

50 rapecrisis.org.uk/historyofrapecrisis.php and www.rapecrisisscotland.org.uk/about/our-story-so-far/.

51 Finn Mackay, *Radical Feminism*, p.73. The towns were Lancaster, Brighton, Bristol, York, Newcastle, London, Bradford, Guildford, Salisbury, Manchester and Leeds.

52 www.tuc.org.uk/sites/default/files/SexualHarassmentreport2016.pdf.

53 Christine Low, email to author, 6 July 2016.

54 Jackie Ford, email to author, 11 October 2016.

55 Dame Janet Smith Review, the Jimmy Savile Investigation report, 2016.

56 www.newstatesman.com/politics/uk/2016/06/culture-enabled-clement-freud-s-abuse-not-yet-defeated.

57 www.bbc.co.uk/programmes/b07vs2ny.

58 www.parliament.uk/business/committees/committees-a-z/commons-select/women-and-equalities-committee/news-parliament-2015/sexual-harassment-and-violence-in-schools-report-published-16-17/.

59 www.parliamentlive.tv/Event/Index/d48c3261-d54f-43bc-a52f-940a9f5c818c.

60 www.universitiesuk.ac.uk/policy-and-analysis/reports/Documents/2016/changing-the-culture.pdf.

61 www.theguardian.com/education/2017/mar/05/students-staff-uk-universities-sexual-harassment-epidemic.

62 www.nspcc.org.uk/what-we-do/news-opinion/child-sex-offence-recorded-every-10-minutes/.

63 Sarah, through Claire Holcombe, email to author, 8 June 2017.

64 Jane, through Claire Holcombe, email to author, 8 June 2017.

65 www.theguardian.com/technology/2016/apr/12/the-dark-side-of-guardian-comments.

66 Shaista Gohir, care of Faeeza Vaid, 12 June 2017.

67 www.bbc.co.uk/mediacentre/latestnews/2016/bbc-wiki; http://www.telegraph.co.uk/news/2017/09/04/female-mps-sent-25000-abusive-twitter-messages-just-six-months/.

68 twitter.com/jk_rowling?lang=en-gb.

69 J. K. Rowling Twitter account, 9 June 2017.

70 www.facebook.com/reclaimtheinternet/ .

71 Elaine De Fries, email to author, 19 July 2016.

72 www.independent.co.uk/news/uk/politics/domestic-violence-istanbul-convention-bill-philip-davies-filibuster-parliament-snp-a7597686.html.

73 E.g. *Nuts* and *Zoo* (2004–2014).

74 Rebecca Whisnant, 'Not your father's Playboy, not your mother's feminist movement: feminism in porn culture', in Miranda Kiraly and Meagan Tyler (eds), *Freedom Fallacy*, p.8.

75 www.cps.gov.uk/publications/docs/cps_vawg_report_2016.pdf.

76 Ana Bridges et al., 'Aggression and sexual behaviour in best-selling pornography videos: A content analysis update' (2010), 16 *Violence Against Women* 1065. Quoted in Meghan Donevan, 'If pornography is sex education what does it teach?' in Miranda Kiraly and Meagan Tyler (eds), *Freedom Fallacy*, p.8.

77 Kat Banyard, *Pimp State: Sex, Money and the Future of Equality,* 2016, p.48.

78 Kat Banyard, *Pimp State: Sex, Money and the Future of Equality,* 2016, p.128.

79 blog.ted.com/cindy_gallop_ma/.

80 Research by Middlesex University into the impact of online porn on young people with the NSPCC and the Children's Commissioner for England, www.nspcc.org.uk/services-and-resources/research-and-resources/2016/i-wasnt-sure-it-was-normal-to-watch-it/.

81 http://blog.cps.gov.uk/2015/08/prosecutors-being-advised-to-learn-from-revenge-porn-cases-across-the-country-to-help-them-tackle-th.html/.

82 www.cps.gov.uk/publications/docs/cps_vawg_report_2016.pdf and www.bbc.co.uk/news/uk-37278264.

83 Kat Banyard, *Pimp State: Sex, Money and the Future of Equality*, 2016, p.32.

84 researchbriefings.files.parliament.uk/documents/SN04751/SN04751.pdf.

85 www.oxforddictionaries.com/definition/english/prostitute.

86 Claire Holcombe, email to author, 13 June 2017.

87 Home Office 2004 report quoted in Kat Banyard, *Pimp State: Sex, Money and the Future of Equality*, 2016, p.25.

88 http://prostitutescollective.net/2016/11/22/facts-sex-work/#_ftn1.

89 Clare Holmes, email to author, 19 July 2017.

90 Home Office 2004 report quoted in Kat Banyard, *Pimp State: Sex, Money and the Future of Equality*, 2016, p.25.

91 Sarah, through Claire Holcombe, email to author, 8 June 2017.

92 Home Office 2004 report quoted in Kat Banyard, *Pimp State: Sex, Money and the Future of Equality*, 2016, p.25.

93 Kat Banyard, *Pimp State: Sex, Money and the Future of Equality*, 2016, pp.23–4, 64, 87.

94 www.newstatesman.com/politics/feminism/2015/10/why-government-charging-more-women-selling-sex-turning-blind-eye-buyers.

95 Meghan Murphy, 'I do what I want, fuck yeah!: moving beyond "a woman's choice"', in Miranda Kiraly and Meagan Tyler (eds), *Freedom Fallacy*, p.16.

96 Kat Banyard, *Pimp State: Sex, Money and the Future of Equality*, 2016, p.142.

97 Kat Banyard, *Pimp State: Sex, Money and the Future of Equality*, 2016, p.89.

98 Iceland, Norway, Northern Ireland, with a variant of it in Canada, and it is being considered in Scotland. France passed a new law that criminalises men in 2016.

99 http://enddemand.uk/about/sex-buyer-law/.

100 appgprostitution.files.wordpress.com/2015/09/appg-prostitution-shifting-the-burden-inquiry.pdf.

101 eur-lex.europa.eu/LexUriServ/LexUriServ.do?uri=OJ:L:2011:101:0001:00 11:EN:PDF.

102 https://www.cps.gov.uk/sites/default/files/documents/publications/ cps-vawg-report-2018.pdf.

103 www.unseenuk.org/about/the-problem/facts-and-figures.

104 Pippa Hockton, email to author, 18 October 2016.

105 Riannah, through Claire Holcombe, email to author, 8 June 2017.

106 www.gov.uk/government/statistics/prison-population-figures-2016; www.womeninprison.org.uk/research/key-facts.php.

107 www.womeninprison.org.uk/research/key-facts.php.

108 www.womeninprison.org.uk/research/key-facts.php.

109 www.prisonreformtrust.org.uk/Portals/0/Documents/sentencing_ mothers.pdf.

110 www.prisonreformtrust.org.uk/Portals/0/Documents/Women/ Sentencing_Mothers_pdf.

111 Shani D'Cruze, 'Crime', in Ina Zweiniger-Bargielowska, *Women in Twentieth-Century Britain*, p.205.

112 www.womeninprison.org.uk/research/key-facts.php.

113 www.prisonreformtrust.org.uk/Portals/0/Documents/sentencing_ mothers.pdf.

114 webarchive.nationalarchives.gov.uk/+/homeoffice.gov.uk/documents/ corston-report/.

115 Mitch Egan CB, email to author, 29 June 2016.

116 Krista Cowman, *Women in British Politics, C.1689–1979*, 2010, p.160.

117 Quoted in Helen Jones, *Women in British Public Life, 1914–1950*, p.195.

118 Helen Jones, *Women in British Public Life, 1914–1950*, pp.188–9.

119 Sue Bruley, *Women in Britain Since 1900*, pp.44–6.

120 Women and the Military during World War One, Professor Joanna Bourke, 2011, BBC History in depth, bbc.co.uk.

121 Dorothy Lawrence, *Sapper Dorothy Lawrence*, 1919 (republished by Kessinger Publishing, 2010).

122 Sue Bruley, *Women in Britain since 1900*, p.103.

123 Mary Turner, *The Women's Century*, p.94.

124 Rita Pankhurst, personal communication, 2 September 2016.

125 https://www.nam.ac.uk/explore/timeline-women-army.

126 Caroline Paige, *True Colours: My Life as the First Openly Transgender Officer in the British Armed Force*, Biteback Publishing, 2017.

127 Patricia, email to author, 23 June 2016.

128 www.whatdotheyknow.com / request / conviction_rate_following_ rape_c; www.theguardian.com/uk/deepcut.

129 Conflicts between families explored in Adam Hochschild, *To End All Wars*, Macmillan, 2011.

130 Mary Davis, email to author, 25 October 2016.

131 Gertrude Carman Bussey and Margaret Tims, *Pioneers for Peace: Women's International League for Peace and Freedom, 1915–1965*, Women's International League for Peace and Freedom, 1980, p.51.

132 Gertrude Carman Bussey and Margaret Tims, *Pioneers for Peace: Women's International League for Peace and Freedom, 1915–1965*, Women's International League for Peace and Freedom, 1980, p.144.

133 Helen Jones, *Women in British Public Life, 1914–1950*, p.81; Brian Harrison, 'Eglantyne Jebb (1876–1928)', *Oxford Dictionary of National Biography* (Oxford University Press, 2004).

134 Lucy Noakes, 'War and peace', in Ina Zweiniger-Bargielowska, *Women in Twentieth-Century Britain*, p.188.

135 Finn Mackay, *Radical Feminism*, p.20.

136 Madeleine Bowyer, email to author, 24 April 2017.

137 Cathy Watson, email to author, 7 May 2017.

138 Joan Ruddock, *Going Nowhere: A Memoir*, 2016, p.261; Women activists of East London: A study of radical female history in Tower Hamlets, Hackney and Waltham Forest', Share UK, p.23.

139 Niamh Moore, 'Ecofeminism as third wave feminism? Essentialism, activism and the academy', in Stacy Gillis, Gillian Howie and Rebecca Munford, *Third Wave Feminism: A Critical Exploration*, Palgrave Macmillan, 2004, pp.227–39.

5. Culture

1 Frances Morris, email to author, 23 January 2017.

2 arementalkingtoomuch.com; www.dailywire.com/news/14294/manter-ruption-feminist-app-detects-when-men-james-barrett.

3 Rebecca Solnit, *Men Explain Things to Me*, 2014, pp.10–11.

4 www.manpanels.org.

5 Louisa Orr, email to author, 23 March 2017.

6 Myra Hird, *Engendering Violence: Heterosexual Interpersonal Violence from Childhood to Adulthood*, 2017.

7 https://www.wsj.com/articles/SB100014241278873247051045781471700
03062856.

8 www.independent.co.uk/voices/comment/i-need-to-sit-that-way-
because-of-my-balls-and-6-other-misguided-defences-of-manspreading-on
-public-9976792.html.

9 Mary, email to author, 8 May 2017.

10 David Gutzke, *Women Drinking Out in Britain Since the Early Twentieth
Century*, 2016.

11 www.theguardian.com/theguardian/from-the-archive-blog/2012/nov/
15/el-vino-women-ban-fleet-street-1982.

12 Diane, email to author via Jackie, 10 May 2017.

13 Fiona Martin, email to author, 21 September 2017.

14 flashbak.com/the-rise-and-fall-of-the-lyons-cornerhouses-and-their-nippy
-waitresses-35186/.

15 www.bbc.com/news/uk-england-london-35688067.

16 Rosina, email to author, 18 May 2017.

17 Isabelle Davies, Hitchin school exercise facilitated by Claire Burnett, 15
June 2017.

18 http://www.bbc.co.uk/news/magazine-35670446.

19 Jo Jowers, Let Toys be Toys, email to author, 3 July 2017.

20 www.telegraph.co.uk/technology/video-games/7037574/Lara-Croft-
picks-up-six-Guinness-world-records.html.

21 The Women's Library, LSE special collection periodicals. Moruzi,
Kristine, and Michelle Smith. "'Learning What Real Work . . . Means":
Ambivalent Attitudes Towards Employment in the "Girl's Own Paper"',
Victorian Periodicals Review 43, no.4 (2010): pp.429-45. www.jstor.org/
stable/41038854.

22 www.friardale.co.uk/Schoolgirls%27%20Own/Schoolgirls%27%20Own.
htm.

23 The Women's Library, LSE special collection periodicals. Moruzi, Kristine,
and Michelle Smith. "'Learning What Real Work . . . Means": Ambivalent
Attitudes Towards Employment in the "Girl's Own Paper"', Victorian
Periodicals Review 43, no.4 (2010): pp.429-45. www.jstor.org/stable/41038854.

24 Beverly Cook, email to author, 6 July 2017.

25 Cynthia White, *Women's Magazine 1693–1968 (Live Issues)*, Michael Joseph, 1970.

26 Penny Tinkler, 'Women and popular literature', in J. Purvis (ed.), *Women's
History: Britain 1850–1945*, pp.131–56.

27 www.penguin.co.uk/series/LBGU/ladybirds-for-grown-ups/.

28 www.theguardian.com/world/2016/dec/12/wonder-woman-un-ambas-sador-gender-equality.

29 www.theguardian.com/books/2017/mar/17/childrens-books-for-girls-publishers-writers-gender-imbalance.

30 Jacqueline Wilson, email to author via Naomi Cooper, 8 May 2017.

31 Sally Nicholls, email to author, 3 April 2017.

32 Laurel Thatcher Ulrich, *Well-Behaved Women Seldom Make History*, 2007, pp.xxxiii.

33 Nomboniso Gasa, *Women in South African History*, p.132.

34 Joan Wallach Scott, *Gender and the Politics of History*, p.18.

35 Data from RAJAR, Lyndsay Ferrigan, email to author, 6–10 April 2017.

36 www.radiotimes.com/news/2016-10-07/womans-hour-was-launched-70-years-ago--but-the-bbc-almost-got-it-totally-wrong.

37 Stephan Collini, *Common Writing: Essays on Literary Culture and Public Debate*, Oxford University Press, 17 March 2016.

38 Jane Garvey, email to author, 11 June 2016.

39 Jane Garvey, email to author, 11 June 2016.

40 www.bbc.com/news/uk-39173398.

41 www.yorkshirepost.co.uk/what-s-on/theatre/coronation-street-only-wrote-in-a-transgender-character-as-a-joke-1-8385575.

42 www.huffingtonpost.co.uk/2013/05/16/harman-highlights-lack-of-older-women-on-television_n_3283989.html.

43 Louisa Orr, email to author, 21 March 2017.

44 www.bbc.co.uk/mediacentre/latestnews/2016/bbc-wiki.

45 Kaitlynn Mendes, email to author, 27 April 2017.

46 https://merchdope.com/youtube-stats.

47 time.com/4258291/30-most-influential-people-on-the-internet-2016/.

48 Kaitlynn Mendes, email to author, 28 April 2017.

49 www.the-mousetrap.co.uk/Online/.

50 Caroline, email correspondence with author, 19 March 2017.

51 Jude Kelly, email to author, 22 May 2017.

52 www.statista.com/statistics/296240/age-and-gender-of-the-cinema-audi-ence-uk/.

53 Bechdeltest.com statistics, 10 April 2016.

54 Holly Tarquini, email to author, 30 May 2017.

55 polygraph.cool/films/.

56 https://en.wikipedia.org/wiki/Roles_of_mothers_in_Disney_media; https://www.theatlantic.com/magazine/archive/2014/07/why-are-all-the-cartoon-mothers-dead/372270/.

57 Julie Walters, email to author via Kate Morgan, 11 May 2017.

58 Sarah Gavron, email to author, 22 November 2016.

59 www.nytimes.com/2015/11/22/magazine/the-women-of-hollywood-speak-out.html?_r=0.

60 www.theguardian.com/film/2016/sep/18/gemma-arterton-it-is-easier-to-conform-and-shut-up-the-girl-with-all-the-gifts.

61 www.newstatesman.com/politics/feminism/2016/03/i-sorted-uk-s-statues-gender-mere-27-cent-are-historical-non-royal-women.

62 Towards the end of 2017 there was some competition around which woman would be honoured in Parliament Square, the media enjoying the tensions between one of Millicent Fawcett or Emmeline Pankhurst; http://www.telegraph.co.uk/women/politics/emmeline-pankhursts-great-granddaughter-millicent-fawcett-should/.

63 barbarahepworth.org.uk/about-barbara-hepworth/alan-bowness-life-and-work.html.

64 www.telegraph.co.uk/culture/art/8523984/The-Hepworth-Wakefield-a-monumental-figure-returns.html.

65 thinkingpractices.wordpress.com/2011/03/30/essay/.

66 Mark Sladen, 'A red mirror', in Mark Sladen, *Helen Chadwick*, 2004, pp.13–32.

67 Frances Morris, email to author, 23 January 2017.

68 www.apollo-magazine.com/abstraction-representation-women-artists-contemporary-art/.

69 www.theguardian.com/education/2015/dec/16/a-level-music-female-composers-students-campaign-jessy-mccabe-edexcel.

70 www.theguardian.com/women-in-leadership/2013/oct/14/blind-auditions-orchestras-gender-bias.

71 The work, by composer Lucy Pankhurst, set a text created by the author from one of Emmeline's speeches. Edwina Wolstencroft, email to author, 5 October 2017.

72 www.huffingtonpost.com/entry/women-music-production-max-martin_us_58b6cb66e4b0a8a9b787aff5.

73 www.dailymail.co.uk/femail/article-3324822/Dame-Shirley-Bassey-says-women-not-pilots-police-officers.html.

74 www.dustyspringfield.org.uk/LTD/index.php/life/memorable-quotes.

75 www.telegraph.co.uk/culture/music/music-news/8224864/Sandie-Shaws
-love-scandal-that-almost-cost-Britain-its-first-Eurovision-victory.html.

76 www.encyclopedia.com/people/literature-and-arts/music-popular-and-
jazz-biographies/marianne-faithfull.

77 Annie Lennox, email to author, 10 February 2017.

78 www.billboard.com/biz/articles/news/1176886/amy-winehouse-owns-
uk-charts-three-albums-in-top-ten-five-singles-in-top.

79 www.telegraph.co.uk/culture/music/music-news/10760558/Lily-Allen-
the-return-of-pops-most-outspoken-star.html.

80 www.huffingtonpost.com/entry/adele-feminism-rolling
-stone_us_5638d7a9e4b00a4d2e0be2d7.

81 Emeli Sandé, email to author via Katie Torrie, 31 May 2017.

82 s.telegraph.co.uk/graphics/projects/paloma-faith/.

83 www.pressreader.com/uk/scottish-daily-mail/20120317/281638187154831.

84 www.bbc.co.uk/news/magazine-30329606.

85 https://www.lewesfc.com.

86 en.wikipedia.org/wiki/Women's_professional_sports#England.

87 www.englandrugby.com/news/rfu-introduce-rugby-100-000-women-and
-girls/.

88 www.theguardian.com/sport/2009/apr/03/andre-strauss-andrew-flower
-england-cricket-st-lucia.

89 womenshistorynetwork.org/women-athletes-are-still-put-in-second-
place-at-the-olympics-its-time-to-sprint-towards-equality/.

90 Quotes from Elli Moody, email to author, 23 March 2017.

91 Karen Walker, email to author, 7 May 2017.

92 Julie Bentley, email to author, 24 February 2017.

93 Sam Morgan, email to author, 8 June 2017.

94 Jane Robinson, *A Force to Be Reckoned With: A History of the Women's
Institute,* 2014.

95 Christine Cowley, email to author, 28 April 2017.

96 Irene Cockroft, email to author, 7 February 2017.

97 www.theguardian.com/media/2010/jul/25/betty-jerman-columnist
-obituary.

98 nwr.org.uk. National Women's Register archives are held in The Women's
Library collection at the LSE Library.

99 Jackie Sayers, email to author, 14 October 2016.

100 Brenda, personal communication, 11 October 2016.

101 www.knittogether.info/find-a-knitting-group/www.stitchlinks.com/
index.html. www.ukhandknitting.com.

102 Juliet Bernard, email to author, 23 May 2016.

103 Susan Hayward and Katherine Marshall (eds), *Women, Religion and Peacebuilding*, 2015, pp.6–7.

104 Mary Magdalene, Mary the mother of Jesus and Mary sister of Martha.

105 https://womenandthechurch.org/resources/maude-royden-1876-1956/.

106 Mrs Rebecca Phillip, Cathedral Archivist, email to author via Jackie Sayers, 2 June 2017. Original source David Welander, Canon of Gloucester, *History, Art and Architecture of Gloucester Cathedral*, (Alan Sutton Publishing, 1991), ISBN: 0-86299-821-2.

107 Susan Hayward and Katherine Marshall (eds), *Women, Religion and Peacebuilding*, 2015, p.8.

108 Susan Hayward and Katherine Marshall (eds), *Women, Religion and Peacebuilding*, 2015, p.8.

109 www.brin.ac.uk/2017/religion-and-the-british-social-attitudes-2015-survey/.

110 Sue Morgan and Jacqueline de Vries (eds), *Women, Gender and Religious Cultures in Britain, 1800–1940*, 2010.

111 http://www.natcen.ac.uk/news-media/press-releases/2017/september/
british-social-attitudes-record-number-of-brits-with-no-religion/.

112 Right Reverend Libby Lane, Bishop of Stockport, email to author, 11 September 2017.

113 Faeeza Vaid, 'Muslim Women and Authorities of Discursive Religious Knowledge Historically-Muslim Women as Re-claimed Authorities Today', MA Dissertation, Warwick University, 2009.

6. Power

1 Rebecca Solnit, www.theguardian.com/world/2017/mar/13/protest-persist
-hope-trump-activism-anti-nuclear-movement?CMP=share_btn_link.

2 Patricia Hill Collins and Sirma Bilge, *Intersectionality*, pp.30–1, 114.

3 Jude Kelly, email to author, 22 May 2017.

4 Audre Lorde, *Sister Outsider*, pp.117–18.

5 Faeeza Vaid, email to author, 7 June 2017.

6 Mitch Egan CB, email to author, 29 June 2016.

7 Adapted from CARE's Women's Empowerment Framework, http://
www.care.org/our-work/womens-empowerment/gender-integration/

womens-empowerment-framework. See also Sarah Mosedale, 'Assessing Women's Empowerment: Towards a Conceptual Framework', *Journal of International Development* 17, no. 2 (2005), pp.243–57. doi:10.1002/jid.1212.

8 Pauline, personal communication, 11 October 2016.

9 Ann Feloy, email to author, 28 February 2016.

10 Mary Evans, *The Persistence of Gender Inequality*, 2016, p.119.

11 Helena Kennedy, 'Eve was framed', in Lisa Appignanesi et al. (eds), *Fifty Shades of Feminism*, p.143.

12 Carlene Firmin, 'Wifey, sket, hoodrat', in Lisa Appignanesi et al. (eds), *Fifty Shades of Feminism*, p.76.

13 Sadiq Khan, press release for #March4Women in 2017.

14 www.womensmarch.com.

15 www.shropshirestar.com/news/emergency-services/2017/01/25/i-was-frightened-by-comments-made-over-womans-march-shock-over-abuse-by-online-trolls-from-shropshire/.

16 Robert E. Goodin, *Explaining Norms*, 2016.

17 www.youtube.com/watch?v=6yQ9a-hJVyo.

18 Anthony Holden and Ben Holden, *Poems That Make Grown Men Cry: 100 Men on the Words That Move Them*, Simon & Schuster Paperbacks, 2015.

19 R. W. Connell's 1995 *Masculinities* unpacked the relationship between different forms of masculinities and power. Jack Urwin's *Man Up*, published in 2016, and Grayson Perry's *The Descent of Man*, explore the dangers of buying into the idealised vision. These are books by men very much talking to men.

20 Cordelia Fine, *Testostorone Rex*, 2017.

21 www.agathachristie.com.

22 www.theatlantic.com/magazine/archive/2016/07/women-are-writing-the-best-crime-novels/485576/.

23 www.telegraph.co.uk/news/2017/01/10/clare-hollingworth-dies-aged-105-telegraph-correspondent-broke/.

24 www.nytimes.com/2006/08/27/books/review/Gray2.t.html.

25 http://mariecolvincenter.org/stories-by-marie-colvin/courage-knows-no-gender/.

26 www.mariecolvincenter.org/?page_id=937.

27 Fiona Martin, email to author, 31 March 2017.

28 Laura Coryton, email to author, 22 May 2017.

29 petition.parliament.uk/petitions/129823   www.theguardian.com/uk-news/
    2016/may/11/receptionist-sent-home-pwc-not-wearing-high-heels-pwc-
    nicola-thorp.

30 petition.parliament.uk/petitions/129823   www.theguardian.com/uk-news
    /2016/may/11/receptionist-sent-home-pwc-not-wearing-high-heels-pwc-
    nicola-thorp.

31 https://publications.parliament.uk/pa/cm201617/cmselect/cmpetitions
    /291/29104.htm.

32 Full report: www.parliament.uk/business/committees/committees-a-z/
    commons-select/petitions-committee/news-parliament-2015/high-heels-
    and-workplace-dress-codes-report-published-16-17/?utm_source=
    petition&utm_campaign=129823&utm_medium=email&utm_content
    =reportstory.

33 Full report: www.parliament.uk/business/committees/committees-a-z/
    commons-select/petitions-committee/news-parliament-2015/high-heels-
    and-workplace-dress-codes-report-published-16-17/?utm_source=
    petition&utm_campaign=129823&utm_medium=email&utm_content
    =reportstory.

34 Full report: www.parliament.uk/business/committees/committees-a-z/
    commons-select/petitions-committee/news-parliament-2015/high-heels-
    and-workplace-dress-codes-report-published-16-17/?utm_source=
    petition&utm_campaign=129823&utm_medium=email&utm_content
    =reportstory.

35 Lucy-Anne Holmes, email to author, 29 November 2017.

36 www.huffingtonpost.co.uk/dr-helen-pankhurst/lad-mags-sell-by-
    date_b_3510343.html.

37 http://www.telegraph.co.uk/men/the-filter/the-end-of-the-lads-mag-
    fhm-and-zoo-magazines-suspended/.

38 Kat Banyard, *Pimp State: Sex, Money and the Future of Equality*, 2016, p.194.

39 www.bbc.co.uk/news/magazine-34649495.

40 www.people.com/article/women-protest-free-bleeding-tampon-tax-uk.

41 www.change.org/p/george-osborne-stop-taxing-periods-period/u/
    15895109.

42 www.independent.co.uk/news/uk/home-news/girls-skipping-school-
    periods-cant-afford-tampons-sanitary-pads-a7629766.html.

43 www.mirror.co.uk/news/ampp3d/tampon-vat-how-much-money
    -5096033.

44 https://www.theguardian.com/uk-news/2018/aug/24/scotland-to-offer-free-sanitary-products-to-all-students-in-world-first..

45 Data from Change.org, email to author through Rima Amin, 21 April 2017.

46 Brie Rogers Lowery, email to author through Rima Amin, 21 April 2017.

47 Lucy-Anne Holmes, *How to Start a Revolution* Corgi, 2015.

48 Caroline Criado-Perez, *Do It Like a Woman: And Change the World* (2015), p.205.

49 Term coined by R. W. Connell, 1996, www.australianhumanitiesreview.org/archive/Issue-Dec-1996/connell.html.

50 www.theguardian.com/world/2017/mar/13/protest-persist-hope-trump-activism-anti-nuclear-movement?CMP=share_btn_link.

How Did We Do?

1 Quoted to me by Doreen Thakoordin, email to author, 20 April 2017.

2 Ailish, email to author, 31 May 2017.

3 Penny Mordaunt, letter to author, 5 October 2016.

4 Justine Greening, email to author via Helen Anderson, 11 October 2017.

5 Jude Kelly, email to author, 22 May 2017.

6 Olivia Newcomb, via Alison Newcomb, email to author, 9 November 2016.

7 Olive Schreiner and Elisabeth Jay, *Dreams Three Works*, p.20.

To 2028 and Beyond

1 Clare Christian, email to author, 26 September 2016.

2 Hilary Spencer, email to author via Helen Anderson, 4 October 2017.

3 Sophie Walker, email to author, 22 June 2017.

4 Clare Bailey, email to author via Elaine O'Neil, 22 June 2017.

5 Leanne Wood, email to author via Danny Grehan, 16 August 2017.

6 Helene Reardon-Bond, email to author, 4 July 2017.

7 Philippa Bilton, email to author, 17 September 2017.

8 Michelle O'Neill, email to author via Carla Campbell, 28 July 2017.

9 Judith Macgregor, email to author, 16 June 2017.

10 Victoria Derbyshire, email to author, 13 June 2017.

11 Anohni, email to author, 28 August 2017.

12 Emily Thornberry, discussion with author, 4 September 2017.

13 Dr Vanessa Ogden, email to author via Lee Davis, 21 June 2017.

14 Muzoon Almellehan, email to author via Hannah Weitzer, 22 May 2017.

15 Fiona Martin, personal communication, 19 October 2016.

16 Amber Lewis, from exercise facilitated by Claire Burnett, Hitchin Girls' School, direct to author, 15 June 2017.

17 Donna Basquille, email to author, 20 April 2017.

18 Cherie Blair, email to author, 1 June 2017.

19 Rosina, email to author, 18 May 2017.

20 Joanna Maycock, email to author, 6 September 2017.

21 Rhea Basra, Hitchin school exercise facilitated by Claire Burnett, 15 June 2017.

22 Janet Cooper, email to author, 10 July 2017.

23 Jane Garvey, email to author, 23 August 2017.

24 Lesley Covington, email to author, 8 June 2017.

25 Nichola Mallon, email to author via Elaine O'Neil, 22 June 2017.

26 Jo Broughton, 13 June 2017.

27 Helen Petrovna, email to author, 5 June 2017.

28 Marica Wainner, email to author, 2 June 2017.

29 Alice Welbourn, email to author, 27 July 2017.

30 Dr Kate Middleton, email to author, 2 May 2017.

31 Laura Bates, email to author, 25 September 2016, changes 14 June 2017.

32 Jo Harrison, email to author, 14 June 2017.

33 Judith Gillespie, email to author, 3 September 2016.

34 Leyla Hussein, email to author, 10 June 2017.

35 Claire Holcombe, email to author, 13 June 2017.

36 Kat Banyard, email to author, 7 September 2017.

37 Nicola Padfield, email to author, 28 May 2017.

38 Hannah Bond, email to author, 5 July 2017.

39 Tamsin Omond, email to author, 3 July 2017.

40 Anita Anand, email to author, 30 June 2017.

41 Elaine De Fries, email to author, 1 July 2017.

42 Olivia Dickinson, email to author, 3 July 2017.

43 Elizabeth Lovegrove, email to author, 1 July 2017.

44 Jacqueline Wilson, email to author via Naomi Cooper, 8 May 2017.

45 Siofra Mawdsley, email to author via Siobhan Jordan, 16 September 2017.

46 SprinkleOfGlitter, Louise Pentland, email to author via Charlotte Street, 23 June 2017.

47 Julie Walters, email to author via Kate Morgan, 11 May 2017.

48 Meryl Streep, email to author, 9 May 2017.

49 Miranda Hart, email to author, via Ellie Cheele, 19 May 2017.

50 Rachel Duckhouse, email to author via Carol Gysin, 25 June 2015.

51 Emeli Sandé, email to author via Katie Torrie, 31 May 2017.

52 Steph Houghton, email to author via Matthew Buck, 30 May 2017.

53 Dame Kelly Holmes, email to author via Andrea Medd, 14 June 2017.

54 Helen Richardson-Walsh, email to author via Lisa Norman, 12 September 2017.

55 Louisa Orr, email to author, 3 June 2017.

56 Right Reverend Libby Lane, Bishop of Stockport, email to author, 11 September 2017.

57 Faeeza Vaid, email to author, 7 June 2017.

58 Emma Watson, email to author via Esme Peach, 19 September 2017.

59 Zoella, email to author via Meghan Peterson, 30 June 2017.

60 Vivienne Abbott, email to author, 3 July 2017.

61 Rhiannon Broome, email to author, 3 June 2017.

62 Nicola Thorp, email to author, 14 March 2017.

63 Laura Coryton, email to author, 25 May 2017.

64 Emma Barnett, email to author, 27 February 2017.

65 Caroline Criado-Perez, email to author, 6 September 2017.

66 Brie Rogers Lowery, email to author via email from Rima Amin, 23 June 2017.

67 Emma Thompson, email to author via Catherine Olim, 22 August 2017.

68 Sandi Toksvig, email to author, 15 March 2017.

69 Claire Sugden, email to author, via Elaine O'Neil, 22 June 2017.

70 Marion Kelly, email to author, 5 July 2017.

71 Adya Ranjan, email to author via Richa Prasad, 7 July 2017.

72 Exercise facilitated by Dorcas Pratt, teacher at Gordon Primary School, email to author, 5 June 2017.

73 Exercise facilitated by Gaynor Symes, email to author via Nick Penn, Deputy Head Pentrepoeth Primary School, 16 June 2017.

74 Exercise facilitated by Myfanwy Lloyd, teacher at St Christopher's Church of England School, email to author, 15 May 2017.

75 Exercise facilitated by Claire Burnett, Hitchin Girls' School, direct to author, 15 June 2017.

BIBLIOGRAPHY

Adichie, Chimamanda Ngozi, *We Should All Be Feminists* (Anchor Books, 2015).

Adichie, Chimamanda Ngozi, *Dear Ijeawele, or A Feminist Manifesto in Fifteen Suggestions* (Alfred A. Knopf, 2017).

Ahmed, Sarah, *Living a feminist Life* (Duke University Press, 2017).

Anand, Anita, *Sophia: Princess, Suffragette, Revolutionary* (Bloomsbury, 2015).

Appignanesi, Lisa et al., *Fifty Shades of Feminism*.

Banyard, Kat, *The Equality Illusion: The Truth about Women and Men Today* (Faber & Faber, 2011).

Banyard, Kat, *Pimp State: Sex, Money and the Future of Equality* (Faber & Faber, 2016).

Barker, Pat, *The Regeneration Trilogy* (Penguin Books, 1992).

Bartley, Paula, *Votes for Women, 1860–1928* (Hodder & Stoughton Educational, 2003).

Bates, Laura, *Everyday Sexism* (Thomas Dunne, 2016).

Beal, Frances, *Double Jeopardy: To Be Black and Female* (Radical Education Project, 1971).

Beard, Mary, *Confronting the Classics: Traditions, Adventures and Innovations* (Profile Books, 2014).

Beard, Mary, *Women & Power: A Manifesto* (Profile Books, 2017).

Beauvoir, Simone de, *The Second Sex* (Knopf, 1953).

Bobel, Chris and Samantha Kwan, *Embodied Resistance: Challenging the Norms, Breaking the Rules* (Vanderbilt University Press, 2011).

Bornstein, Kate and S. Bear Bergman, *Gender Outlaws: The Next Generation* (Seal Press, 2010).

Boyd, Nina, *From Suffragette to Fascist: The Many Lives of Mary Sophia Allen* (History Press, 2013).

Braybon, Gail, *Women Workers in the First World War: The British Experience* (1981).

Bressey, Caroline and Claire Dwyer, *New Geographies of Race and Racism* (Ashgate Publishing Group, 2008).

Brownmiller, Susan, *Against Our Will: Men, Women and Rape* (Simon & Schuster, 1975).

Bruley, Sue, *Women in Britain Since 1900* (St Martin's Press, 1999).

Bryson, Valerie, *Feminist Political Theory: An Introduction* (Macmillan, 1992).

Budgeon, Shelley, *Third Wave Feminism and the Politics of Gender in Late Modernity* (Palgrave Macmillan, 2011).

Bussey, Gertrude Carman and Margaret Tims, *Pioneers for Peace: Women's International League for Peace and Freedom 1915–1965* (WILPF British Section, 1980).

Butler, Simon and Olive Hockin, *Land Girl Suffragette: The Extraordinary Story of Olive Hockin* (Halstar, 2016).

Campbell, Beatrix, *End of Equality: The Only Way is Women's Liberation*.

Caputi, Mary, *Feminism and Power: The Need for Critical Theory* (Lexington Books, 2013).

Carson, Rachel Louise, *Silent Spring* (Hamish Hamilton, 1962).

Castle, Barbara, *Sylvia and Christabel Pankhurst* (Penguin, 1987).

Chadwick, Helen et al., *Helen Chadwick* (Hatje Cantz, 2004).

Chakrabarti, Shami, *Of Women: In the 21st Century* (Allen Lane, 2017).

Chamberlain, Mary and Justin Partyka, *Fenwomen* (Full Circle, 2011).

Chaney, Sarah, *Psyche on the Skin: A History of Self-Harm* (Reaktion Books Ltd, 2017).

Childs, Sarah *New Labour's Women MPs: Women Representing Women* (Routledge, 2004).

Childs, Sarah, *The Good Parliament Report* (Bristol University, 2015).

Childs, Sarah and Rosie Campbell, *Deeds and Words: Gendering Politics after Joni Lovenduski* (ECPR Press, 2015).

Chilton, Denise, *Suddenly Single* (Fernlea Publishing House, 2017).

Christie, Bridget, *A Book for Her* (Arrow Books, 2016).

Cochrane, Kira, *All the Rebel Women: The Rise of the Fourth Wave of Feminism* (Guardian Books, 2013).

Coleman, Verna, *Adela Pankhurst: The Wayward Suffragette, 1885–1961* (Melbourne University Press, 1996).

Collini, Stefan, *Common Writing Essays on Literary Culture and Public Debate* (Oxford University Press, 2016).

Collins, Patricia Hill and Sirma Bilge, *Intersectionality* (Polity Press, 2016).

Connell, Raewyn W., *Masculinities* (University of California Press, 1995).

Connelly, Katherine, *Sylvia Pankhurst: Suffragette, Socialist and Scourge of Empire* (Pluto Press, 2013).

Cook, Hera, *The Long Sexual Revolution: English Women, Sex, and Contraception, 1800–1975* (Oxford University Press, 2004).

Cornwall, Andrea et al., *Masculinities under Neoliberalism*.

Cowman, Krista, *Women in British Politics, c.1689–1979* (Palgrave Macmillan, 2010).

Cowman, Krista and Louise A. Jackson, *Women and Work Culture Britain c.1850–1950* (Routledge, 2017).

Crewe, Emma, *Lords of Parliament: Manners, Rituals and Politics* (Manchester University Press, 2005).

Crewe, Emma, *Commons and Lords: A Short Anthropology of Parliament* (Haus, 2015).

Crewe, Emma, *The House of Commons: An Anthropology of MPs at Work* (Bloomsbury Academic, 2015).

Criado-Perez, Caroline, *Do It Like a Woman: And Change the World* (Granta Books, 2016).

Currell, Melville, *Political Woman* (Croom Helm, 1974).

Davies, Margaret Llewelyn and Virginia Woolf, *Life as We Have Known It* (Virago, 1990).

Davis, Angela Yvonne, *Women, Race & Class* (Vintage Books, 1983).

Davis, Mary, *Sylvia Pankhurst: A Life in Radical Politics* (Pluto Press, 1999).

Dillwyn, E. A. and Kirsti Bohata, *Jill* (Honno, 2013).

Dyhouse, Carol, *Glamour: Women, History, Feminism* (Zed Books, 2011).

Dyhouse, Carol, *Girl Trouble: Panic and Progress in the History of Young Women* (Zed Books, 2014).

Evans, Mary, *The Persistence of Gender Inequality* (Polity Press, 2016).

Evans, Sian, *Queen Bees: Six Brilliant and Extraordinary Society Hostesses Between the Wars – A Spectacle of Celebrity, Talent, and Burning Ambition* (Two Roads, 2016).

FitzSimons, Peter, *Nancy Wake: A Biography of Our Greatest War Heroine 1912–2011* (HarperCollins Publishers, 2011).

Fleming, Jacky, *The Trouble with Women* (Square Peg, 2016).

Ford, Robert Anthony and Matthew Goodwin, *Revolt on the Right: Explaining Support for the Radical Right in Britain* (Routledge, 2014).

Freeman, Esther, *Women Activists of East London* (Share UK, 2016).

Friedan, Betty, *The Feminine Mystique* (W.W. Norton, 1963).

Gasa, Nomboniso, *Women in South African History: Basus'iimbokodo, Bawel'imilambo = They Remove Boulders and Cross Rivers* (South Africa Human Science and Research Council, 2007).

Gawthorpe, Mary Eleanor, *Up Hill to Holloway* (Traversity Press, 1962).

Gay, Roxane, *Bad Feminist: Essays* (Corsair, 2014).

Gillis, Stacy et al., *Third Wave Feminism: A Critical Exploration* (Palgrave Macmillan, 2004).

Goodin, Robert E., *Explaining Norms* (Oxford University Press, 2016).

Gottlieb, Julie V. and Richard Toye, *The Aftermath of Suffrage: Women, Gender, and Politics in Britain, 1918–1945* (Palgrave Macmillan, a Division of St Martin's Press LLC, 2013).

Grant, Jane W., *In the Steps of Exceptional Women: The Story of the Fawcett Society 1866–2016* (Francis Boutle Publishers, 2016).

Green, Duncan, *How Change Happens* (Oxford University Press, 2016).

Greer, Germaine, *The Female Eunuch* (Fourth Estate, 2012).

Grosse, Robert E., *International Business and Government Relations in the 21st Century* (Cambridge University Press, 2005).

Gutzke, David, *Women Drinking Out in Britain Since the Early Twentieth Century* (Oxford University Press, 2016).

Haig, Margaret Viscountess Rhondda, *This Was My World* (Macmillan, 1933).

Hall, Radclyffe et al., *The Well of Loneliness* (Covici Friede, 1929).

Hamer, Emily, *Britannia's Glory: A History of Twentieth-Century Lesbians* (Cassell, 1996).

Harman, Harriet, *A Woman's Work* (Allen Lane, 2017).

Harrison, Shirley, *Sylvia Pankhurst: Citizen of the World* (Hornbeam, 2009).

Heilbron, Hilary, *Rose Heilbron: The Story of England's First Woman Queen's Counsel and Judge* (Hart, 2012).

Hird, Myra, *Engendering Violence: Heterosexual Interpersonal Violence from Childhood to Adulthood* (Routledge, 2017).

Hochschild, Adam, *To End All Wars: How the First World War Divided Britain* (Macmillan, 2011).

Holden, Anthony and Ben Holden, *Poems That Make Grown Women Cry: 100 Women on the Words that Move Them* (Simon & Schuster, 2017).

Holdsworth, Angela, *Out of the Doll's House: The Story of Women in the Twentieth Century* (BBC Books, 1988).

Holmes, Lucy-Anne, *How to Start a Revolution* (Corgi, 2015).

Holmes, Rachel, *Sylvia Pankhurst: Natural Born Rebel* (Bloomsbury, 2018).

Holton, Sandra Stanley, *Feminism and Democracy: Women's Suffrage and Reform Politics in Britain, 1900–1918* (Cambridge University Press, 2002).

Hooks, Bell, *The Will to Change: Men, Masculinity, and Love* (Washington Square Press, 2004).

Howes, Maureen, *Emily Wilding Davison: A Suffragette's Family Album* (The History Press, 2013).

Hughes, Bettany, *Helen of Troy: Goddess, Princess, Whore* (Pimlico, 2013).

Hunter, Rosemary C. et al., *Feminist Judgments: From Theory to Practice* (Hart, 2010).

Jacey, Helen, *The Woman in the Story: Writing Memorable Female Characters* (Michael Wiese Productions, 2010).

Janmohamed, Shelina Zahra, *Generation M: Young Muslims Changing the World* (I.B. Tauris, 2016).

Jónasdóttir, Anna G. and Kathleen B. Jones, *The Political Interests of Gender Revisited: Redoing Theory and Research with a Feminist Face* (Manchester University Press, 2009).

Jones, Helen, *In Her Own Name: A History of Women in South Australia from 1836* (Wakefield Press, 1994).

Jones, Helen, *Women in British Public Life, 1914–1950: Gender, Power, and Social Policy* (Longman, 2000).

Kelly, Audrey, *Lydia Becker and the Cause* (Centre for North-West Regional Studies, University of Lancaster, 1992).

Kennedy, Helena, *Eve Was Framed: Women and British Justice* (Vintage, 2005).

Kiraly, Miranda and Meagan Tyler, *Freedom Fallacy: The Limits of Liberal Feminism* (Connor Court Publishing, 2015).

Lawrence, Dorothy, *Sapper Dorothy: The Only English Woman Soldier in the Royal Engineers 51st Division, 79th Tunnelling Co. During the First World War* (Leonaur, 2010).

Lawrence, Emmeline, *My Part in a Changing World* (1976).

Lewis, Jane, *Women in Britain Since 1945: Women, Family, Work, and the State in the Post-War Years* (Blackwell, 1992).

Lewis, Jane, *Before the Vote Was Won: Arguments for and Against Women's Suffrage 1864–1896* (Routledge, 2001).

Liddington, Jill, *Rebel Girls: Their Fight for the Vote* (Virago, 2006).

Liddington, Jill and Elizabeth Crawford, *Vanishing for the Vote: Suffrage, Citizenship and the Battle for the Census* (Manchester University Press, 2014).

Liddington, Jill, and Jill Norris, *One Hand Tied behind Us: The Rise of the Women's Suffrage Movement* (Rivers Oram, 2000).

Lorde, Audre, *Zami: A New Spelling of My Name* (Crossing Press, 1982).

Lorde, Audre, *Sister Outsider: Essays and Speeches* (Crossing Press, 2007).

Lyndsey, Jenkins, *Lady Constance Lytton: Aristocrat, Suffragette, Martyr* (Biteback Publishing, 2015).

Mackay, Finn, *Radical Feminism: Feminist Activism in Movement* (Palgrave Macmillan, 2015).

MacKinnon, Catharine A., *Toward a Feminist Theory of the State* (Harvard University Press, 1989).

MacKinnon, Catharine A., *Butterfly Politics* (The Belknap Press of Harvard University Press, 2017).

Maguire, G. E., *Conservative Women: A History of Women and the Conservative Party, 1874–1997* (Macmillan, 2000).

Mantel, Hilary, *Hilary Mantel Collection* (HarperCollins Publishers, 2014).

Marshall, Katherine, and Susan Hayward, *Women, Religion, and Peacebuilding: Illuminating the Unseen* (United States Institute of Peace Press, 2015).

Mayer, Catherine, *Attack of the 50 Ft. Women: How Gender Equality Can Save the World!* (HQ, 2017).

McDowell, Linda, *Migrant Women's Voices: Talking about Life and Work in the UK Since 1945* (Bloomsbury Academic, 2016).

Mead, Margaret and M. Mok, *Seksualiteit En Temperament* (Het Spectrum, 1963).

Miles, Rosalind, *The Women's History of the World* (Salem House, 1989).

Millett, Kate, *Sexual Politics* (University of Illinois Press, 2000).

Moalem, Sharon, *Inheritance: How Our Genes Change Our Lives, and Our Lives Change Our Genes* (Sceptre, 2015).

Moran, Caitlin, *How to Be a Woman* (Harper Perennial, 2012).

Moran, Caitlin, *How to Build a Girl* (Harper Perennial, 2015).

Morgan, Sue, *The Feminist History Reader* (Routledge, Taylor & Francis, 2006).

Morgan, Sue, *Women, Gender and Religious Cultures in Britain, 1800–1940* (Routledge, 2010).

Morley, Edith J. and Barbara Morris, *Before and After: Reminiscences of a Working Life* (Two Rivers Press, 2016).

Murray, Jenni, *A History of Britain in 21 Women: A Personal Selection* (Oneworld Publications, 2016).

Norris, Pippa and Joni Lovenduski, *Blair's Babes: Critical Mass Theory, Gender, and Legislative Life* (John F. Kennedy School of Government, Harvard University, 2001).

Oakley, Ann, *Taking it Like a Woman* (Flamingo, 1985).

Oakley, Ann, *Sex, Gender and Society* (Arena, 1993).

Offen, Karen M., *European Feminisms, 1700–1950: A Political History* (Stanford University Press, 2000).

Orbach, Susie, *Fat is a Feminist Issue* (Arrow, 1989).

Paige, Caroline, *True Colours: My Life as the First Openly Transgender Officer in the British Armed Forces* (Biteback Publishing, 2017).

Pankhurst, E. Sylvia, *Save the Mothers: A Plea for Measures to Prevent the Annual Loss of about 3000 Childbearing Mothers and 20000 Infant Lives . . .* (Alfred A. Knopf, 1930).

Pankhurst, E. Sylvia, *The Suffragette: The History of the Women's Militant Suffrage Movement, 1905–1910* (Source Book Press, 1970).

Pankhurst, Emmeline, *My Own Story* (Source Book Press, 1970).

Pankhurst, Emmeline, *Suffragette* (Hesperus Press, 2016).

Pankhurst, Helen, *Gender Development & Identity: An Ethiopian Study* (Zed Books, 1993).

Pankhurst, Richard, *Sylvia Pankhurst: Artist and Crusader – An Intimate Portrait* (Paddington Press, 1979).

Paoletti, Jo Barraclough, *Pink and Blue: Telling the Boys from the Girls in America* (Indiana University Press, 2012).

Paseta, Senia, *Irish Nationalist Women, 1900–1918* (Cambridge University Press, 2013).

Pedwell, Carolyn, *Feminism, Culture and Embodied Practice: The Rhetorics of Comparison* (Routledge, 2010).

Pepe, Victoria et al., *I Call Myself a Feminist* (Virago, 2016).

Perry, Grayson, *The Descent of Man* (Penguin Books, 2017).

Phillips, Jess, *Everywoman: One Woman's Truth about Speaking the Truth* (Hutchinson, 2017).

Pizzey, Erin and Alison Forbes, *Scream Quietly or the Neighbours Will Hear* (Penguin, 1983).

Pugh, Martin, *The Pankhursts* (Allen Lane, 2001).

Purvis, June, *Women's History: Britain 1850–1945: An Introduction* (Routledge, 2000).

Purvis, June, *Emmeline Pankhurst: A Biography* (Routledge, 2002).

Purvis, June, *Christabel Pankhurst: A Biography* (Routledge, 2018).

Rackley, Erika, *Women, Judging and the Judiciary: From Difference to Diversity* (Routledge, 2013).

Radford, Jill and Diana E. H. Russell, *Femicide: the Politics of Woman Killing* (Twayne, 1992).

Raw, Louise, *The Bryant and May Matchwomen and Their Place in History* (Continuum Publishing Corporation, 2009).

Reeves, Rachel, *Alice in Westminster: The Political Life of Alice Bacon* (I.B. Tauris, 2016).

Reeves, Rachel, *Picking Your Battles* (I.B. Tauris, 2016).

Reeves, Rachel and Richard Carr, *Alice in Westminster: The Political Life of Alice Bacon* (I.B. Tauris, 2017).

Reger, Jo, *Different Wavelengths: Studies of the Contemporary Women's Movement* (Routledge, 2005).

Robinson, Jane, *A Force to Be Reckoned With: A History of the Women's Institute* (Virago, 2014).

Rosaldo, Michelle Zimbalist, *Woman, Culture, and Society* (Stanford University Press, 2006).

Rowbotham, Sheila, *Hidden from History: Rediscovering Women in History from the 17th Century to the Present* (Vintage Books, 1976).

Rowbotham, Sheila, *The Past is Before Us: Feminism in Action since the 1960s* (Pandora Press, 1989).

Rubinstein, David, *A Different World for Women: The Life of Millicent Garrett Fawcett* (Harvester Wheatsheaf, 1991).

Ruddock, Joan, *Going Nowhere: A Memoir* (Biteback Publishing, 2016).

Sandberg, Sheryl, *Lean In* (W.H. Allen, 2014).

Schreiner, Olive and Elisabeth Jay, *Dreams Three Works* (University of Birmingham Press, 2003).

Scott, Joan Wallach, *Gender and the Politics of History* (Columbia University Press, 1988).

Scutt, Jocelynne A. (ed.), *Women, Law and Culture Conformity, Contradiction and Conflict* (Springer International Publishing, 2016).

Seldon, Anthony et al., *The Coalition Effect, 2010–2015* (Cambridge University Press, 2015).

Short, Clare et al., *Dear Clare – This is What Women Feel about Page 3* (Hutchinson Radius, 1991).

Shortfall, S. 'Farming, Identity and Well-Being: Managing Changing Gender Roles within Western European Farm Families', *Anthropological Notebooks*, Vol. 20, no. 3, 2014, pp. 67–81.

Sladen, Mark and Helen Chadwick, *Helen Chadwick* (Hatje Cantz, 2004).

Solnit, Rebecca, *Men Explain Things to Me and Other Essays* (Granta Publications, 2014).

Sparrow, Andrew, *Obscure Scribblers: A History of Parliamentary Journalism* (Politico's, 2003).

Spender, Dale, *There's Always Been a Women's Movement this Century* (Pandora Press, 1983).

Spender, Dale, *Man Made Language* (Pandora, 2001).

Stopes, Marie Carmichael, *Wise Parenthood: A Treatise on Birth Control for Married People* (Jaico, 1957).

Stopes, Marie Carmichael, *Married Love: A New Contribution to the Solution of Sex Difficulties* (Phoenix, 2000).

Stroud, Rick, *Lonely Courage: The True Story of the SOE Heroines Who Fought to Free Nazi-Occupied France* (Simon & Schuster, 2018).

Sugg, Zoe, *Girl Online: Going Solo* (Keywords Press, 2016).

Summerfield, Penny, *Reconstructing Women's Wartime Lives: Discourse and Subjectivity in Oral Histories of the Second World War* (Manchester University Press, 1998).

Summerfield, Penny, *Women Workers in the Second World War: Production and Patriarchy in Conflict* (Routledge, 2014).

Summers, Anne, *Christian and Jewish Women in Britain, 1880–1940: Living with Difference* (Palgrave Macmillan, 2017).

Turner, Mary, *The Women's Century: A Celebration of Changing Roles* (National Archives, 2006).

Ulrich, Laurel, *Well-Behaved Women Seldom Make History* (Knopf, 2007).

Urwin, Jack, *Man Up: Surviving Modern Masculinity* (Icon Books, 2017).

Vakoch, Douglas A., *Ecofeminism and Rhetoric: Critical Perspectives on Sex, Technology, and Discourse* (Berghahn Books, 2011).

Vallely, Vanessa, *Heels of Steel: Surviving & Thriving in the Corporate World* (Panoma Press, 2013).

Waihong, Choo, *The Kingdom of Women: Life, Love and Death in China's Hidden Mountains* (I.B. Tauris, 2017).

Walby, Sylvia, *Gender Segregation at Work* (Open University Press, 1988).

Walby, Sylvia, *Theorizing Patriarchy* (Blackwell, 1991).

Walby, Sylvia, *The Future of Feminism* (Polity Press, 2011).

Walmsley-Johnson, Helen, *The Invisible Woman: Taking on the Vintage Years* (Icon, 2016).

Watkins, Sarah-Beth, *Ireland's Suffragettes: The Women Who Fought for the Vote* (The History Press Ireland, 2014).

Webster, Juliet and Keith Randle, *Virtual Workers and the Global Labour Market* (Palgrave Macmillan UK, 2016).

Weir, Alison, *The Marriage Game: A Novel of Queen Elizabeth I* (Thorndike Press, 2015).

Whelehan, Imelda, *Modern Feminist Thought: From the Second Wave to 'Post-Feminism'* (Edinburgh University Press, 2005).

Whitmore, Richard, *Alice Hawkins: And the Suffragette Movement* (DB, 2012).

Wolf, Naomi, *The Beauty Myth* (Vintage, 1991).

Wollstonecraft, Mary, *A Vindication of the Rights of Women* (Prometheus Books, 1989).

Zweiniger-Bargielowska, Ina, *Women in Twentieth-Century Britain* (Longman, 2001).

INDEX

Page numbers in **bold** refer to figures.